RHYTHM IN
KHAJURAHO

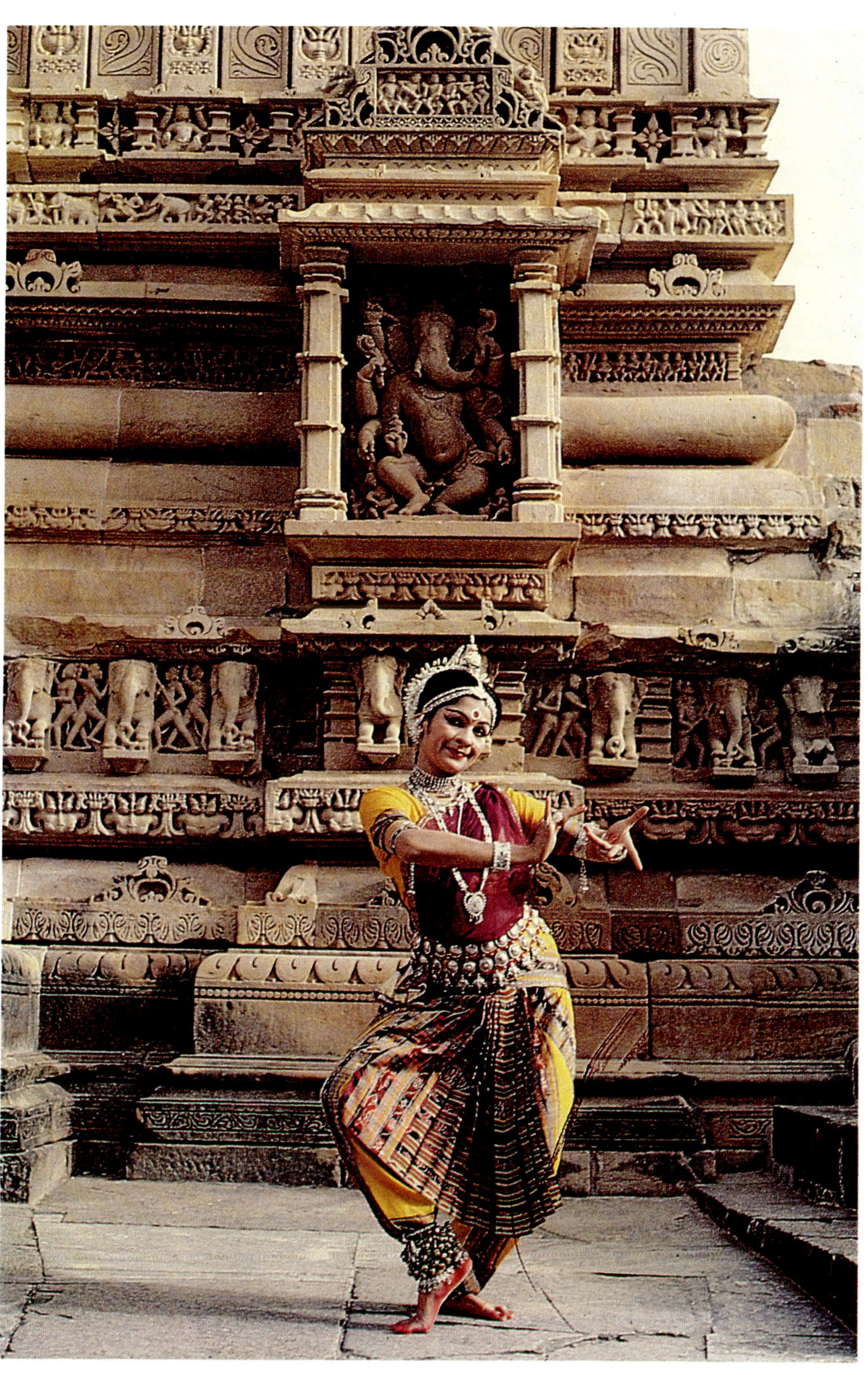

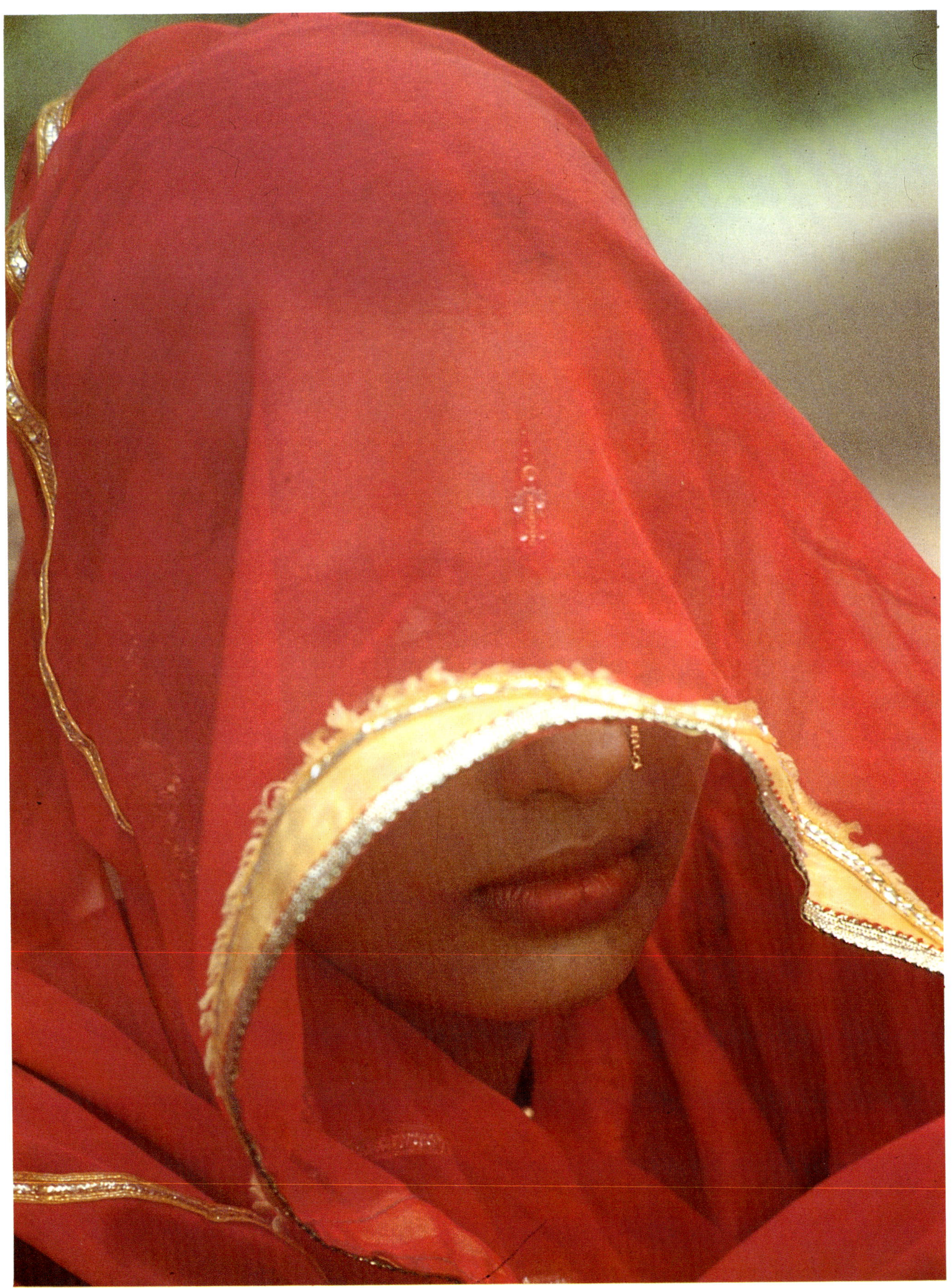

R H Y T H M I N

K H A J U R A H O

Text and Photo
ASHOK KHANNA

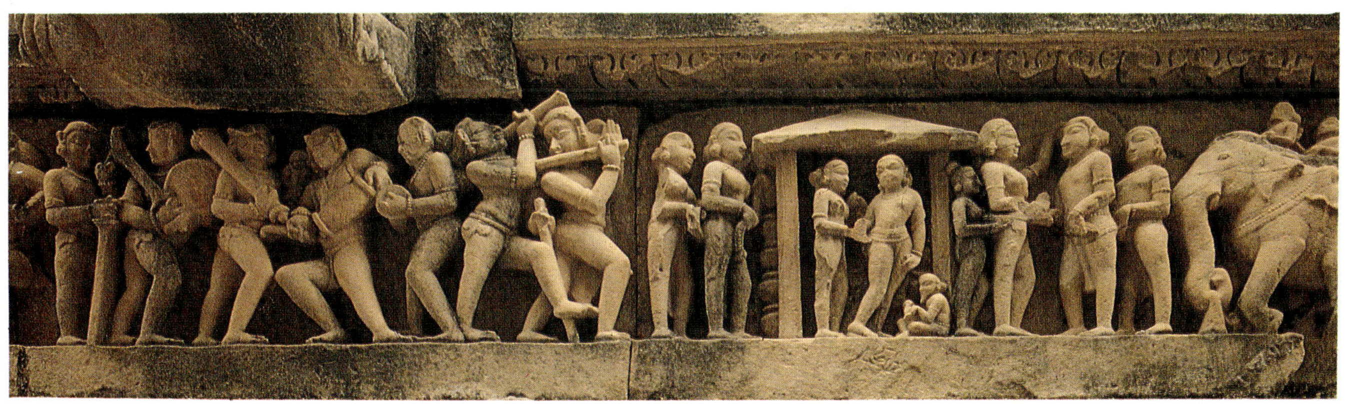

South Asia Publications
Delhi 110052

Published by
South Asia Publications
29, Central Market, Ashok Vihar I
Delhi 110052 [INDIA]

First Edition 1997

ISBN 81-7433-016-X

Layout
Tulika

Processed at
Laser Graphics Pvt. Ltd., New Delhi

Printed at
Rakesh Press, New Delhi

Back Cover

Khajuraho's holy traditions have a continuous link with their past. Sadhus, Hathayogis and Tantra practitioners used to visit and stay at Khajuraho known during the ancient times as Vatsa and in medieval times as Jejakabhukti and Khajuravatika.

Inside Cover

Ganesh—the elephant headed god of wisdom. Pious Hindus begin all religious rites and sacrifices, or any wordly affair of importance with an invocation of Ganesh, who removes all obstacles. Sanjukta Panigrahi, an exponent of Guru Kelu Charan Mahapatra, saluting Ganesh with her Odissi dance.

P R E F A C E

आङ्गिकं भुवनं यस्य वाचिकं सर्ववाङ्मयम्।
आहर्यं चन्द्रतारादि तं नमः सात्विकं शिवम्॥

"We bow to Lord Shiva whose body is the Universe, whose speech is the entire literature and whose decoration or adornments are the moon and the stars."

(Source : Nadikesvara's *Abhinayadarpanam)*

From the ancient times, the temple, music and dance — twin tools of concentration — have been an inseparable part of Indian Culture and Religion. Tinkling anklets, flashing expressions, evocative mudras (poses) pay obeisance to the Patron of the Arts --- Lord Nataraja. The spirit of Satyam, Shivam, Sundaram drives us to conclude, what is Sundaram (Charming) is Satyam (Truth) and which is Satyam might be the God — Shivam. The Khajuraho epitomises this mantra. A small village once hidden in impenetrable jungles, Khajuraho now attracts people in search of charm, truth or God.

On my photographic explorations across India in search of Satyam...Shivam... Sundaram, I was captivated by the sculptural art of Khajuraho. Present volume is the result of ceaseless clicking of innumerable pictures by my camera, my eyes and my soul. Treasure of art is everyone's right and it compels me to share the Rhythm in Khajuraho with you. Perhaps nowhere else in the world has such a hymn to the beauty of woman been sung.

My effort has been to present Khajuraho in Indian social and mythological perspective, giving due importance to Erotica. Since pictures' silence speaks louder than words, text has been restricted. I wish the present effort will quench the readers' thurst for art and ecstasy.

In the journey of my photographic explorations I owe gratitude to Dr Mulk Raj Anand, Dr Sunil Kothari and Dr Bhanu Shanker Mehta who inspired, guided and encouraged me. I am thankful to Mr Francis Leeson, Dr Krishna Deva, Mr Raghu Rai and Rana P. Singh whose research work nourished my thoughts. I cannot forget inspiration and encouragement extended by Swami Brahm Dev Upadhyaya, Mr R.P. Srivastava, Mr V.K. Mehrotra, Mr S. Chintamani, Mr V.C. Mehrotra, Mr S.T. Das, Mr Pramod Kapoor, Mr Gyan Chandra Mehrotra. During my Khajuraho visits the help extended by Mr Pramod Chandel, Mr S.P. Khandelwal and the renowned guide, Mr Brijendra Singh cannot be expressed in words. My heartfelt gratitude to my wife Swayam Prabha, and friends Sanjay P. Garg, Gyanendra Pandey and Mirza Mahboob Alam for helping me in editing and planning of the book.

Very special thanks are also due to the world renowned Indian classical dancers who extended their very kind and patient cooperation to me in completing this book with a colour of Indian dance form.

Ashok Khanna

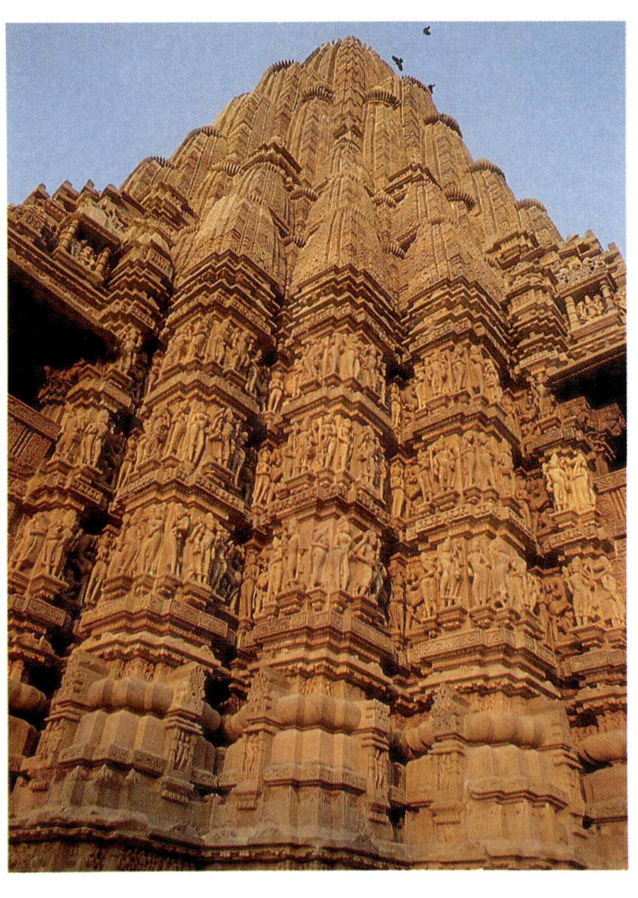

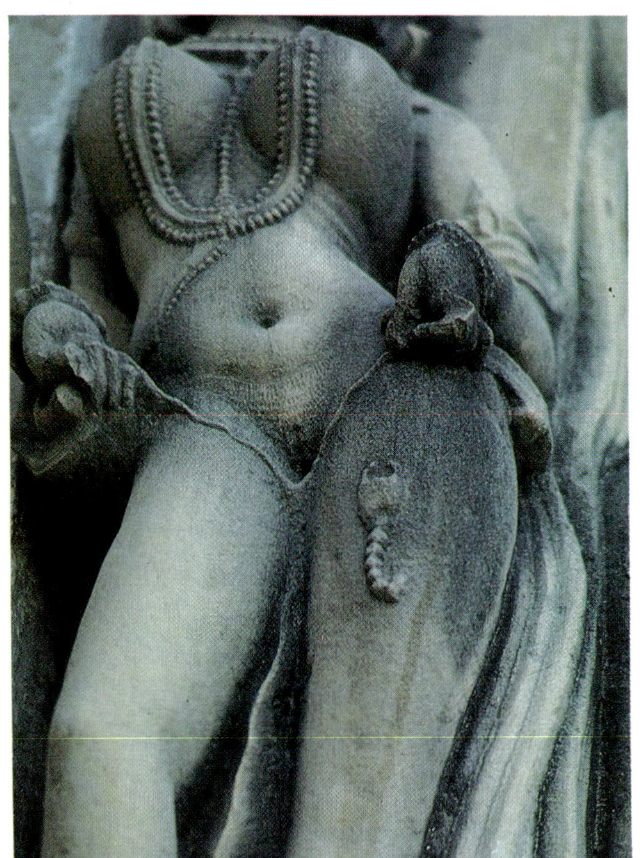

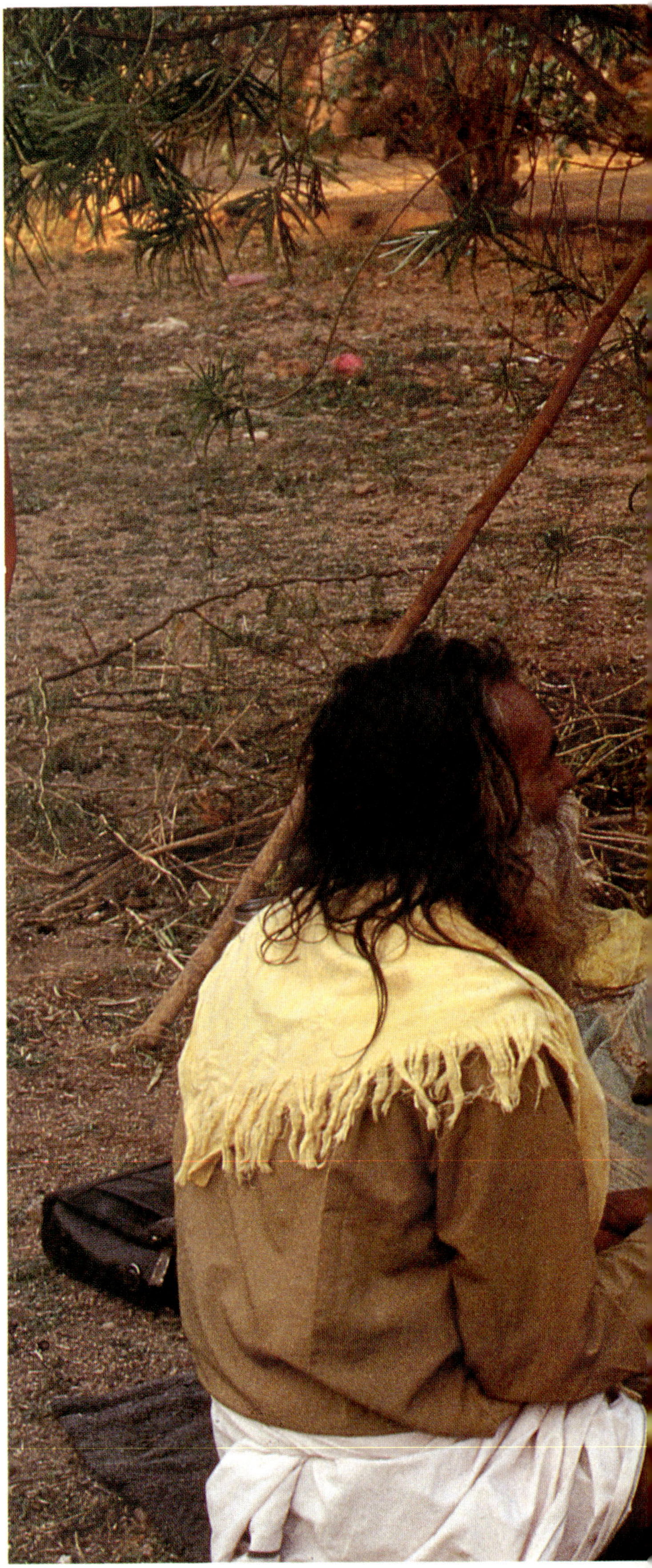

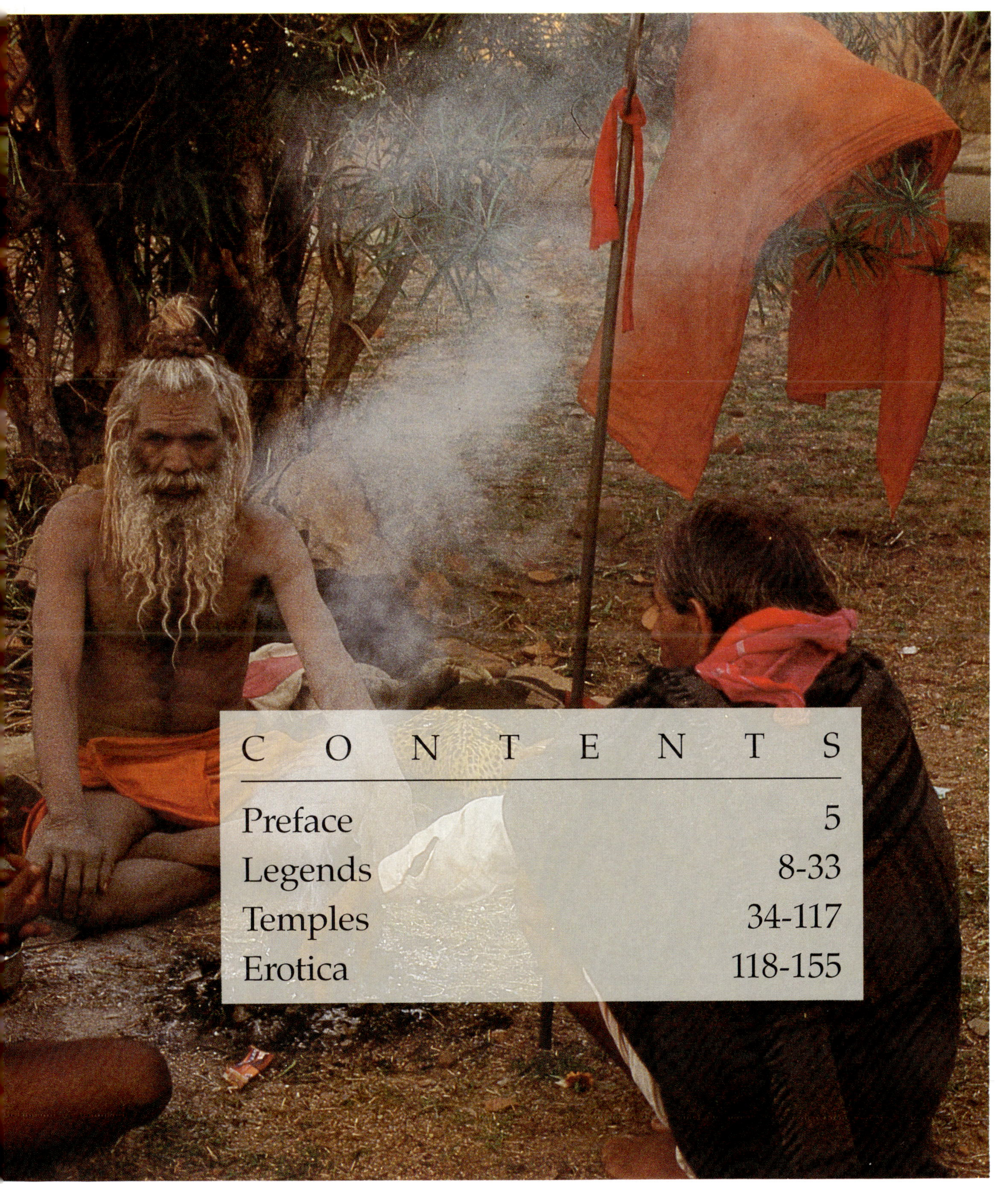

CONTENTS

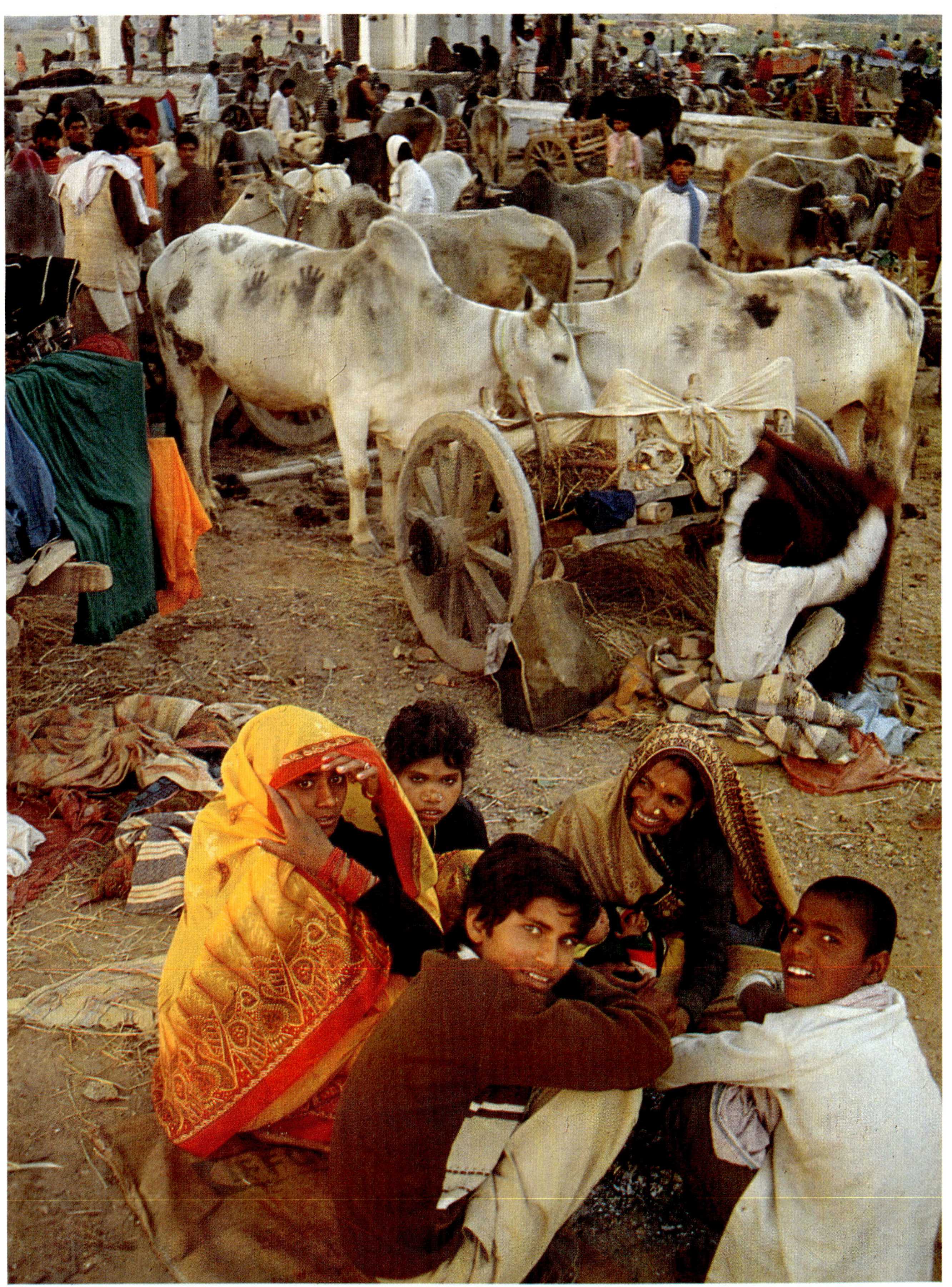

L E G E N D S

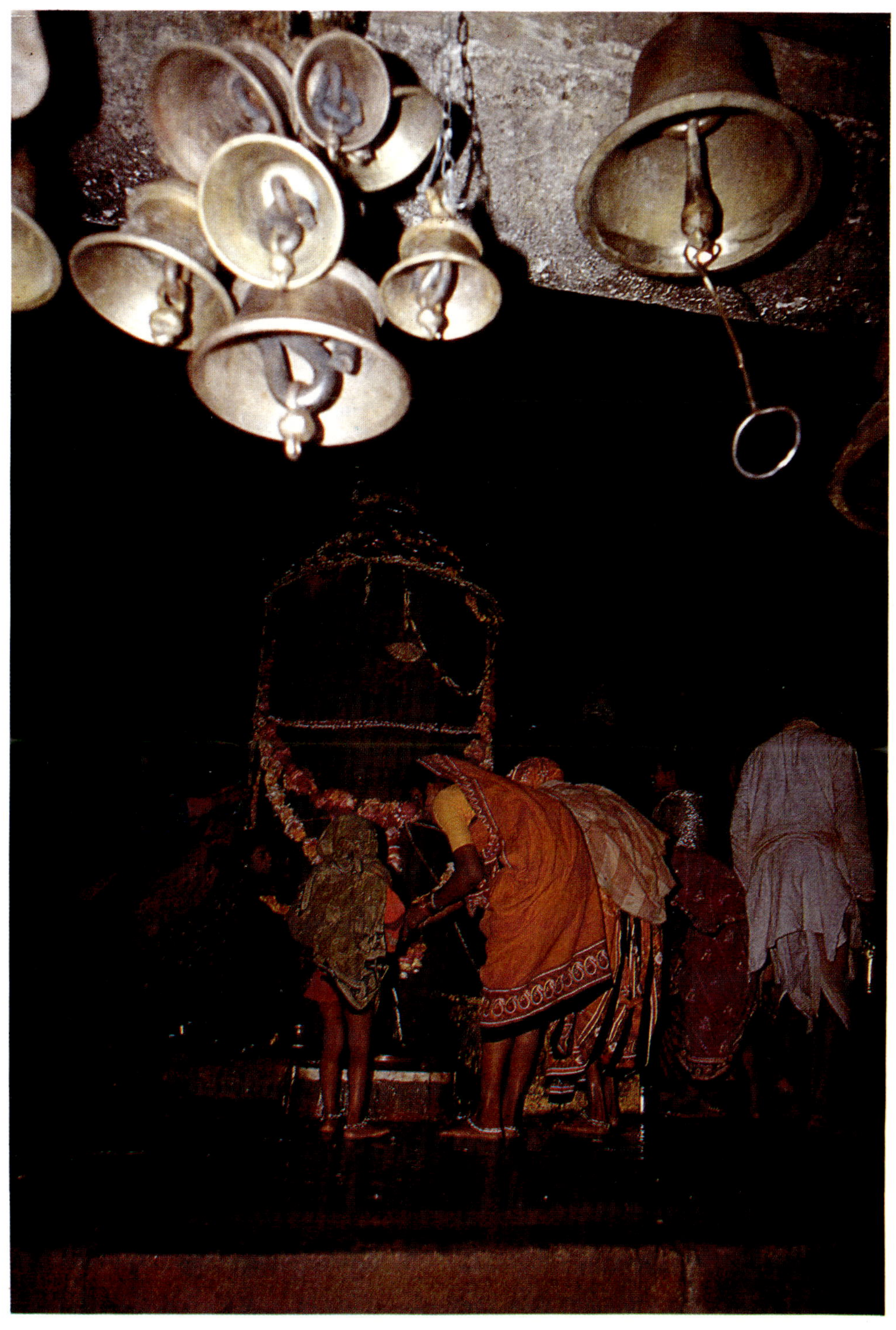

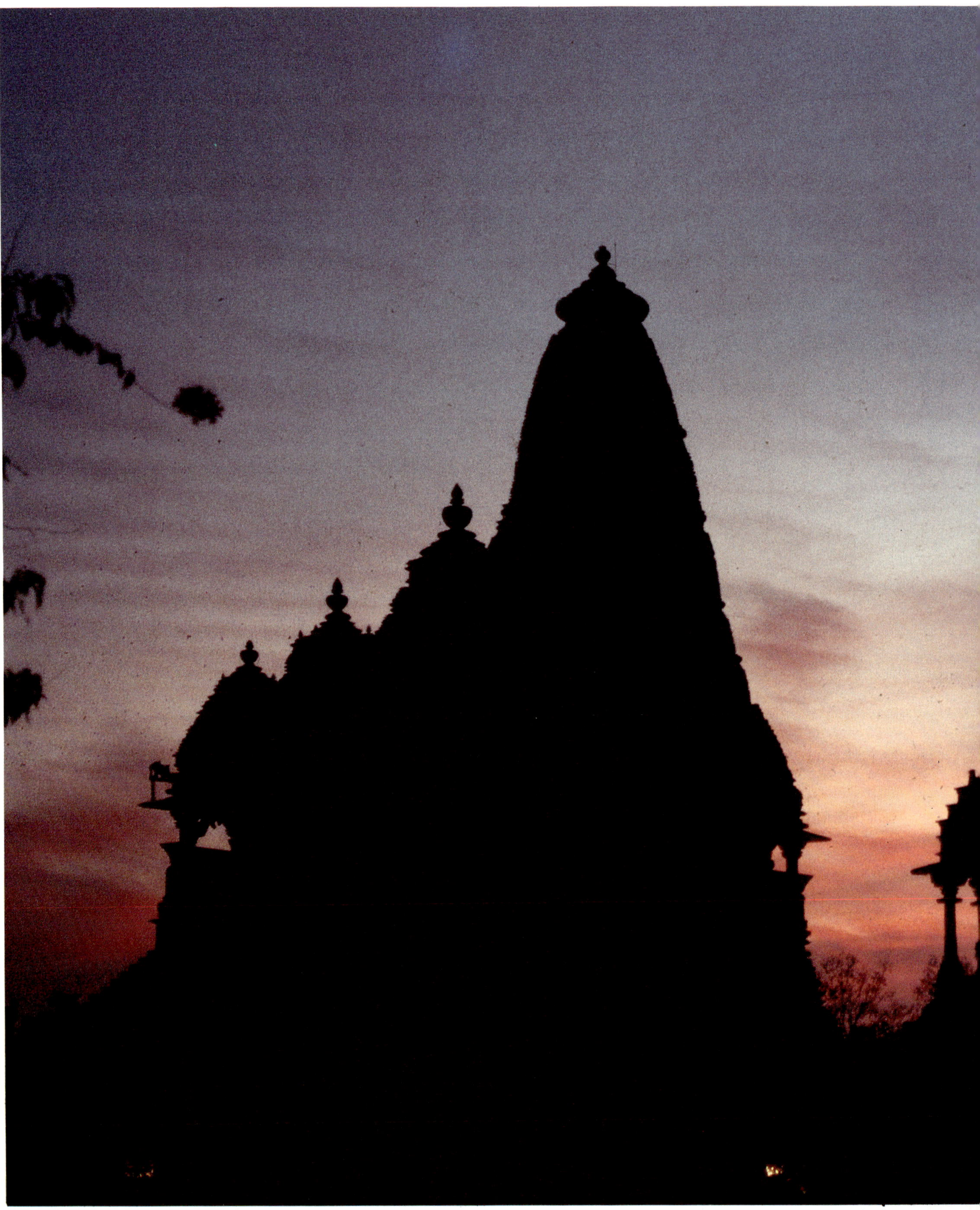

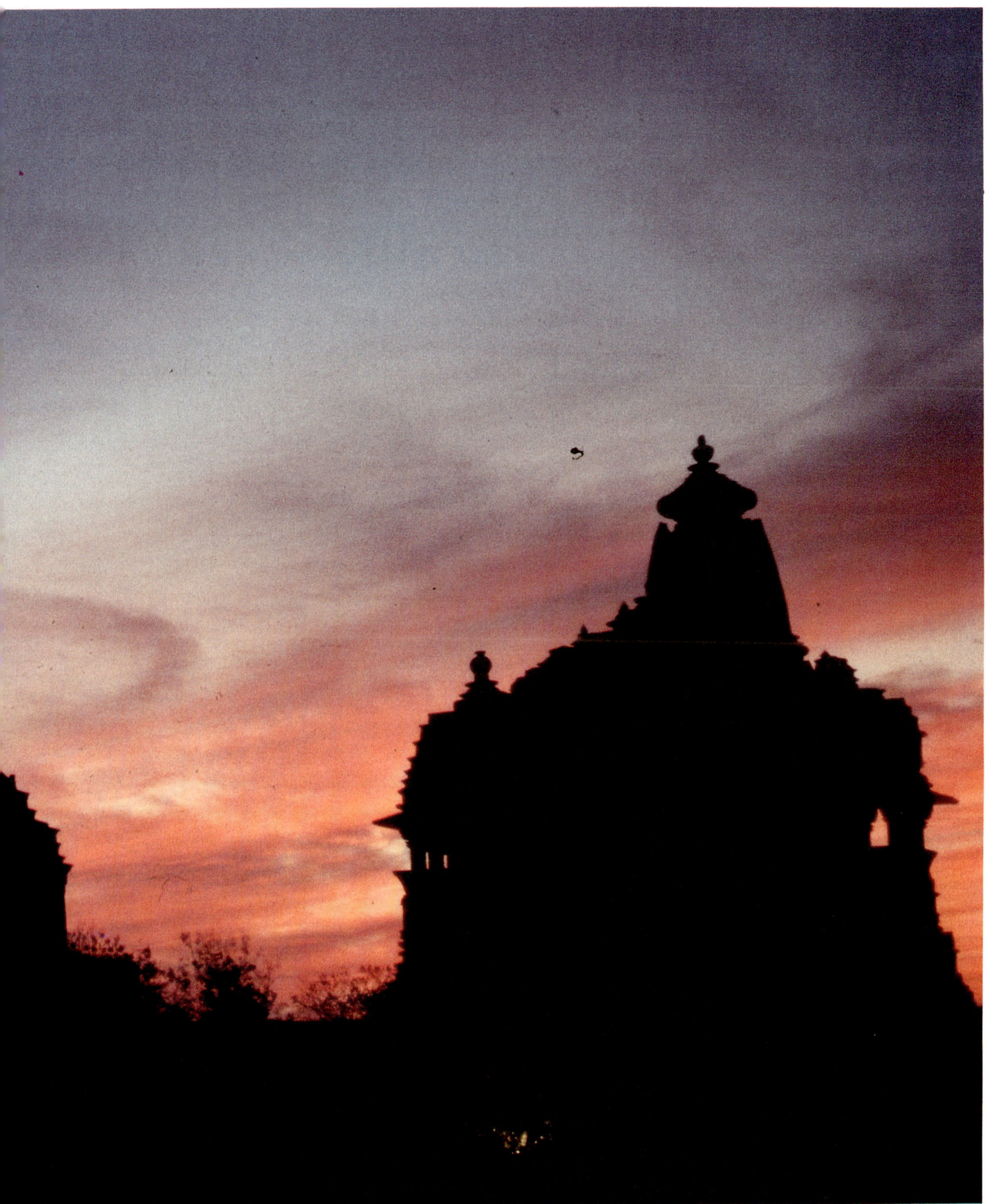

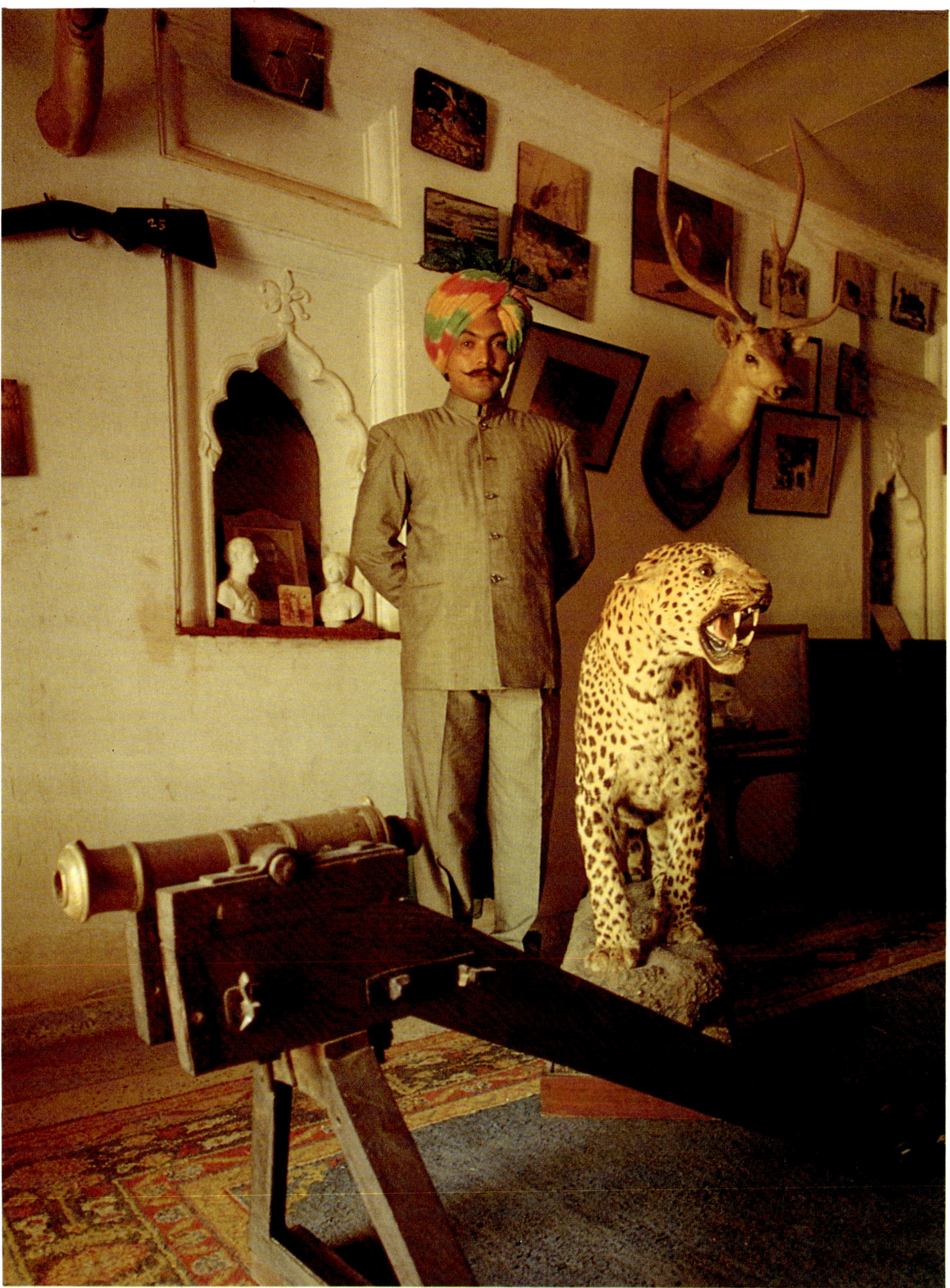
25

L E G E N D S

Khajuraho shines as a north star in the sky of splendid cultural legacy of India. The superb mix of art and religion, the Mecca of art connoisseurs housing the mystries in stone, Khajuraho has been the cynosure of the world, teaching the lessons in materialistic pleasures of life and in attaining salvation thereafter. Here we find the religion in art and art in religion.

Khajuraho, a small village in the heart of Central India, falls in Chhatarpur District of Madhya Pradesh. Inhabited by merely 3000 and odd people, the place is visited by persons in much larger number with varying taste. It seems to be the only village in India to have an airstrip catering to flights connecting it with far off places, where signboards in foreign languages explain its place on the world scene. The carved stones justify its protection and preservation under 'World Heritage' programme of the United Nations.

Known as 'Vatsa Janpad' in 400 B.C. Khajuraho was named 'Jejakabhukti' in medieval times. We trace its name 'Khajura' from the chronicles of Ibn Batutta, the Moroccan traveller who visited the place in 1335 AD. He writes, "Kajarra is the place where there is a great pond about a mile in length near which are temples containing idols which the Muslims have mutilated. In the centre of that pond there are three cupolas of red stone, each of three storeys; and at the four corners of the pond are cupolas in which live a body of the *jogis* who have clotted their hair and let them grow so that they become as long as their bodies, and on account of their practising asceticism their colour had become extremely yellow. Many Musalmans follow them in order to take lessons from them. It is said that whoever is subjected to a disease like the leprosy or elephantiasis lives with them for a long period of time and is cured by the permission of God." Even in the 7th Century the famous Chinese traveller Huien Tsang came across a number of Buddhist monasteries in Khajuraho. Since the area had Khajur (Palm) trees in abundance, it gave a justification to its name. The Vishvanath Temple inscriptions of Dhanga King dated 1002 A.D. also call the place as 'Kharjura Vahak'.

Pages 10-11 : Nature's piece of art, enchanted by the beauty of Khajuraho sculptures even the God becomes sentimental.
At the sunset, watching the western groups of temples is a unique experience. Each evening at dusk the silhouette of the temples tunes with the changing hour to give a new look.
Page 12 : Rajkumar Vikram Singh with his forefathers' hunting 'trophies', the evidence of past splendour when hunting and war were significant parts of daily life.

Originally related to the aboriginal tribes of the Bhars and the Gonds, the Chandelas trace their descent from the Moon God, The Chandra. In absence of historical inscriptions or other evidences, myths and legends are woven around the Chandela legacy. However, their aboriginal affiliation is revealed by the fact that they continued to regard Maniya Dev, a tribal divinity enshrined on a hill near Khajuraho, as their tutelary deity. As per traditions, they are the descendants of mythical sage Chandratreya, himself born of Moon. In the Mahoba *Khand* of *Parimal Raso* (a text of 17th Century in the Bundelkhandi dialect) the legacy has been narrated with traditional fragrance. Hemvati was a beautiful but unfortunate young widowed daughter of a Brahmin, Hemraj, the royal priest of Kashi. One summer night she felt uneasy and went for a bath in the sparkling waters of a lotus-filled pond. The Moon-god appeared in the sky. Awestruck by her beauty, He descended to earth in human form and embraced her passionately. The distressed Hemvati threatened to curse the Moon for outraging her chastity. To make amends for His folly the Moon-god blessed her, "Hemvati! you will be the mother of an invincible hero, the originator of a golden dynasty who will perform Bhandya Yajna to restore your chastity." On the bank of the Karnavati river, she gave birth to a son as handsome as moon. The son was called Chandravarman. At his birth, Brihaspati, the preceptor of the gods, descended on earth to prepare the horoscope of the child, and the Moon-god too appeared to celebrate the birth of his son. When he grew as a teenager, Chandravarman became a brave youth who could kill a tiger barehanded. The Moon-god blessed him with a kingship and gave him a touchstone to ensure an inexhaustible treasure. In course of time, Chandravarman performed Bhandya Yajna with prescribed rituals which included the depiction of erotic figures and built eightyfive temples flanked by pond or lake and trees. At the conclusion of the Yajna all sins of Hemvati were washed away and she proceeded to heaven.

A variation of the same legend introduces Hemvati as the widowed daughter of Mani Ram, the royal priest of Kalinjar. As a result of a mistake in his calculations the priest advised his King a particular night as Puranmasi, the fullmoon night contrary to the fact that it was the dark night. In her concern for her father's reputation the beautiful Hemvati prayed to the Moon-god who was gracious enough to uphold the word of the priest. But in return of His favour the Moon-god ravished Hemvati. Shame strickened the grieving priest cursed himself and turned into a stone. This stone had been worshipped by the Chandelas as their deity — Maniya Dev. Hemvati gave birth to a son, the sage Chandratreya, who became the progenitor of the Chandela dynasty.

Chandravarman, who is believed to be the first ancestor of the Chandelas, was consecrated as the King of Khajuraho. He is also credited with the foundation of the Kalinjar fort and the capital town of Mahoba. The available inscriptions designate Nanuka, the first prince of Chandela dynasty who appears to have ruled from Khajuraho since beginning of the ninth century. Subsequently the region was known as Bundelkhand. After the death of Harsh, the Chandelas might have accepted sovereignty of the Pratiharas. When Pratiharas were weakened by Rastrakutas, Yashovarman carved a territory for Chandelas. In due course of time the capital was shifted to Kalinjar to face the wrath of Muslim invaders, but Khajuraho continued to be their religious capital.

Lying in the region of legendary Bundelkhand, Khajuraho is surrounded by a fairly picturesque upland, dotted by hummocky hills, well covered with trees and shrubs. Augmenting the charm of the region are Panna diamond mines, Rajgarh Palace, Pandava and Raneh falls in the vicinity. Bounded on the south by river Ken and its tributaries, the area forms a sort of transition between the Vindhya Mountains and the Ganga, the holiest amongst holy rivers. With the granite, sandy land and average annual rainfall of 40 inches, the once fertile tract permits only patchy cultivation. However, the activities in the field intense up during the monsoon. When comparing Khajuraho with its surroundings one finds it as an oasis in the desert. The village, once decorated with lakes, forts and palaces of Chandelas now bears a modified face. Whereas the forts and palaces succumbed to the raiders and the elements, other activities of village life have been subjected to the modern development. The village once watered by lakes now has only wells. Although, women still gather and gossip around the wells before they fetch water for daily needs, the men enjoy their evenings with friends, smoking and talking on issues ranging from personal problems to national and international politics. What has not yet changed is the place of Khajuraho temples in their heart. Each morning people take a holy dip in Shiv Sagar lake and have a divine glimpse of Shiva Lingam consecrated in Matangeshwar Temple centuries ago. Day after day their life continues at the same rhythm, calm and slow. Though their lifestyles may look awkward to outsiders visiting the place, they appear undeterred, satisfied in the lap of nature.

Khajuraho has bravely faced many upheavels in its past. Beginning from the narrations by Xvang Zang who visited the place in 601 A.D., it was inhabited by numerous scholars and monks belonging to Hindu, Buddhist, Jain and even Muslim sects. In Puranas, the ancient scriptures, the place finds a mention as a favourite resort of sages and ascetics. The region had its cultural glory at height during the Sunga period (200 B.C.) with Bharhut as centre, and also during the Gupta period, when it had a remarkable efflorescence of sculptural and architectural art. The glory of Khajuraho reached the pinnacle when Chandelas in the 10th Century adorned it with many world class temples, tanks, lakes, forts and palaces. The almost barren sandy land was thus transformed into fertile land by the waters of lakes and ponds. The abundance of rich mineral ores provided copper and iron for melting and to make weapons. The Panna mines gave plenty of diamonds making the region a centre of business activities. However, it is hard to ascertain the motive of Chandelas for constructing such masterpieces of art.

In the later part of Chandela regime, the iconoclast Muslim invaders — Mahmud of Ghazni, Mohammed Ghori, Lodi and others started invading their territory. Vidyadhar, the most powerful of Chandelas, faced them bravely but his successors could not withstand. They somehow managed to keep the temples away from the greed of the invaders though forts and palaces were annihilated. However, some of the temples must have been destroyed either by the invaders or by the ravages of time and nature leaving behind only twenty out of eighty-five built during the golden period of Chandela dynasty. The village lost its importance by 16th Century finding no mention in *Aina-e-Akbari*. Having lesser force to fight Muslims and to regain lost territories, the place was abandoned by the Chandela rulers. It proved a blessing in disguise paving the way for preservation of the temple art, though the place fell into oblivion burying itself in the depth of jungle only to be rediscovered later.

The neglect of centuries combined with the vandalism of man resulted in further disintegration of these monuments. In 1838, T.S. Burt, an adventure loving Englishman, braving the hazards of barbaric terrain, unearthed the lost legacy of Chandelas. Sites of Khajuraho were studied in detail by Alexander Cunningham, whose observations published in the Archaeological Survey Reports (1871-1885), made the world rediscover the exquisite art of Khajuraho temples. The free India gave Khajuraho its present form. By building roads, airstrip, the museum and hotels the place has been converted into one of the most important tourist centres. Though temple art is as new as it was, the fortresses and palaces have been replaced by five star hotels. The silence, which soothed the Khajuraho for centuries, has been occupied by cacophony of any modern village.

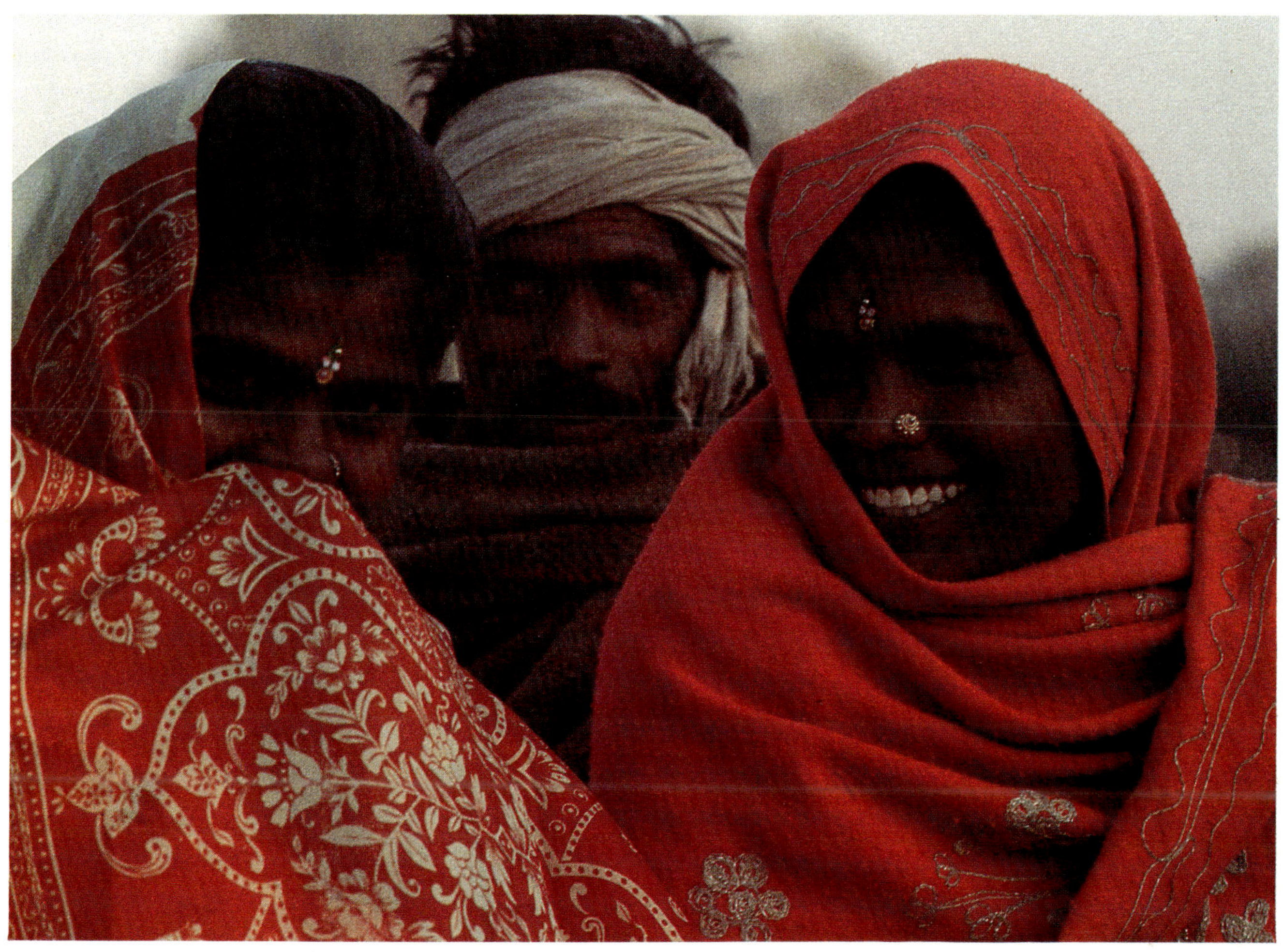

Every festival in India has its own fervour — rural folk have been instrumental in preserving the traditions and the rhythm of Indian cultural heritage.

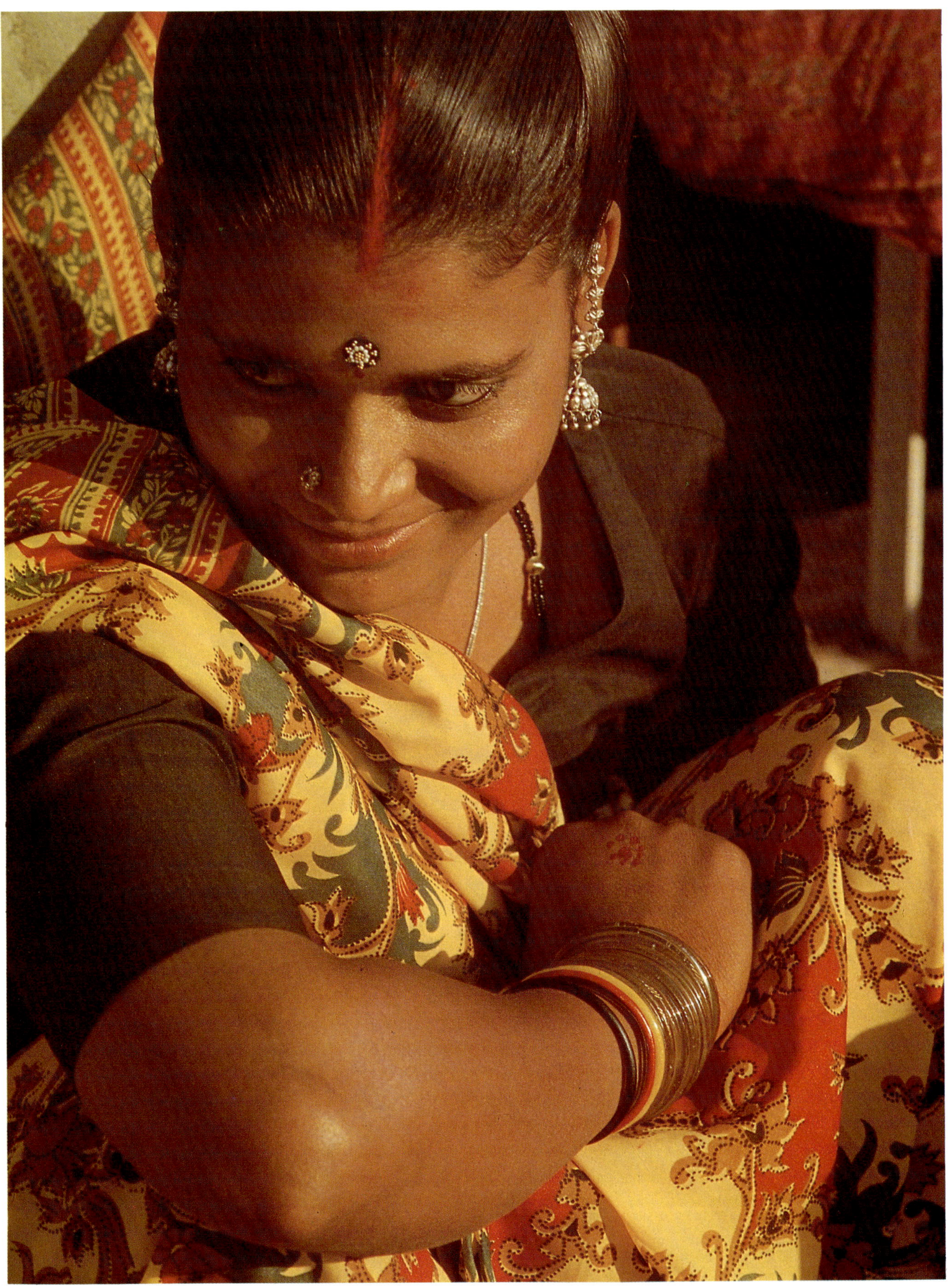

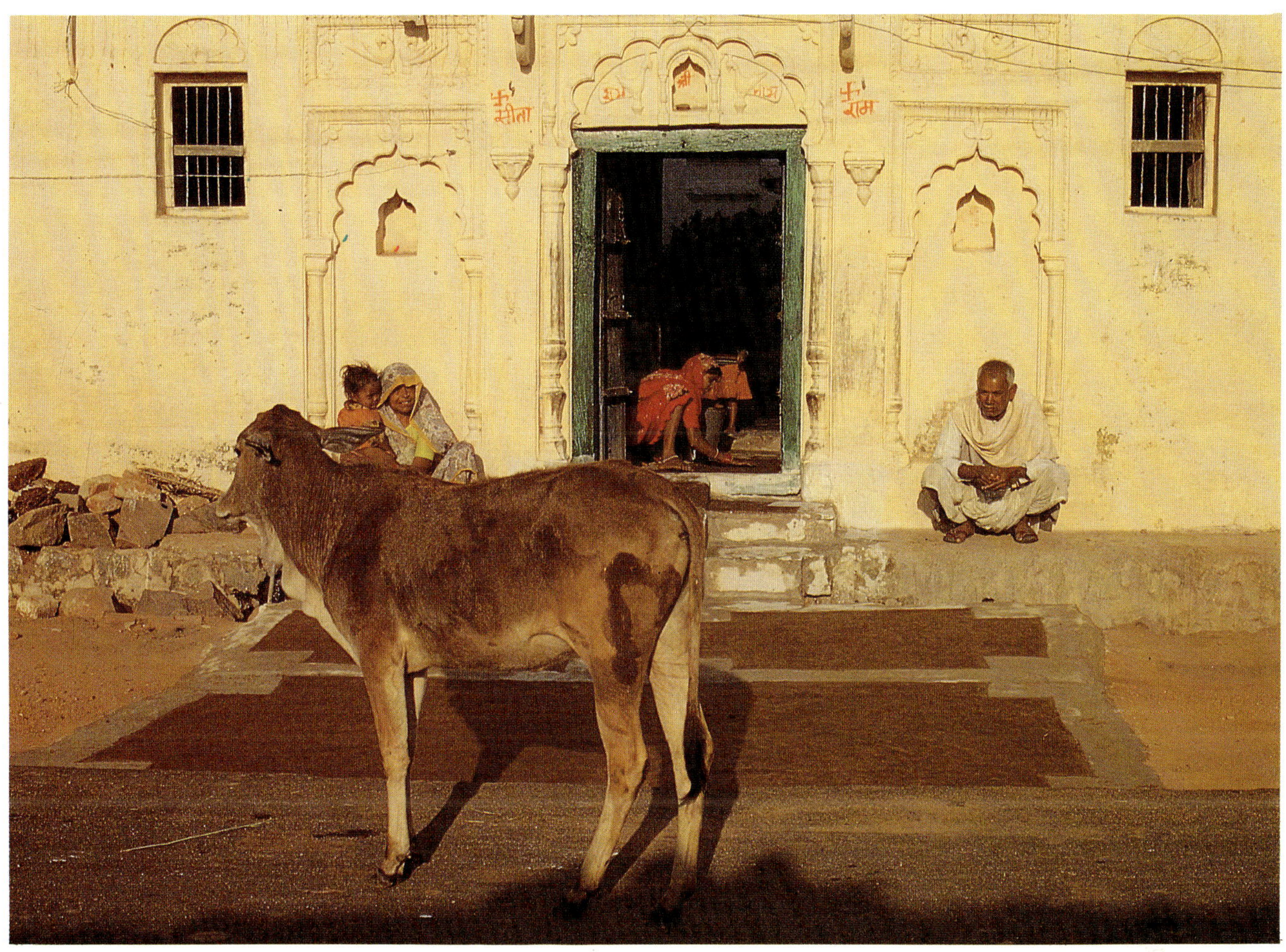

A woman from Khajuraho village seems to be contended with her life. The festivities fill her life with joy. The rural folk live with the vigour of traditions. Cow is worshipped and cow-dung and cow-urine are considered pious. Each morning the women adorn the door of their home and kitchen with cowdung. Her parents-in-law enjoy the warmth of sunrays outside the house. *Pages 20-21*: A mother applies Kajal (collyrium) to her son's eyes and on the forehead to keep evil spirits away from the child.

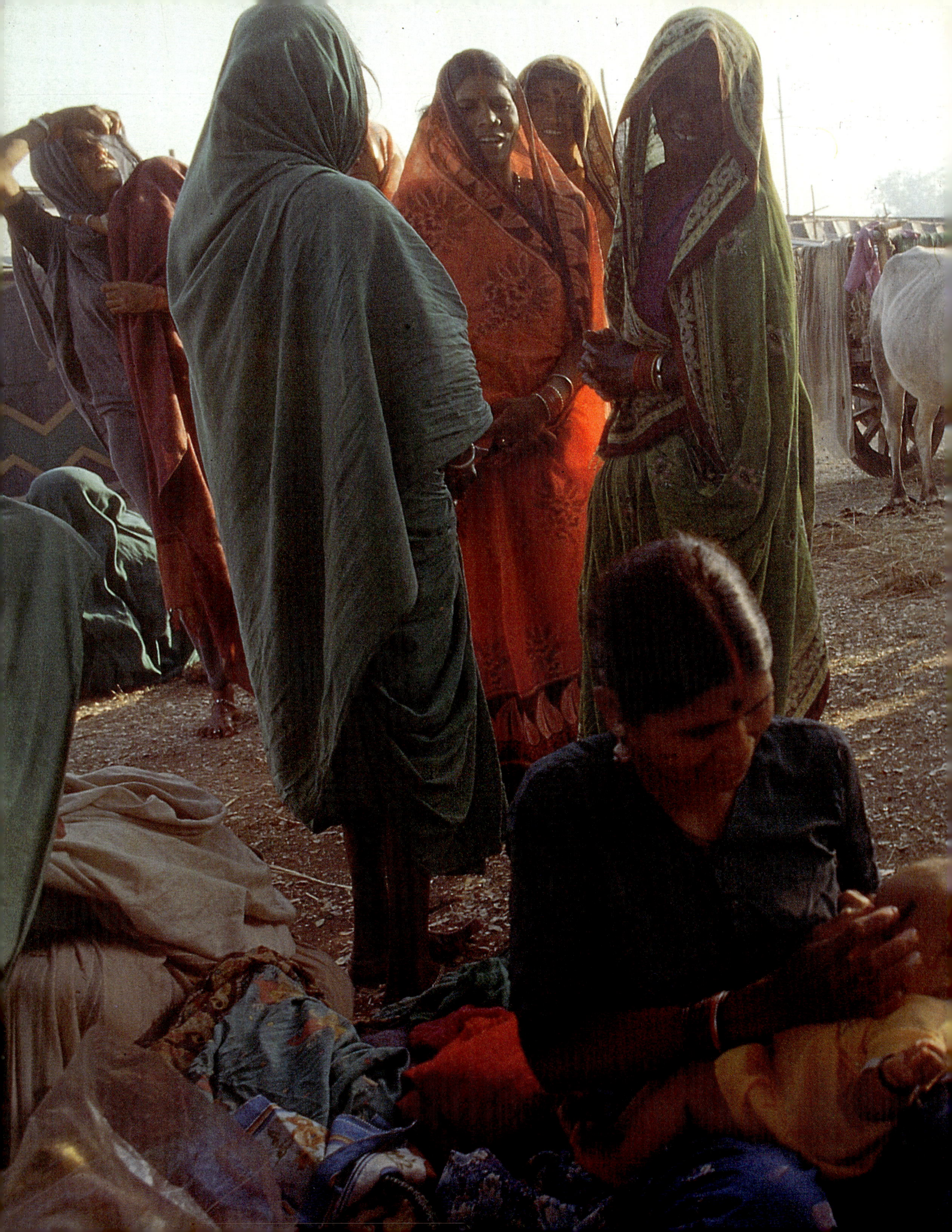

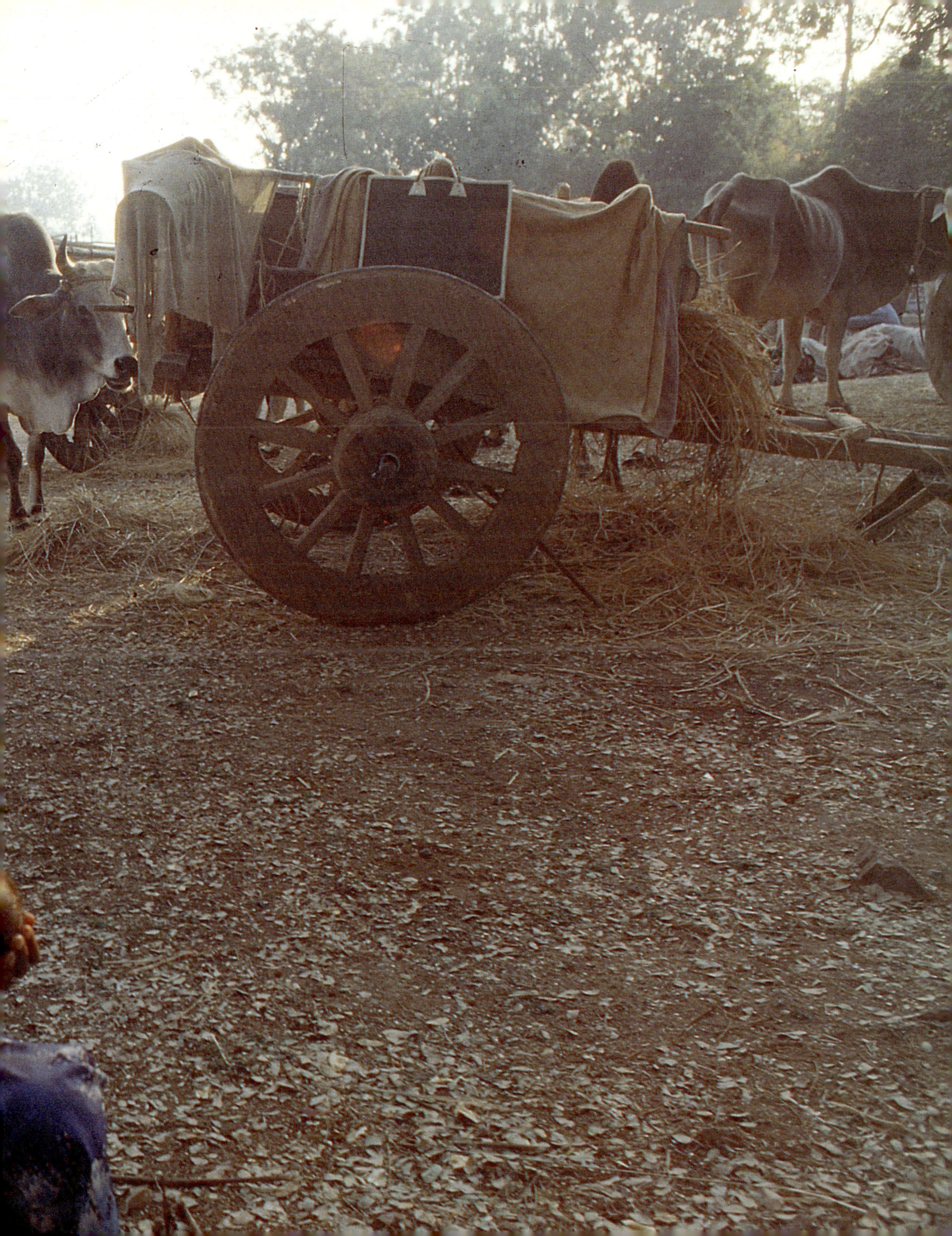

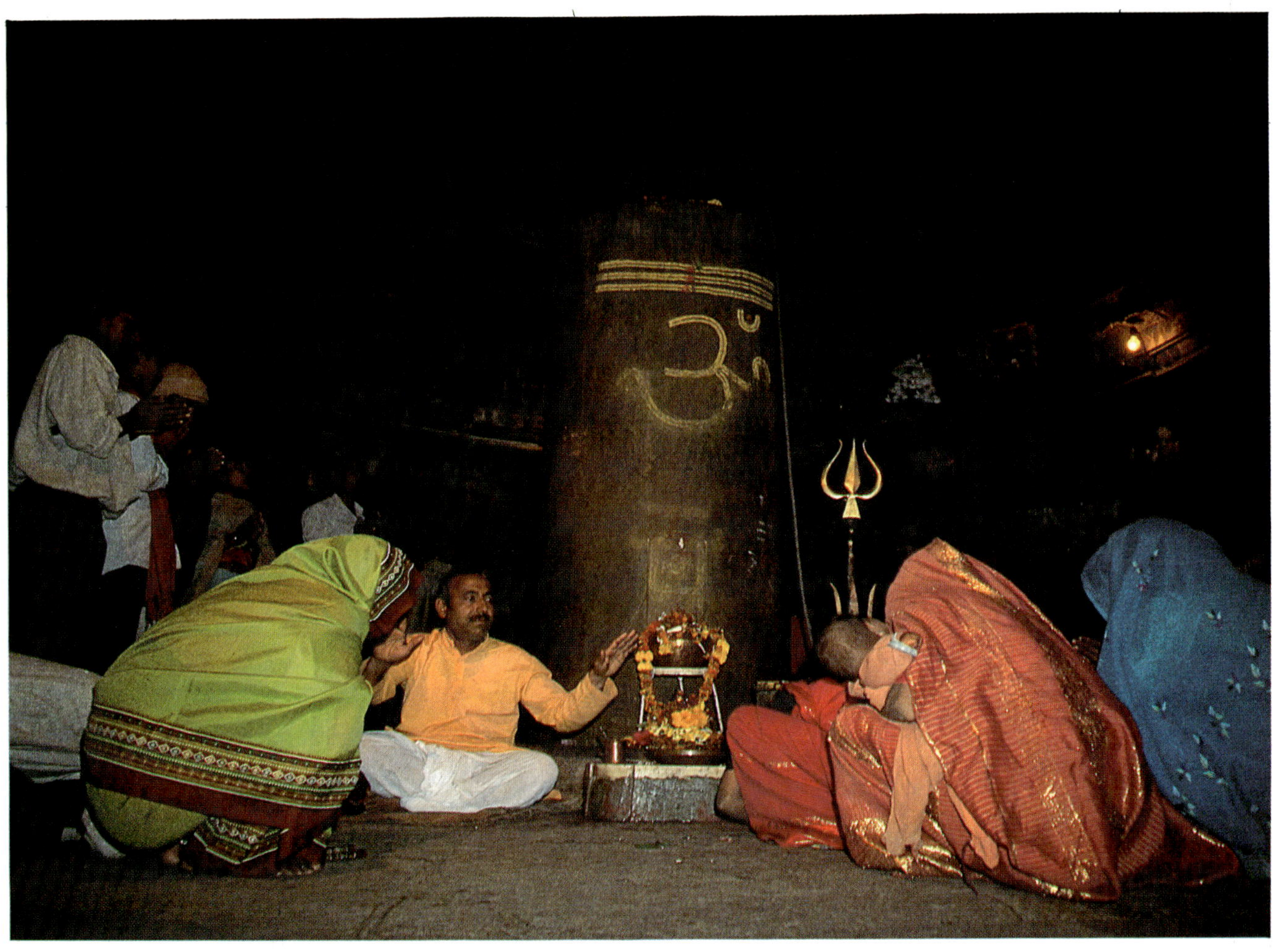

The priest of Matangeshwar Temple blesses the devotees. *Page 23* : The rooftop of a fort (Rajgarh Palace) which once enjoyed the royal glory, now left under the supervision of an old Chaukidar (watchman).

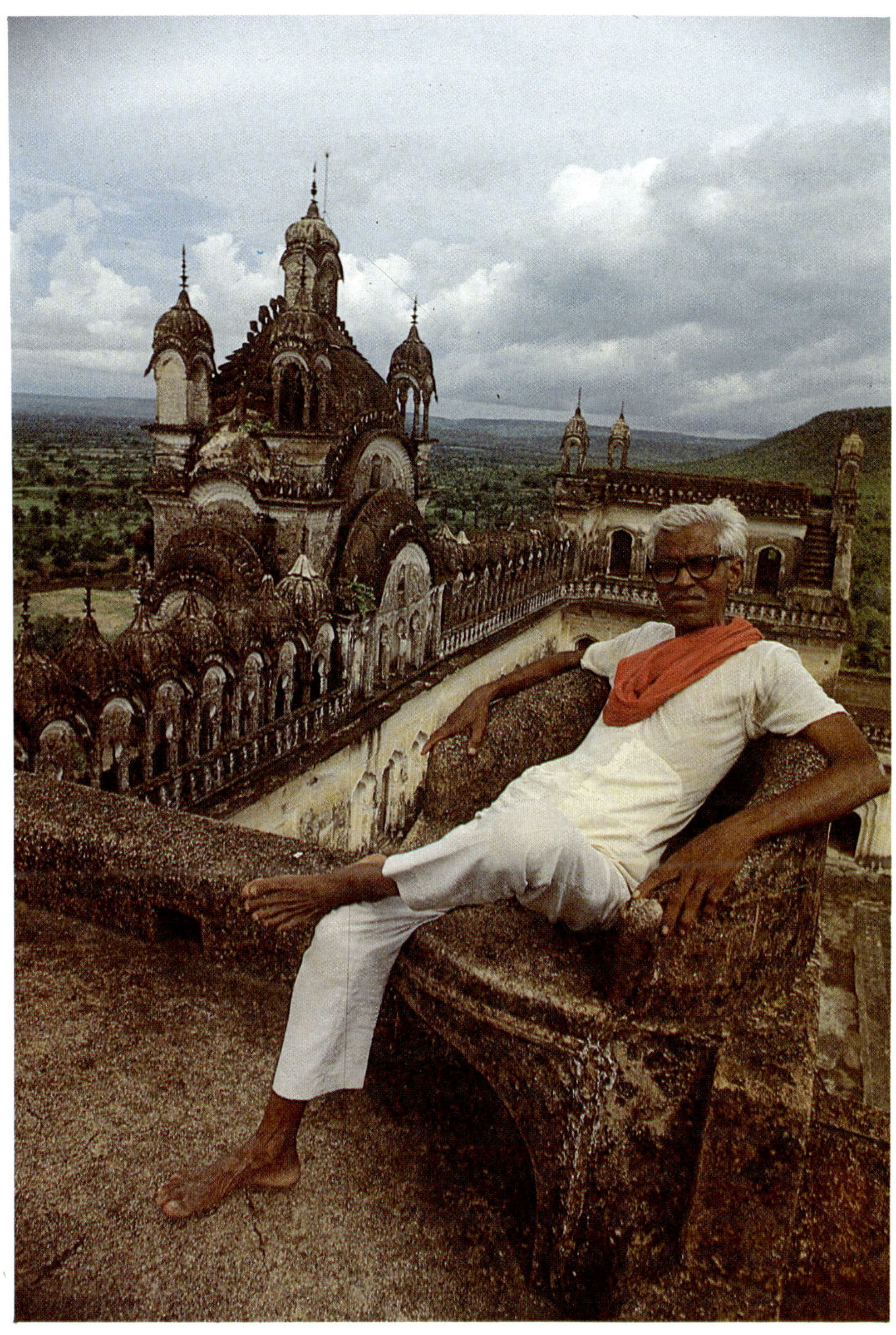

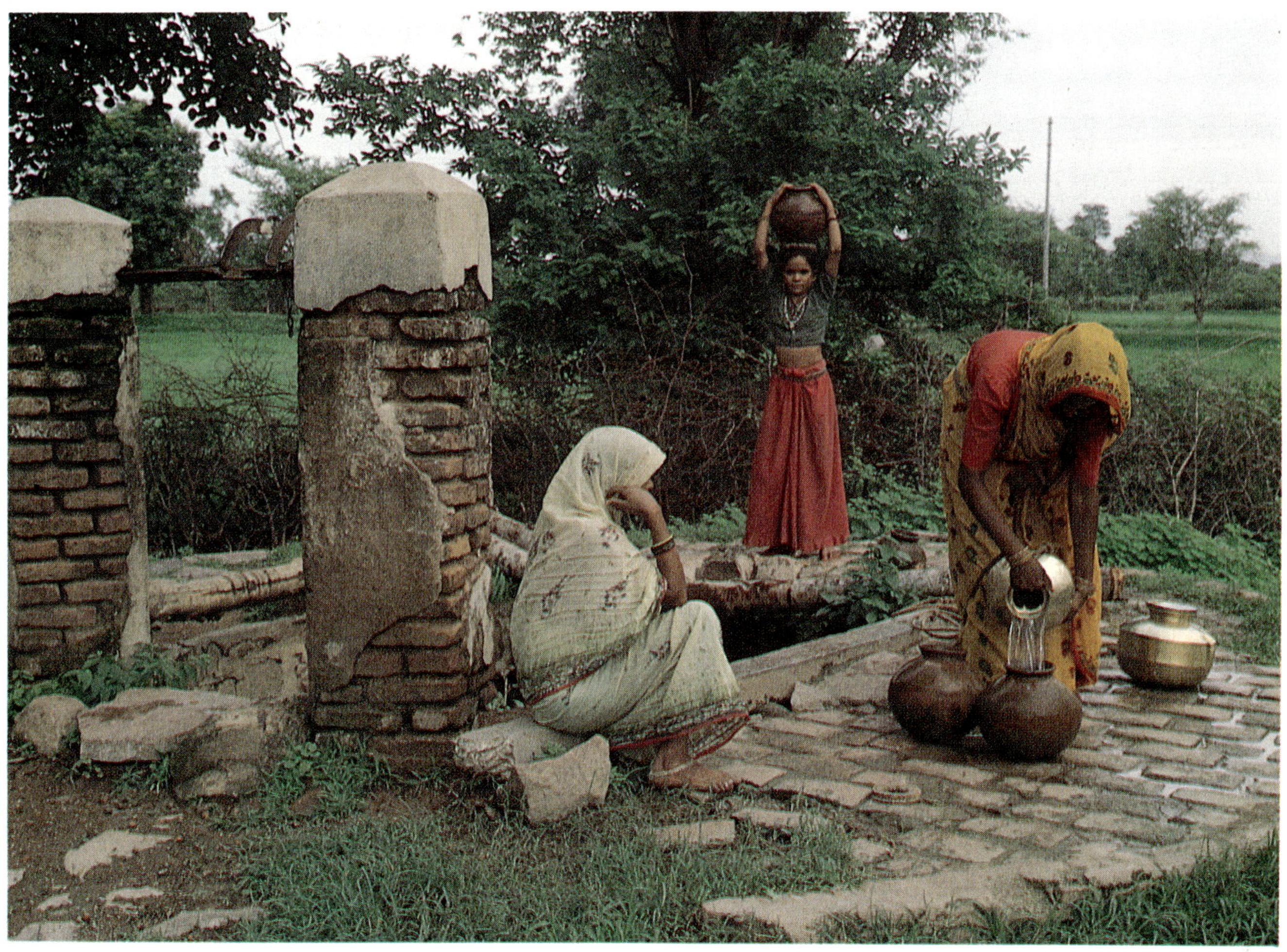

The hubub of modern world cannot disturb daily life of the villagers at Khajuraho. *Facing page* : The Raneh falls, some 19 kilometers east of Khajuraho, is a centre of attraction specially during monsoon. The vibrant force of Ken River enchants and takes the spectator into a different world. The sandstone brought by the river was transformed to a piece of art by the sculptors of Khajuraho temples.

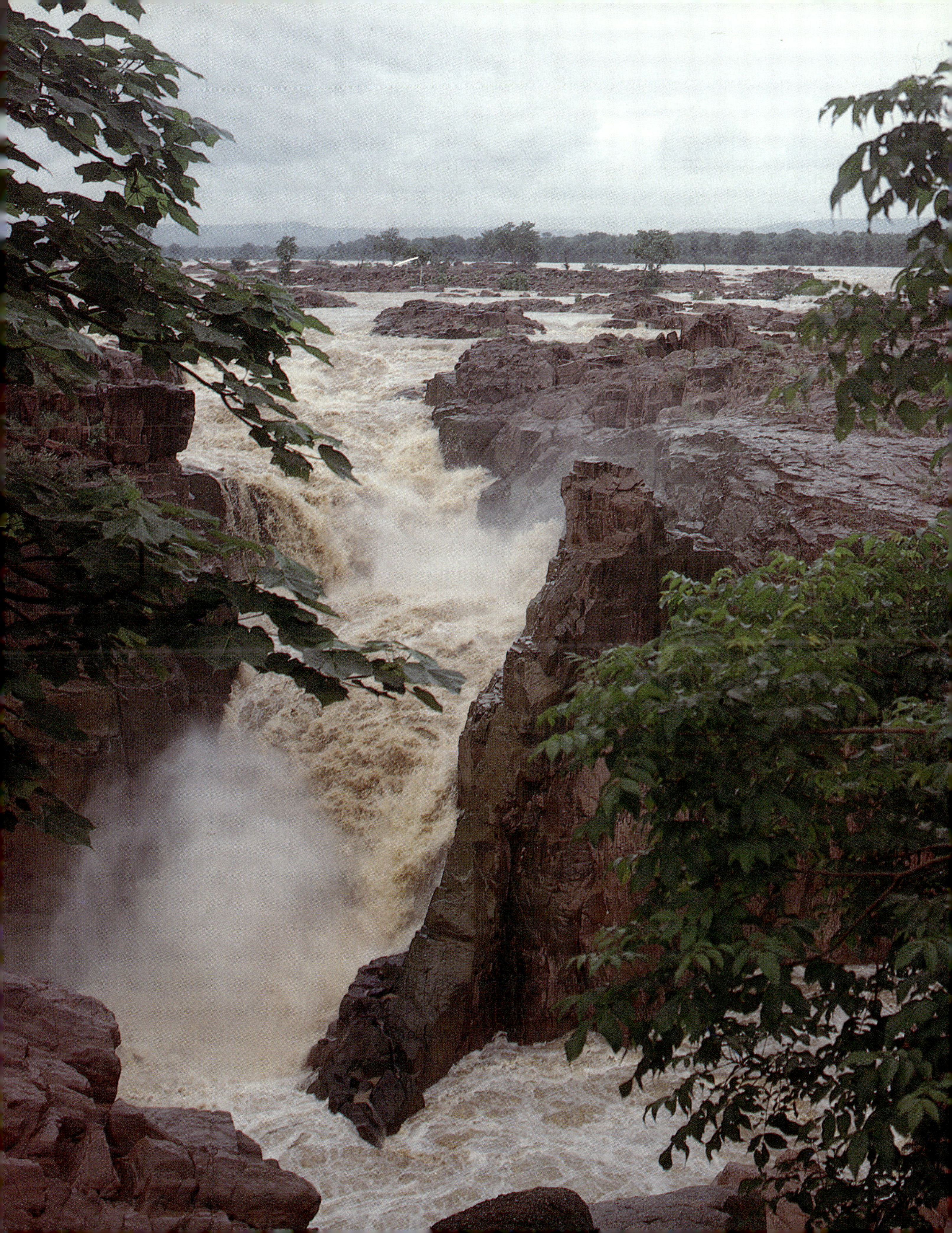

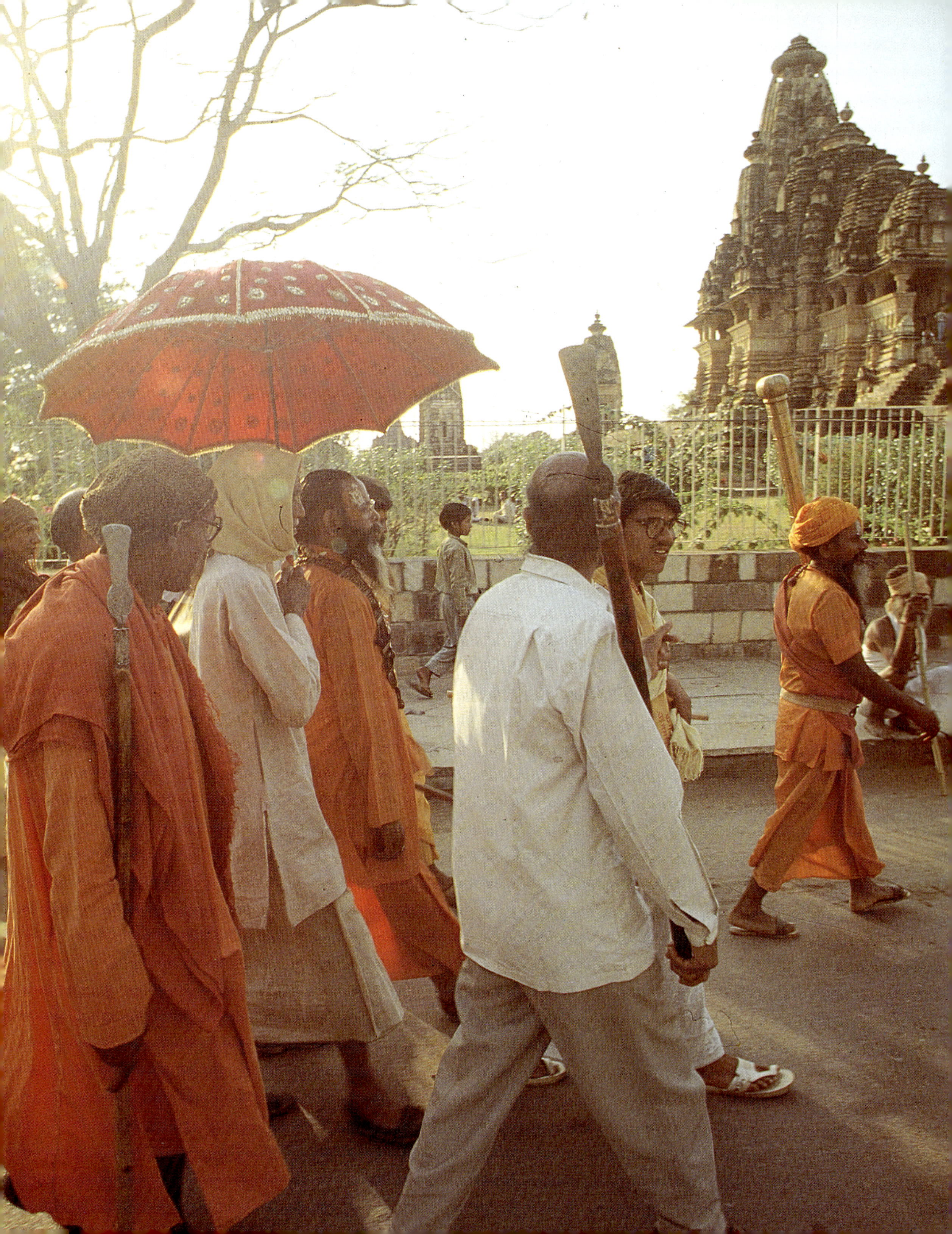

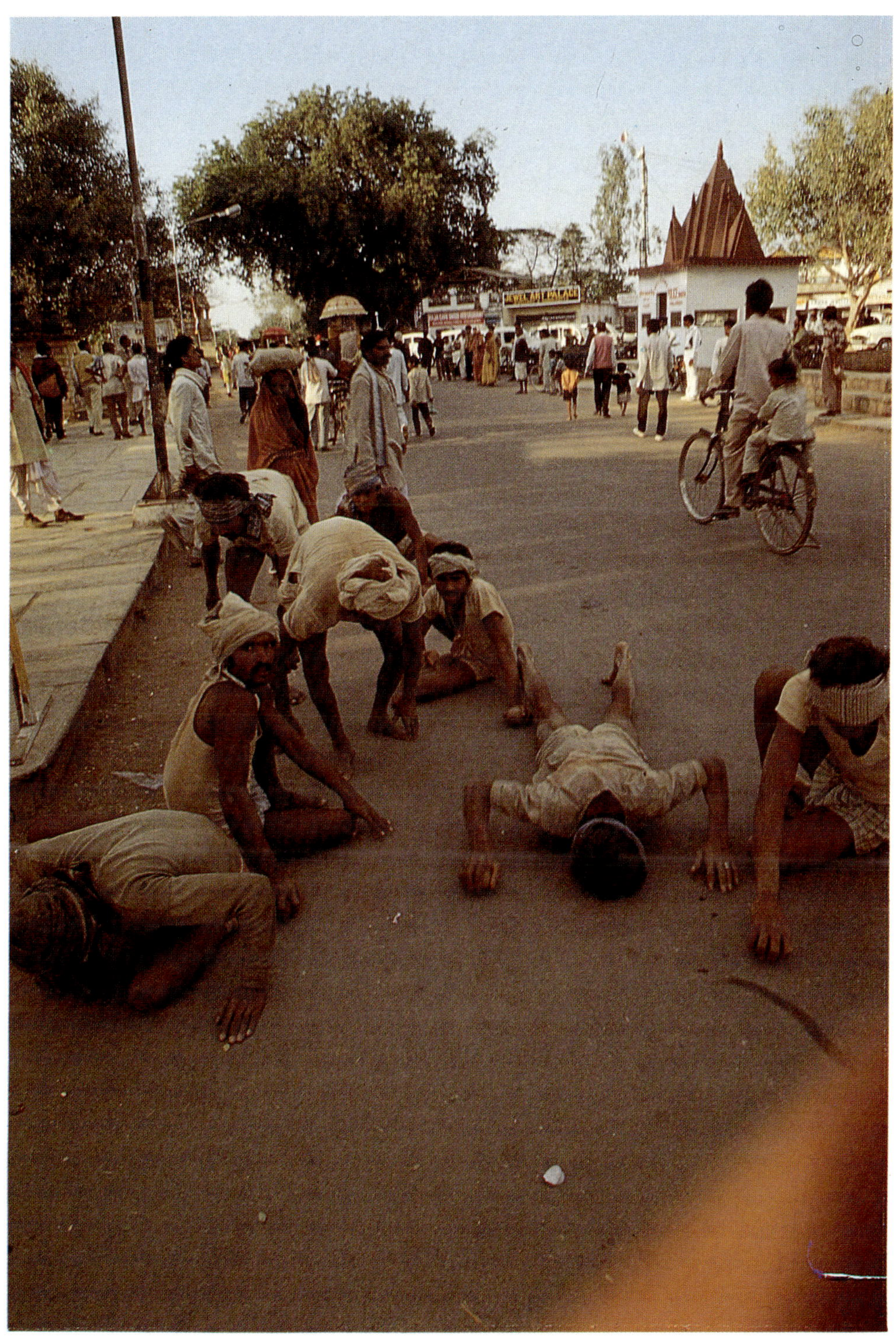

The holymen visit the temple on Shivaratri and other festivals in grand processions with all pomp and show. The common rural folk contend themselves with paying homage to the sadhus, sometimes by prostrating before them.

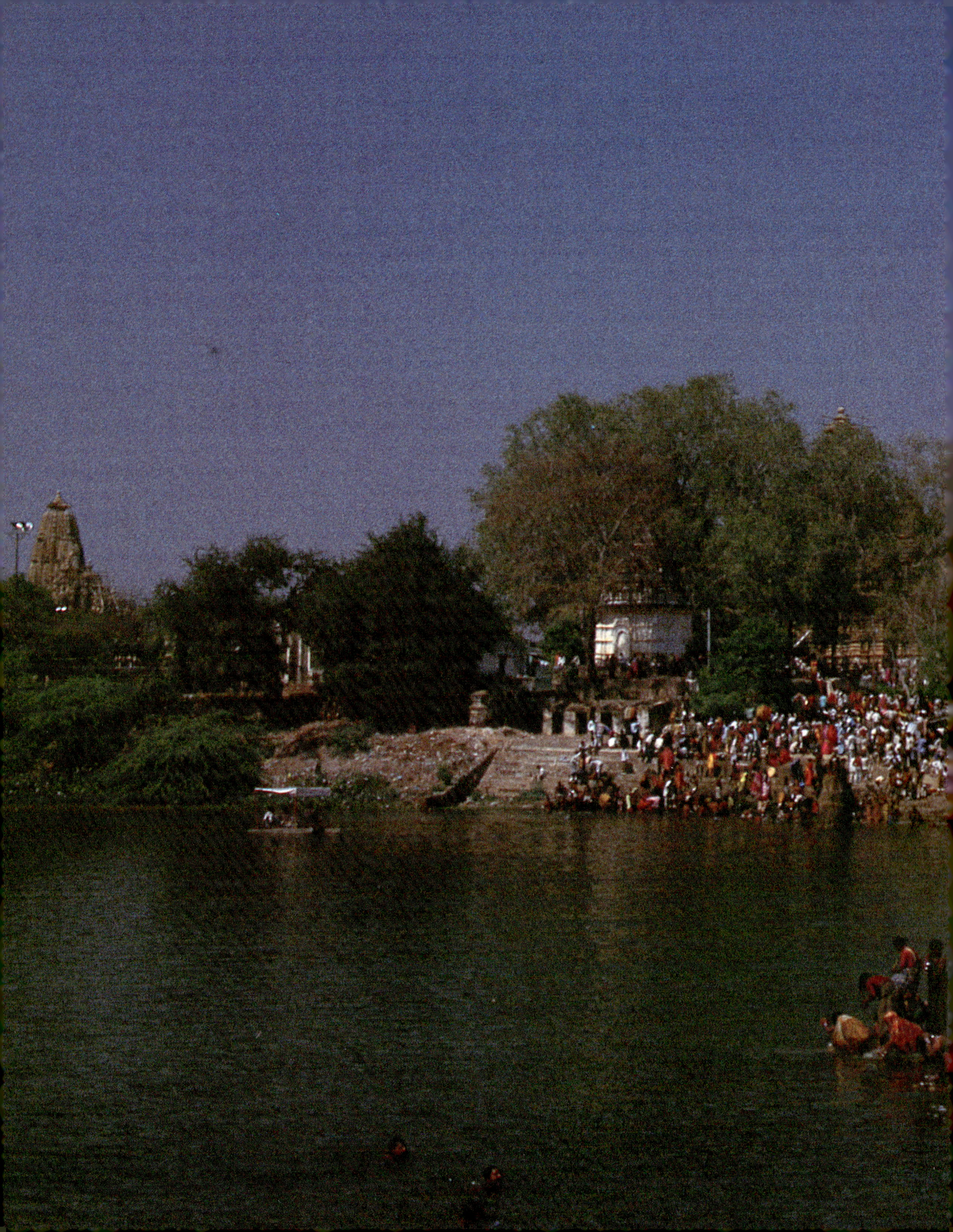

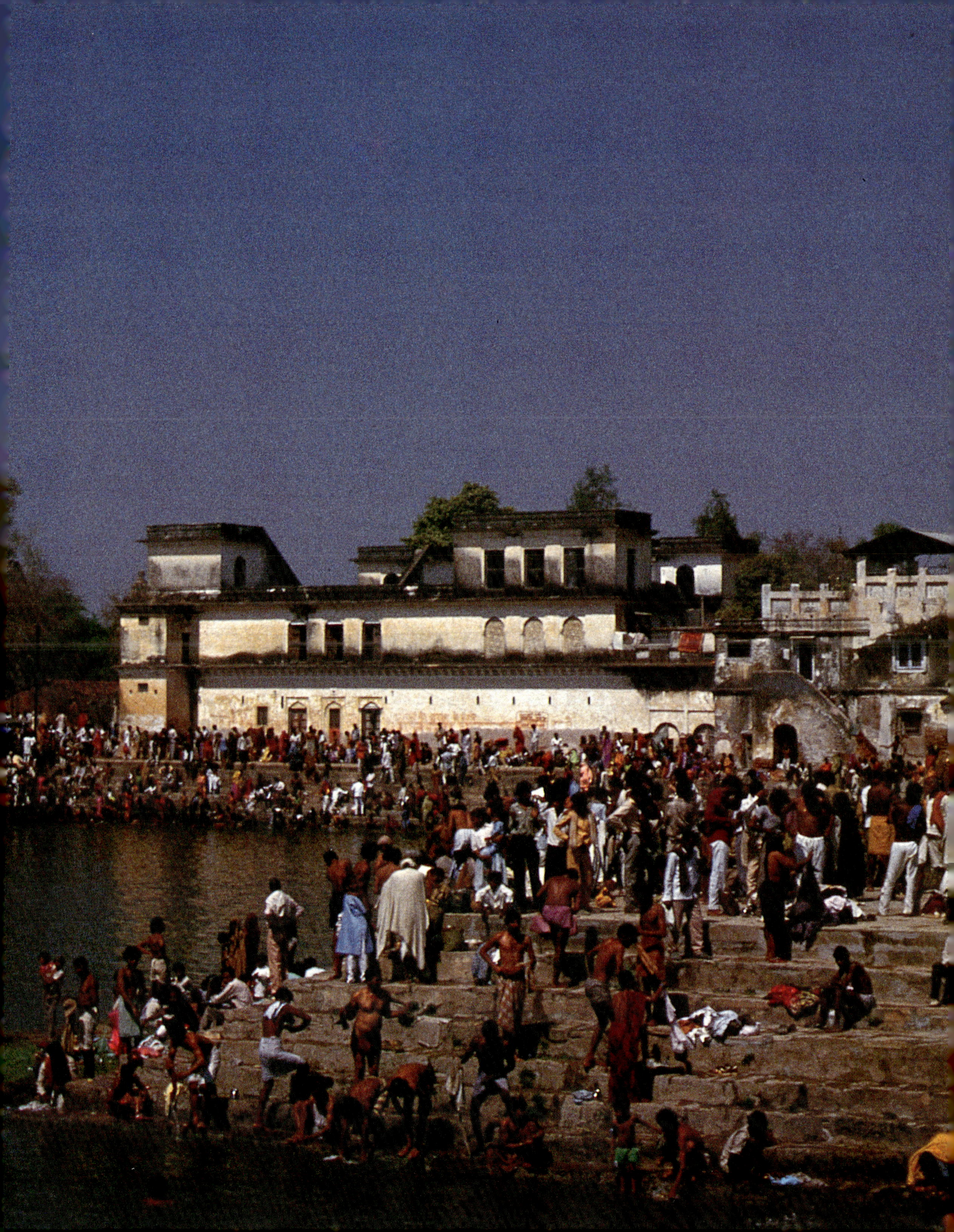

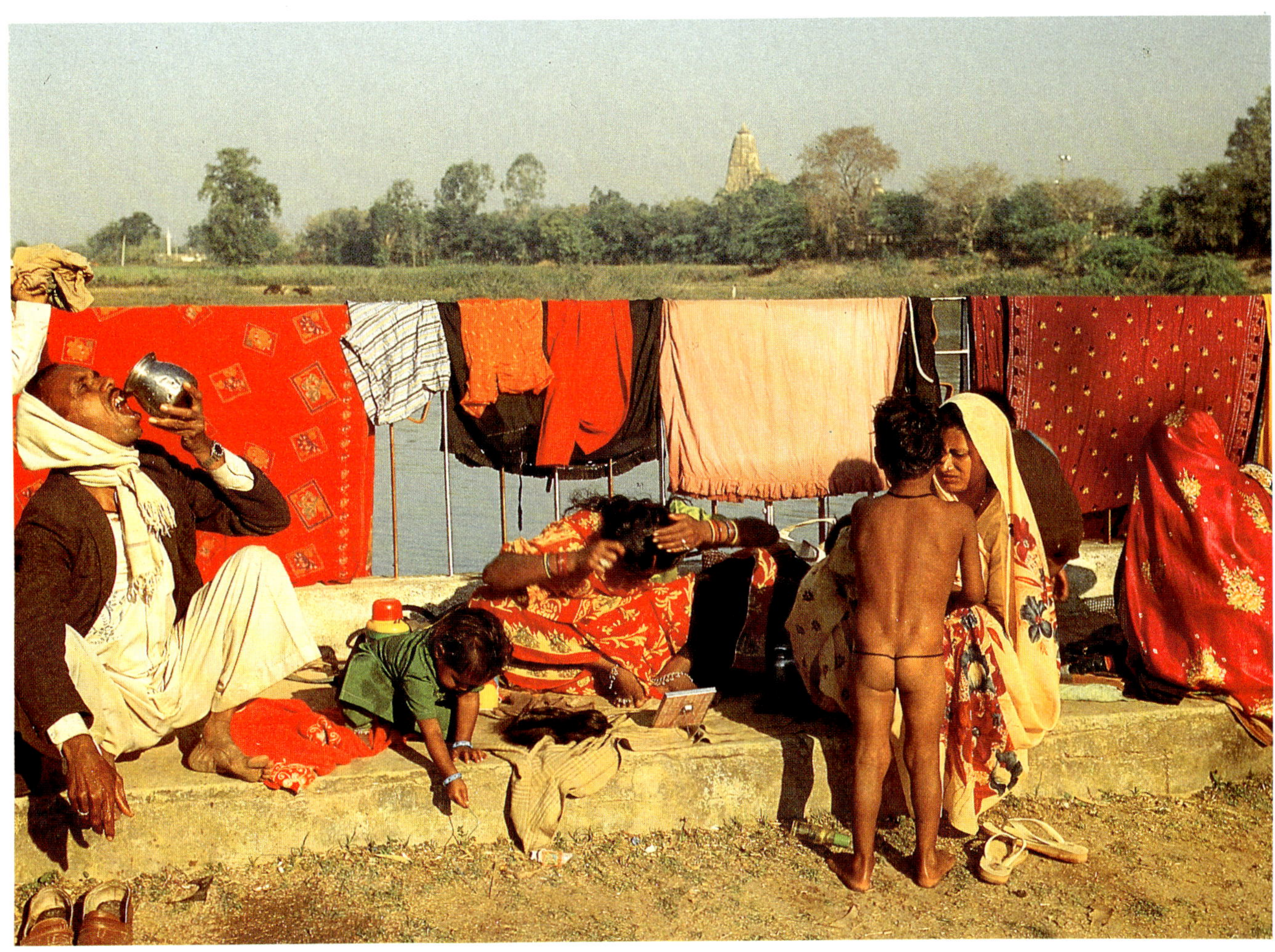

The Khajuraho lake crowded with rural folk who spread vista of colours and a unique rhythm. Shivaratri, the auspicious day for Shiva worship, attracts a large number of people to take a holy dip in the lake to wash away their sins and recharge themselves to face the ups and downs of their daily life. After completing the ritual of bathing in Shivsagar lake and worshipping Matangeshwar Mahadev they take rest at the banks of the lake. Having spread their wet clothes they dressup for the Shivaratri Mela.

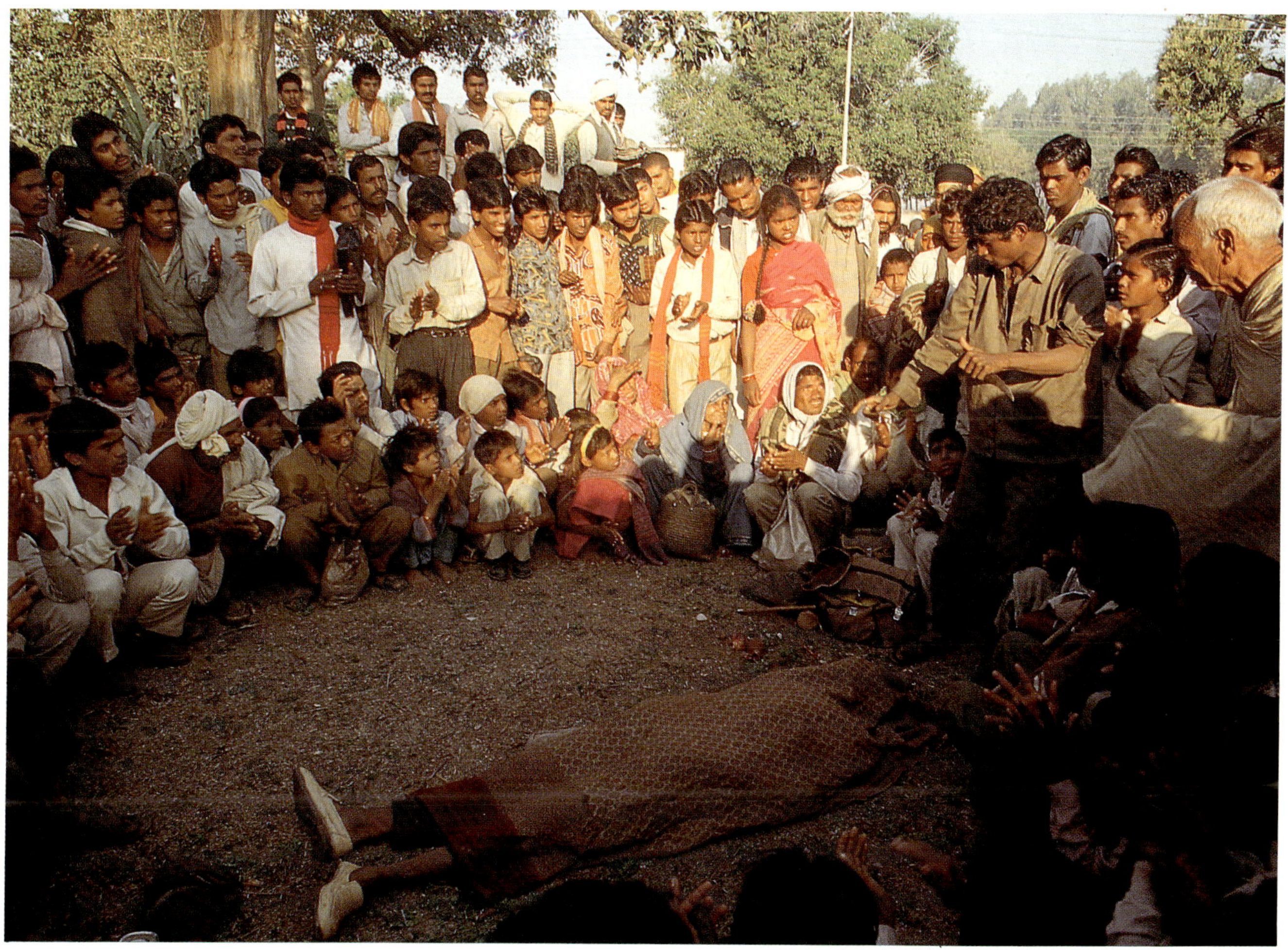

Though a large number of souvenir shops, restaurants and hotels have come up around the temples, plenty of open space is still left for the rural folk to enjoy their traditional 'Melas'. The villagers love to witness acrobatic shows and wrestling bouts and sing folk lores in praise of the great Bundelkhand warriors.

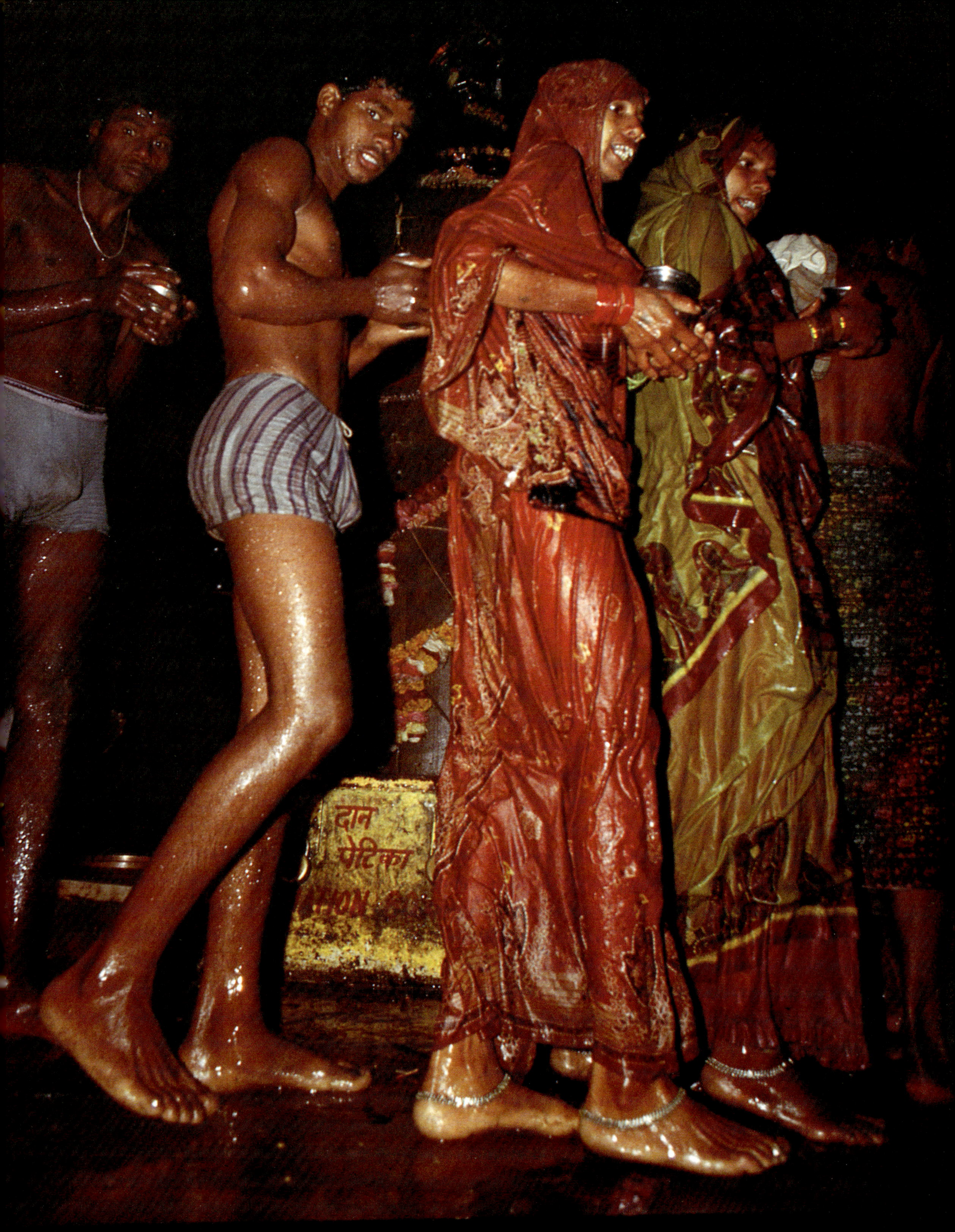
दान
पेटिका

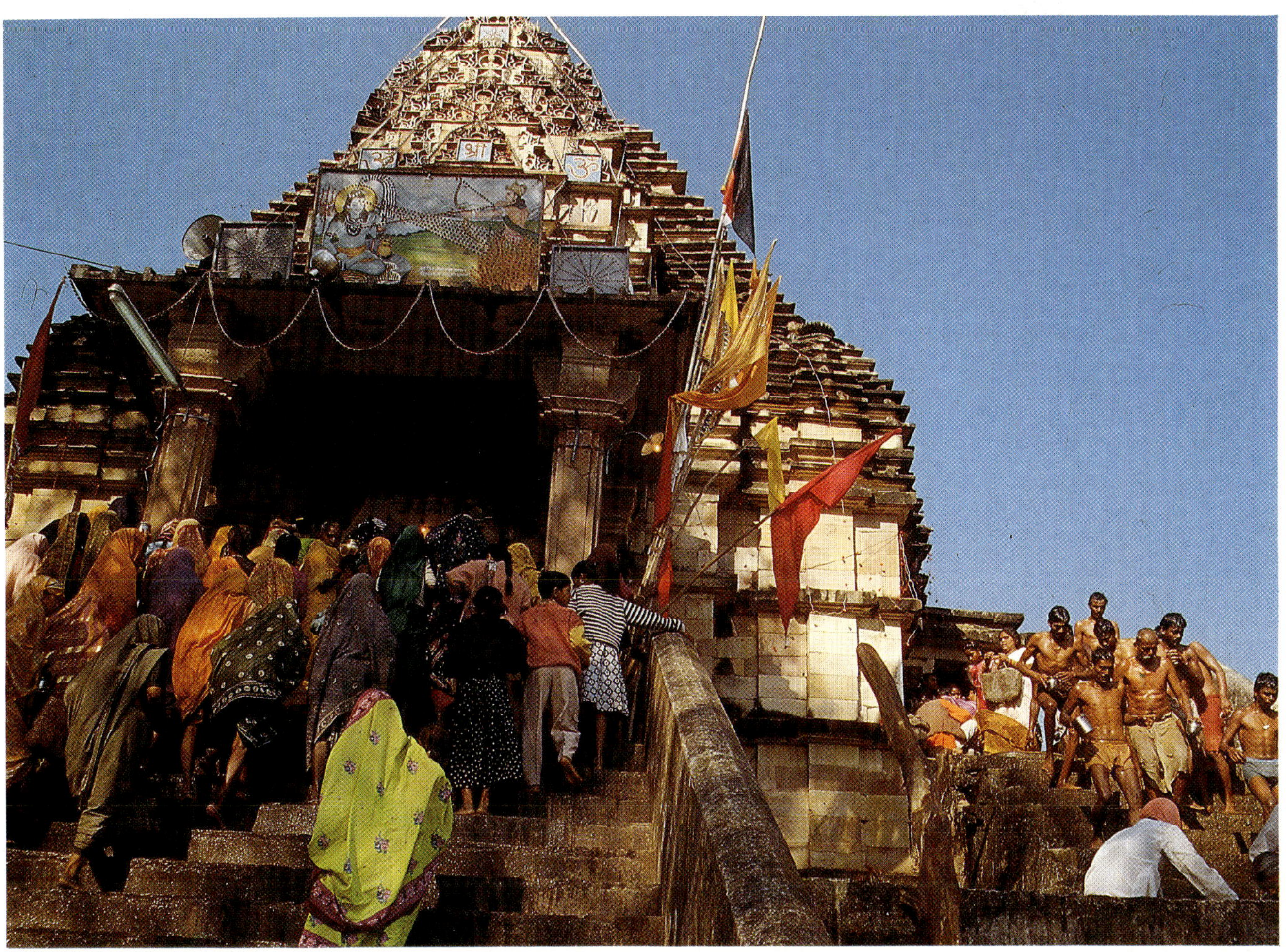

Shivaratri (the night of Shiva) is both a festival and a time to keep a vow. Celebrations held in February/March every year have their own significance at Matangeshwar temple. The devotees spend the whole night at the temple, on the banks of Shivasagar Lake and the sprawling open space near the western group of Khajuraho temples. Here the Shiva's marriage is celebrated on the auspicious night. Shiva's union with Parvati is regarded as the fountain head of cosmic energy. Lord's marriage procession passes through the village and ultimately reaches the Matangeshwar temple where the wedding rituals are performed as per almost thousand years old living traditions. When a devotee approaches the steep stairway and enters the sanctum, he sees a cross-shaped room entirely dominated by a huge (8.5 feet high and 3.5 feet wide) *lingam* rising out of an enormous stone pedestal about 20 feet in diameter. The devotee has to move in a clockwise direction around the pedestal (Yoni) and climb the stairs to reach the top where sits the priest. Lingam is washed with the holy water, milk, curd, honey and ghee, and flower petals are poured over it. The rituals with chanting mantras fill the arena with a divine bliss. Many devotees abstain from food, ending the fast with a meal of dates, fruits, nuts, sweet potatoes and milk. Charged with emotions, the devouts offer holywater brought from Shivsagar lake to Shiva lingam, and get wet by the splash of water spread all over inside the sanctum. Unlike other temples, Shiva *lingam* is accessible even to a common man who offers flowers, belva leaves and water, and hug and touch it with endearing affection, as if to partake the power of Shiva.

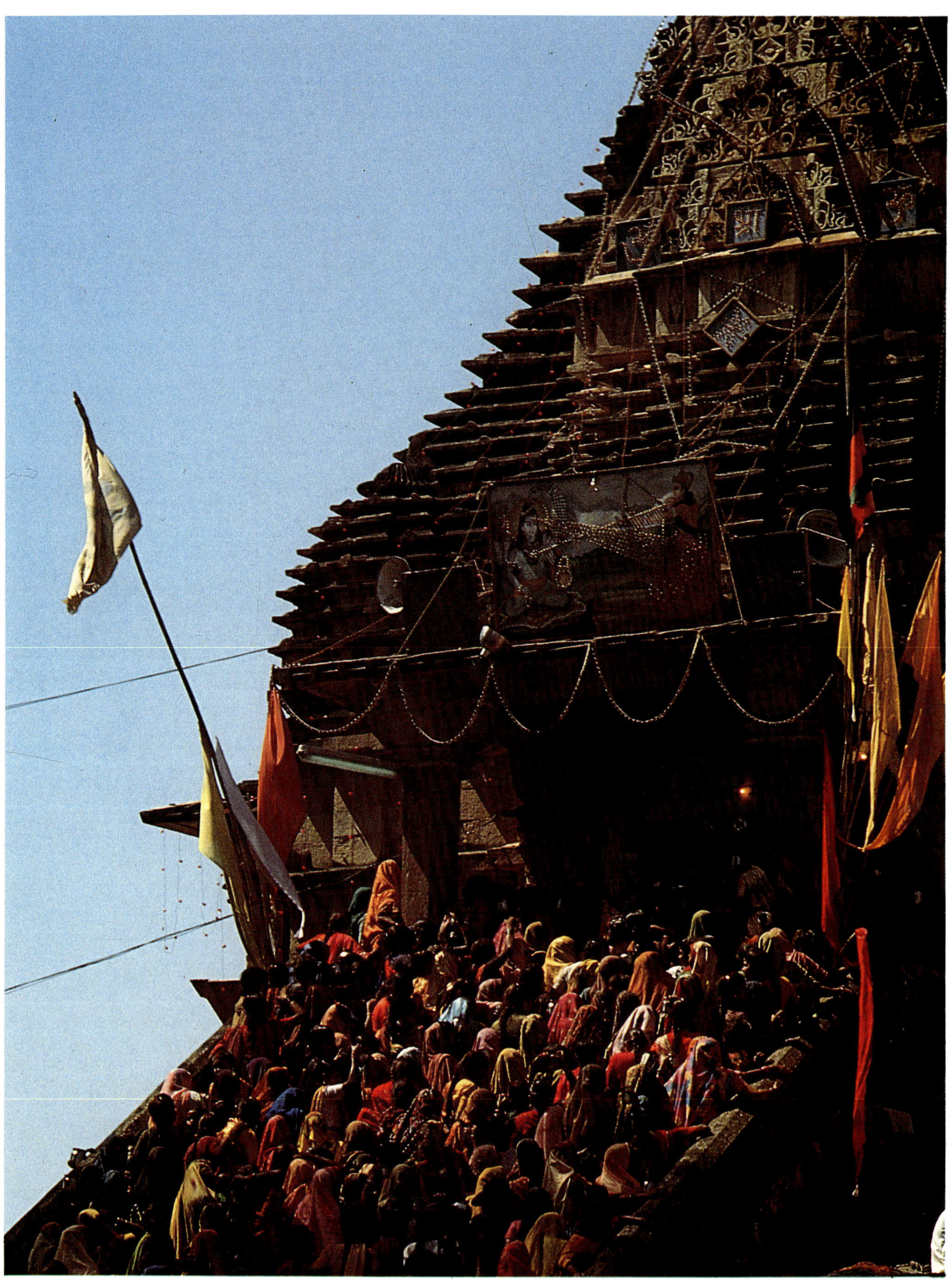

T E M P L E S

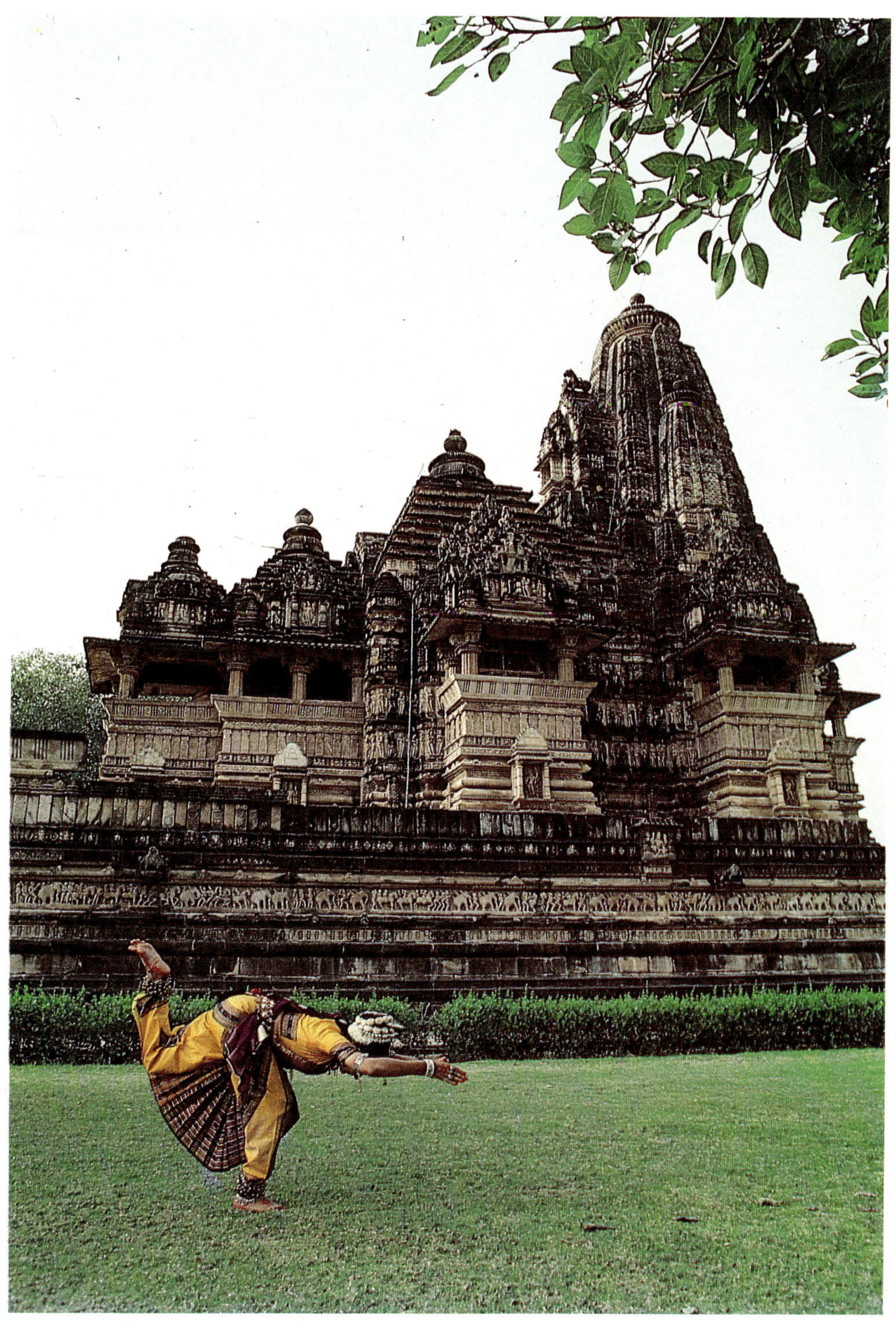

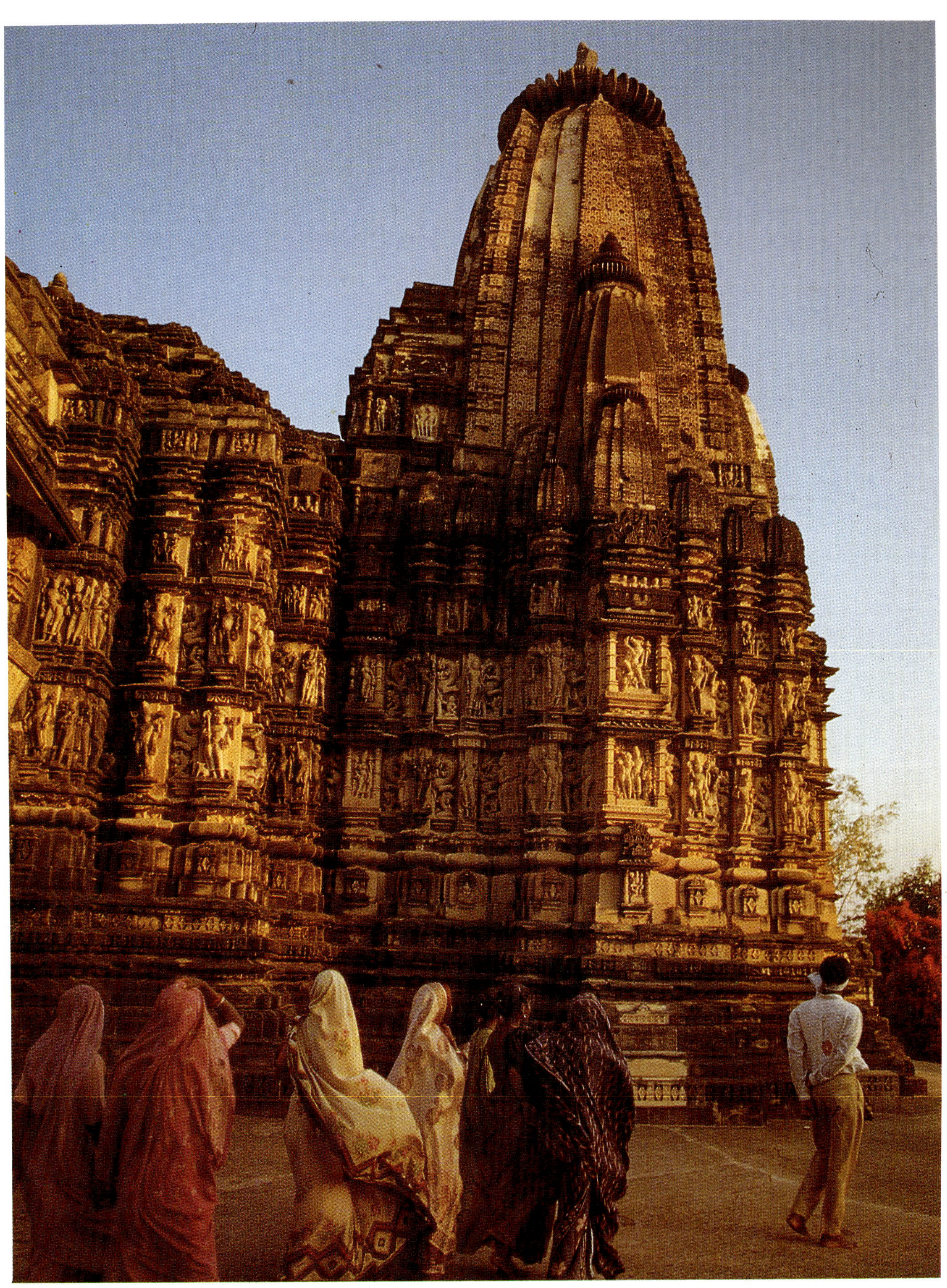

T E M P L E S

The Khajuraho Temples are known for their elegance, graceful contours and rich sculptural treatment. They represent the zenith of Indian architecture. Historians believe that eighty-five temples once existed. Only twenty-five have survived the ravages of time, and stand testament to the glory and splendour of the place.

Temples, the holy home of worship, mirror significant socio-philosophical attitudes of the age. With the presumption that a person's lifespan is a century, Hindu philosophy divides it into four stages — 'Ashramas' of twenty-five years each — *Dharma, Artha, Kama* and *Moksha*. 'Dharma' stage referes to Brahmacharya or Celibacy when the student receives instruction about scriptures, learns self control and prepares himself for shouldering responsibilities of life. 'Artha' stage of life is the period to earn and to enjoy the delights of material wealth, while 'Kama' stage indicates the period of life to enjoy sensual pleasures. The three stages were considered essential by the sages for detachment from all desires and ultimately achieve 'Moksha' (liberation) or, God-realization. Hindu Temples' plan match the ultimate goal of Hindu philosophy — the gradual ascent to self-fulfilment where there is no room for reluctance or regret.

Mayamata, one of the architectural treatises, describes the religious norms governing the foundation and organization of a town plan and building a temple in it. The choice and consecration of the site was ascertained as per sacred norms. The ritually prepared site had ponds, streets, houses, trees and all requisites related to the divinity which presided over the temple. Khajuraho temples had numerous lakes, ponds and pools around it making the arena picturesque. The aroma of flowers blossomed and the breeze passing through the groves must have inspired the Chandela Kings to build 85 or more temples in their capital city. The artists, craftsmen, architects, sculptors, brahmins thronged the rich territory of Chandelas. The reputation of the ancient Jejakabhukti (Khajuraho) attracted saints and sages, tantriks (tantra-practitioners), Yogis (Yoga practitioners) as well as artist-priests like Shri Kana, Satana, Chitanka whose names found engraved on the stones and of numerous others embedded in the layers of unrevealed history. The migration process being a historical phenomena refers to the human psychology to fulfill the urge of creativity.

The erotic sculpture art attracts the foreigners as also the rural folk from Indian villages who do not find it easy to fathom the motive behind the incomparable sculptural art of the medieval India.

It is difficult to assign a very precise date to these masterpieces of art yet the recent studies reveal their period of construction between early ninth century and early twelth century. The temples of Khajuraho, with their contemporaries in Gujarat, Orissa and Rajasthan, have a sharply defined architectural character, akin to Nagara, the general northern Indian style. Khajuraho temples are built on high terraces which either isolate them or group them together. This style is in contrast with other temples in India which are usually enclosed by walls and built at ground level.

The blocks of beige and pinkish fine-grained sandstone from the quarries at the neighbouring place Panna, situated on the banks of the river Ken, was raw material for the sculptors. Once transported to the site the split blocks of rocks were trimmed to the desired shape and size. Most of them were sculpted before being hoisted onto the place with winches and wooden ramps, then secured without use of cement, resting on one another simply by their weight. The architects bound the sculpted stone pieces together with wrought-iron clamps. They made the Shikhars (Towers) hollow in order to reduce their weight, piling series of columned rooms on top of one another. These rooms were completely inaccessible having no religious use. To strengthen the Shikhars, a whole series of buttresses, rising in tiers one above the other on each side of the main Shikhar. The construction on the stable and rigid foundation of the elevated terraces, and the scientific approach of the traditional architects and sculptors enabled the Khajuraho temples to face and withstand the onslaught of time and the elements.

The interior plan of temples is quite remarkable as that of the exteriors. The structure of each Khajuraho temple is based on Shilp Shastra principles. A small 'garbha-griha', where the image of the deity is installed, is enfolded in darkness. Usually square in shape this has only a single entrance. No one except the brahmin priest appointed to perform daily rituals can enter. Its entrance gate has two columns or piers adorned with auspicious motifs like the anthropomorphic effigies of the Ganga and Yamuna rivers and their symbols, Makara (the sea monster) and the tortoise. This is the heart of the temple and the dome on spire is normally above 'garbha griha'. Circumbulance (in clockwise) after prayers is an important ritual. Hence a passage for circumbulation 'Pradakshinapatha' around 'garbha griha' is an essential part of temple structure. This passage is, therefore, lit by balconies with small windows.

Antarala (Vestibule) is a small passage which connects the 'garbha griha' to the 'Mandapa' or the pillared hall. The devotees gather in Mandapa for worship. The pillars normally have carvings of minor gods and goddesses, incidents related to the main deity and sometimes scenes from the epics.

The entrance porch Ardhamandapa, is allegorised as 'dharma', the Mandapa as 'Arth', the 'Antarala' as 'Kama' and 'Garbh-griha' symbolizes 'Moksha'. The divinity flows into the faithful when they touch the outer wall of 'garbha-griha' during the ritual circumbulation.

The interior plan of the temple is designed so that the devotee progresses from the full daylight (worldly attractions) of the *ardh-mandapa*, to the dimmer light of the *mandapa* and *mahamandapa*, and *antarala* (which contains most of the erotic sculptures) to the partially lighted *pradikshna path* (Corridor for circumbulance), before finally getting a glimpse of divine consecrated in the dimmer light of 'grabha-griha'. Thus the devotee penetrates gradually to the heart of the divine mystry.

The 'Shikhars' have one or two or three inverted lotus blossoms and a 'Kalash' vase placed in ascending order on the top of the temple exterior. These represent Mount Meru, in Indian cosmogony the world's axis, or Mount Kailasa in the temples dedicated to Shiva which symbolizes His celestial palace. The ascending arrangment of the Shikhars also has a hidden expression of Hindu philosophy of life -- the gradual ascent to self-fulfilment and ultimately achieve liberation 'Moksha'.

Khajuraho temples are not affiliated to any single sect. For example, Kandariya Mahadeo and Matangeshwar temples are dedicated to Shiva, while Lakshmana temple is dedicated to Vishnu, the Adinath and Parsvanath to Jain Tirthankaras. But all of them are almost similar in composition and architectural style. Fergusson and Kapila Vatsayan, the authorities on ancient Indian architecture, say these temples were built in an age of extreme toleration. The temples at Khajuraho may be divided in three broad groups, viz. Western, Eastern and Southern.

Reaching Khajuraho the visitor encounters first the **Western Group of Temples.** The Lakshmana, the Matangeshwar and the Varah temples form one complex. The Visvanatha and Nandi temples are quite near to this complex. While about 600 feet to their west, the trinity of Kandariya Mahadeo, Devi Jagadamba and Chitragupta temples share a common platform raised at about ten feet height from the ground. Apart from these, Chaunsath Yogini and Lalguan Mahadeo temples are the farthest ones of the group. Though they are not spectacular but claim historical and architectural significance.

The Eastern Group of Temples are situated in close proximity to the Khajuraho village. Three Brahmanical temples — Brahma, Varuna and

Javari are located near the Khajuraho Sagar, while three Jaina temples — Ghantai, Adinath and Parsvanath are situated farther south.

The Southern Group of Temples comprise the Duladeo and Chaturbhuja temples. The Duladeo temple is about one mile south of the village and south-west of the Jaina temples complex. The Chaturbhuja temple is a mile further south near the Khajuraho airport.

LAKSHMANA TEMPLE c.954 A.D. *pages. 35, 51, 69, 83, 85* : built by Yasovarman, is one of the best preserved Khajuraho temples. The quincuncial plan of the temple has the main shrine at the centre surrounded by four subsidiay shrines at the four corners of the same platform. A flight of steps leads to an high terrace facing east. The raised walls of the terrace is profusely ornamented showing erotic motifs, scenes of bestiality, huntings, battle and even scenes from daily life. These processional friezes must have been planned in a proper sequence. But in due course, during restoration of the Khajuraho temples, they seem to have been arranged, atleast some of them, as per convenience. The interior carvings are most elegant. Entrance porch has *makar-torana* (crocodile arch) flanked by gladiators. The ceiling, depiction of the *navagraha*, (Nine Planets), *panchagni* (five fires). In a frieze above the lintel, the image of gods and goddesses, the sculptural depiction of the mythological churning of the ocean are few examples of the exquisite carvings. The main shrine measures about 98 feet in length and 45 feet in width having a beautiful four-armed image of Vishnu, the main deity.

MATANGESHWAR TEMPLE c.900-925 A.D. *pages 9, 32-34, 45* : the only one amongst Khajuraho temples being used for worship. There are no figurative decorations on the exterior walls except in the niches on the cardinal sides. When a devotee approaches the steep stairway and enters the sanctum, he sees a cross-shaped room entirely dominated by a huge (3.8 feet diameter and 8.4 feet high) *lingum* rising out of an enormous circular stone pedestal about 22 feet in diameter. The devotee has to move in a clockwise direction around the pedestal (Yoni) and climb the stairs to reach the top where sits the priest.

VARAH TEMPLE c.900-925 A.D. *pages 58-59* : a simple oblong structure which enshrines a huge statue of the boar, an incarnation of Vishnu. Measuring 8.5 feet long and 5.6 feet high, the body of the sculpture has encarved 674 figures of the Hindu pantheon such as Brahma — the creator, Vishnu — the preserver, Shiva — both the creator and the destroyer, Saraswati — the goddess of learning, Ganga — the mother river, the navagraha — the nine planets, nagas (male snakes) and nagins (female snakes) etc. The image together with its pedestal is carved out of single piece of yellow sandstone with exquisite finish to a glory lustre. On the proper left of this image are two ornamental female feet of probably Bhudevi (the earth goddess) whose main figure would have chipped off alongwith the tusk of the boar. The image faces the south-east side of the Lakshmana temple. Its pyramidal roof having receding tiers, and supported by twelve pillars while entrance projection has another two pillars.

VISHVANATH TEMPLE *pages 54-55, 80-81* : dedicated to Shiva, the temple is on a raised platform. It was built in the form of Panchayatna complex and consecrated in A.D. 1002 during King Dhangai's period. Its platform has only two subsidiary shrines amongst the original four made on the four corners. Main shrine has *ardh-mandap, mandap, maha-mandap* with transepts, *antaral, garbha-griha* with *pradakshina path.* Its ceiling has carved design of many petalled flowers and hanging stamens. The inner wall is adorned with fine examples of erotic and other noteworthy sculptures viz. women playing flute, mother caressing child, women with fruit in one hand and parrot in the other and dancing celestial nymphs. One subsidiary shrine contains a four faced *lingam* and the other an image of goddess Durga.

NANDI TEMPLE *page 86* : a separate pavilion forming part of Vishvanath complex. One of the rare temples open to the west, its *mandapa* houses a colossal image of Shiva's vehicle, 'Nandi' the bull. Situated to the east of Vishvanath temple, Nandi faces to its entrance on the same platform. Its huge pyramid shaped roof is supported by a series of twelve pillars resting on a low wall. The symbol of bull has a link with the fertility cult of Indus Valley civilisation.

CHITRAGUPTA TEMPLE c. 1000 A.D., *page - 60* : dedicated to Surya (The Sun God) it has an impressive image of the deity in the sanctum. Surya riding his chariot with seven horses representing seven days of a week. The temple is an exception being without an ambulatory passage around the *garbha-griha.* The exterior walls are adorned with the images of nymphs, erotic couples, gods and goddesses.

DEVI JAGDAMBA TEMPLE *page 72-73* : dedicated to Parvati, the Consort of Shiva, shares the same platform on which the Kandariya Mahadev temple is built. Measuring about 73 feet by 42 feet, it has exterior wall adorned with remarkable images of gods and goddesses, erotic figures, some of the fine carvings of celestial nymphs whose faces depict expressions of utter bliss. However, the sanctum has a crude image of Parvati, also called Kali, as it is painted black. The prominence shown to Vishnu on the sanctum doorway indicates the temple being originally dedicated to Him.

KANDARIYA MAHADEO c. 1025 A.D. *pages 56-57, 61, 62-63, 72-73, 115:* one of the largest, architecturally most impresive amongst Khajuraho temples. Its magnificence, perfection of design and sculptural profusion claims it being the culmination of temple architecture in Central India. The word 'Kandariya' means a cave and 'Mahadeo' — one of the numerous names of Shiva. The Shikhars (Pinnacles) surge upwards, spire upon ornate spire look as the peaks of Mount Kailash, the abode of Shiva in the Himalaya. The temple is about 101 feet high, 101 feet long and 66 feet wide. Its lavish display of sculptures adds to the richness of its architectural design. Every inch of the available space of inner as well as exterior walls and pillars has been fully embellished and adorned. The exquisitely carved arch of the entrance gate, the figures of gods and goddesses, nagas and nagins, mythical animals, musicians, loving couples, intricate carvings on the ceilings are peerless. Stella Kramrich was compelled by the exquisite architectural beauty to write, 'Its surface vibrates at every moment of the day and the clear Indian nights with an ever responsive play of light and shade, a chiaroscuro of the widest range.'

CHAUNSATH YOGINI TEMPLE c. 900 A.D. *pages 114-115*: dedicated to Shakti, the monument is a unique open-air quadrangular structure, consisting of a courtyard, measuring 102 feet by 60 feet which was originally enclosed by sixty-four peripheral chapels, each dedicated to a Yogini or an allied deity, each representing different aspect of Shakti. Entire temple was built by local granite stones. Only three images surviving are, Mahishasurmardini, Maheshwari and Brahmani.

LALGUAN MAHADEO TEMPLE c. 900 A.D. : was dedicated to Shiva; however there is no image at present. In respect of plan this shrine is Pancharatha, having a pyramidal roof of stepped horizontal tiers.

BRAHMA TEMPLE : Dating to about AD 900, it was originally dedicated to Vishnu as evidenced by the image of Vishnu carved in the lintel of a sanctum doorway. However, there is a four-faced Shiv-lingam in the sanctum now. One of the earliest Khajuraho temples it has a simple structure comprising a porch and a sanctum.

VAMANA TEMPLE c. 1050-1075 A.D. *page 74* : dedicated to Vamana, the dwarf incarnation of Vishnu. Though it differs from the Khajuraho temple style for not having an ambulatory path, it is similar in having a raised platform. The Shikhar of the temple is of the curvilinear type. The carved images of the holy trinity — Brahma, Vishnu and Mahesh (Shiva) — with their consorts have been placed in the upper row of the main niches of the sanctum. A carved depiction of Buddha inside the sanctum mirrors intermingling of Hinduism and Buddhism and religious tolerance in the Chandela dynasty. The exterior walls of the temple have two rows of sculptures contrary to three in other temples. The celestial apsaras vaunting their voluptuous charms in different attitudes and displaying more provocative erotica are confined to subsidiary niches of roof pediments. The main diety's statue of four-armed Vamana is a unique sculpture amongst the Khajuraho art.

JAVARI TEMPLE c. 1075-1100 A.D. : dedicated to Vishnu, it has magnificent architectural design. A lofty terrace, having no ambulatory path it measures 39 feet by 21 feet. The sanctum is enshrined with four headed (Chaturbhuj) image of Vishnu. Its entrance porch flanked by exquisitely carved crocodiles and having exterior walls adorned with three bands of sculptures comprising graceful images.

GHANTAI TEMPLE (End of 10th Century A.D.) *page - 68* : one of the Jain temples situated a little far from the other ones in the village. Only a few pillers are adorned with bell and chain motifs, ornate ceiling with the carved doorway panel depicting sixteen dreams of Jina Mahavira's mother. Its hanging bell column has encarved floating celestial beings — Gandharvas, Kinnaras and Vidyadharas.

ADINATH TEMPLE 11th Century A.D. *page - 53* : dedicated to Jain Tirthankar Adinath has an image of the deity installed in place of the original one missing. Three bands of sculptural decorations depiciting celestial beauties nd deities. The topmost band is smaller than the lower two and carries figures of apsaras, attendants with garlands and musical instrumnts.

PARSVANATH TEMPLE c. 950-970 A.D. *page - 94* : The oblong shaped (68 feet by 35 feet) temple considered to be the best amongst the Jain temples of Khajuraho. Its architectural plan and design resembles that of a Hindu temple. Although the temple is affiliated to the Jain sect, the deities of the Hindu pantheon have been conspicuously protrayed. The sanctum has a statue of Parsvanath flanked by a nude male figure on the left and a nude female figure on the right. The presence of the figure of a bull on a pedestal reveals the original dedication to Adinath. Some of the masterpieces of Khajuraho sculptural art are beautifully displayed on the exterior wall panels, viz. an apsara writing a letter, another one extracting a thorn from her foot, yet another applying collyrium to her eyes, and the Hindu gods with their energy partners — the goddesses, ten armed Chakreshwari, Parasuram, Balram-Revati, Ram-Sita, depict astonishing delicacy and divine expressions.

DULADEO TEMPLE c. 1100-25 A.D. *page 75* : now dedicated to Shiva while considered to be originally dedicated to Kartikeya, commander of the divine army. According to a local legend the temple acquired its name from 'dulha' (bridegroom), to commemorate the death of a young man who died on way to his marriage. Although restored and renovated, the temple retains its original character, like other Khajuraho temples, the only exception being the absence of circumbulatory passage inside the sanctum. The exterior wall of the temple has been adorned with the celestial nymphs moulded with grace and elegance, rich ornamental carvings, musicians and dancers heralding the presence of the gods. An *Apsara* holding an intricate waist ornament on outer wall and seven mother goddesses in dancing postures at the entrance of sanctum are noteworthy. The sunset pours a golden glow on the sculptures symbolizing the golden era of the Chandela dynasty.

CHATURBHUJ TEMPLE c. 1100 A.D. *pages 64-65, 104-105* : also known as Jatkari, the temple has an remarkable 10.3 feet high monolithic statue of four-armed Vishnu having a crown and vivid ornamentation. West facing entrance and absence of erotic sculptures are the peculiarities of the temple. Though the images of nymphs appear to be lifeless, the sculptures of Narsingh (partly man and partly lion) and Ardha-narishwar (half male and half female) incarnations of Lord Vishnu and Shiva respectively are noteworthy. Facial expression of the main deity reveals Buddhist influence. Some scholars consider the deity as a rare manifestation of Shiva.

Khajuraho, the then religious capital of Chandela dynasty, as famous as Varanasi, now has twenty odd temples, moot observers of the ravage of time whose magnificent ornamentation recalls the fervour of the the art-loving valiant rulers who created them.

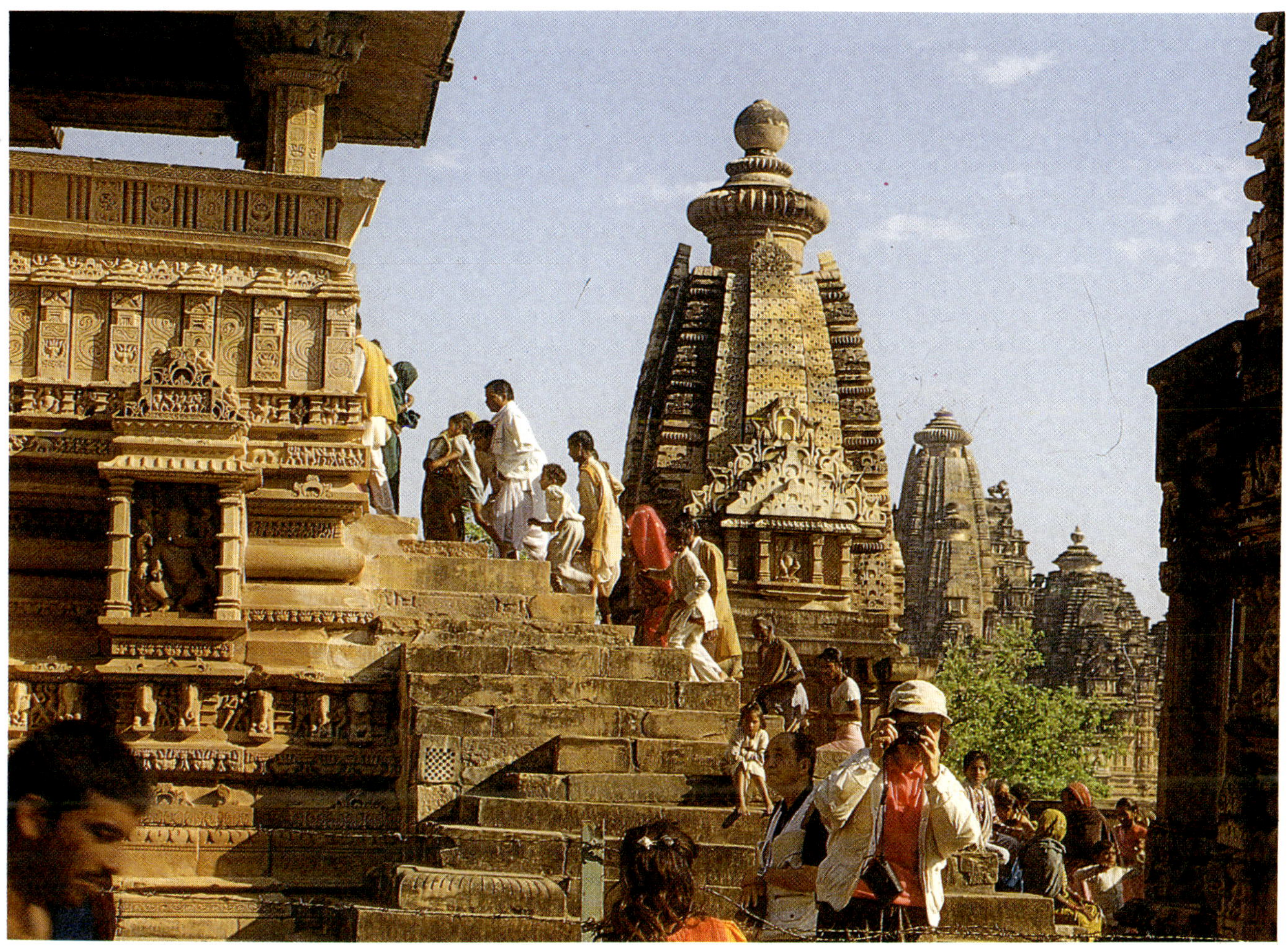

But for Matangeshwar Temple, none of the Khajuraho temples are now worshipped, yet the visitors especially the Hindu rural folk, never forget to pay homage to their ancestors and offer supplication with a belief that the divinity still prevails all over there. Do they come to worship or to fulfil their sensual desire or, just for curiosity, about their golden era, or for all intermingled reasons.

LAKSHMANA TEMPLE KHAJURAHO

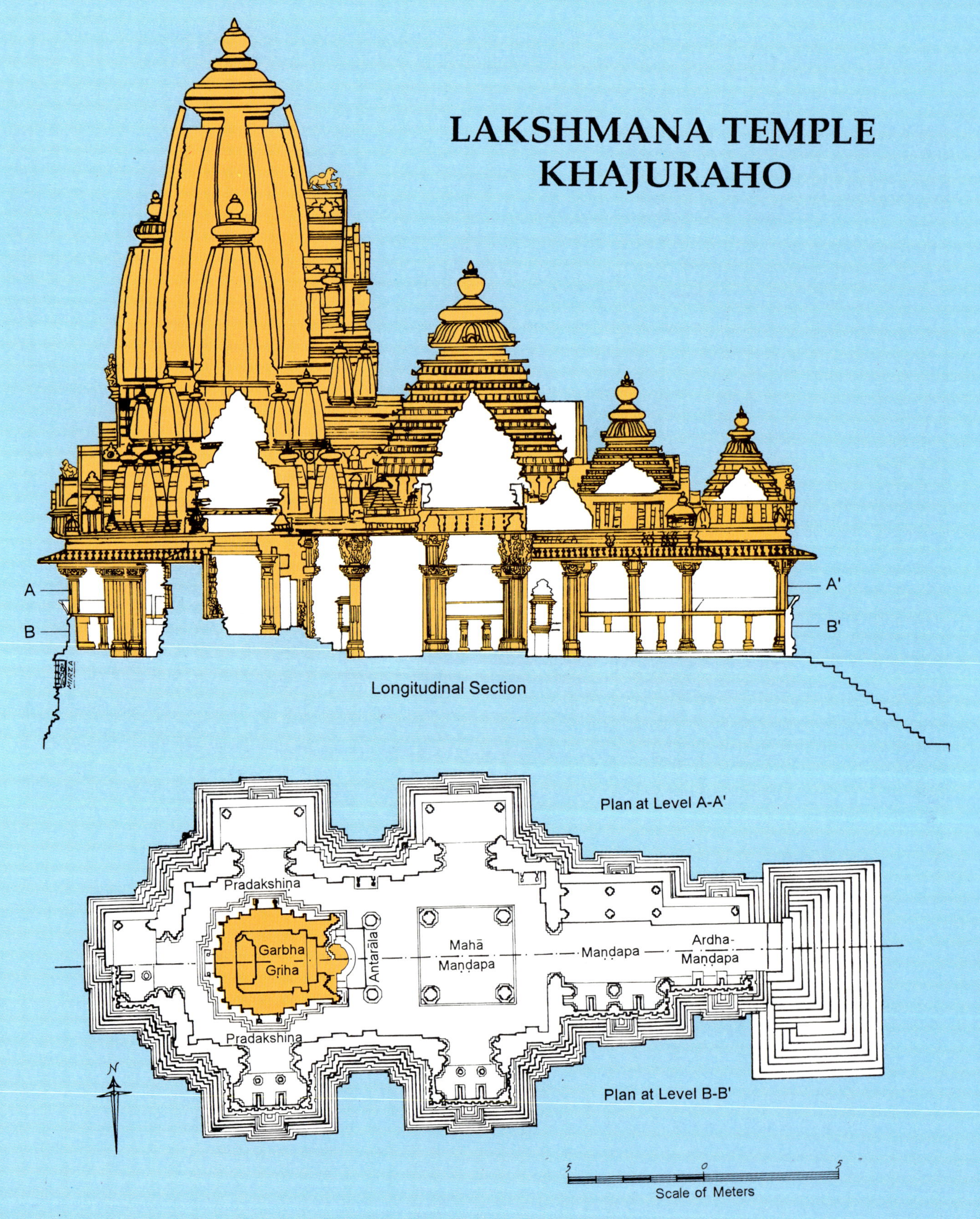

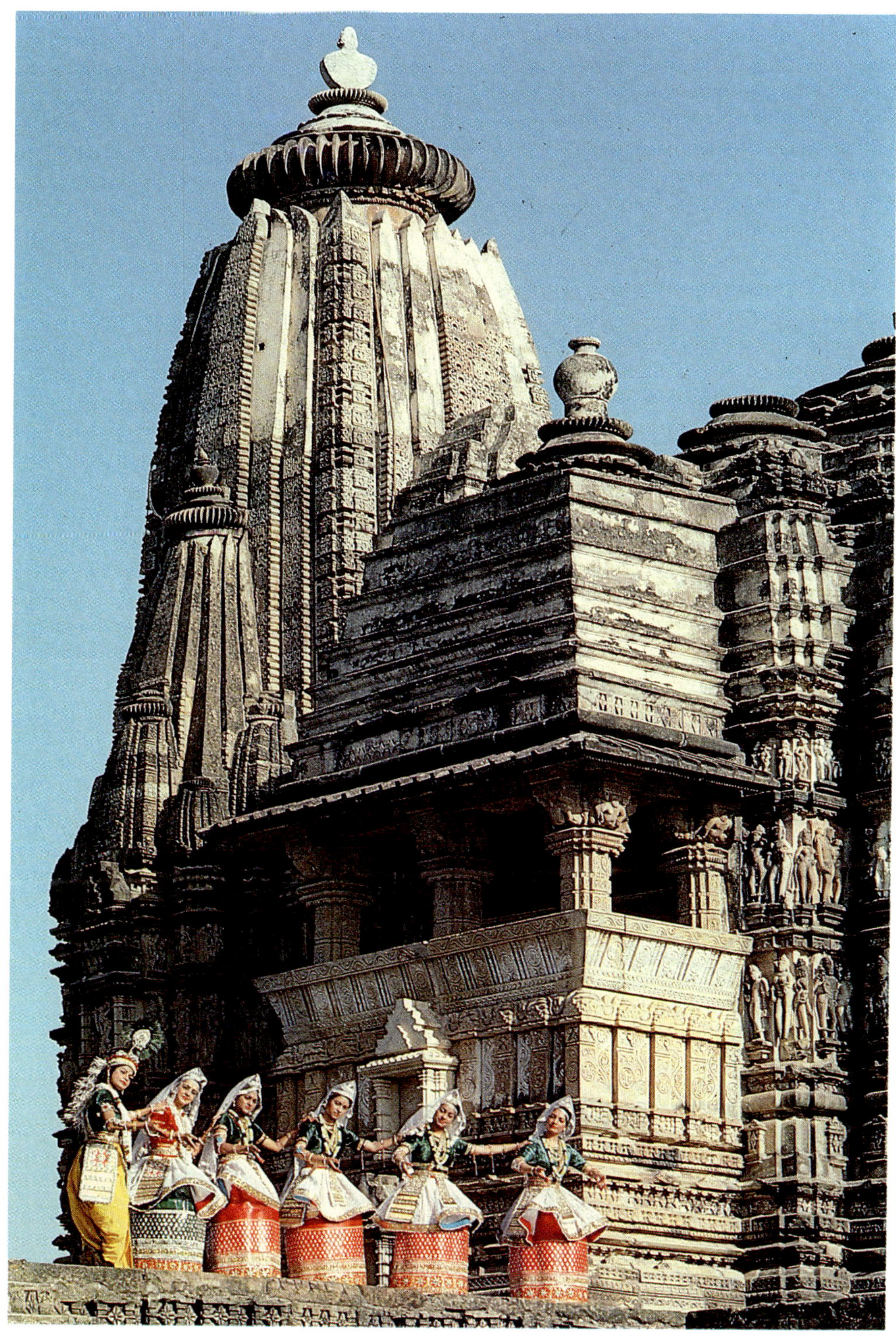

Jhaveri sisters and the desciples offer homage to the gods and goddesses. Odissi dance performance by the internationally renowned dancers merges with the celestial beauties adorned on the Jagdamba Temple walls. The unique rhythm created enchants the spectator with divine bliss.

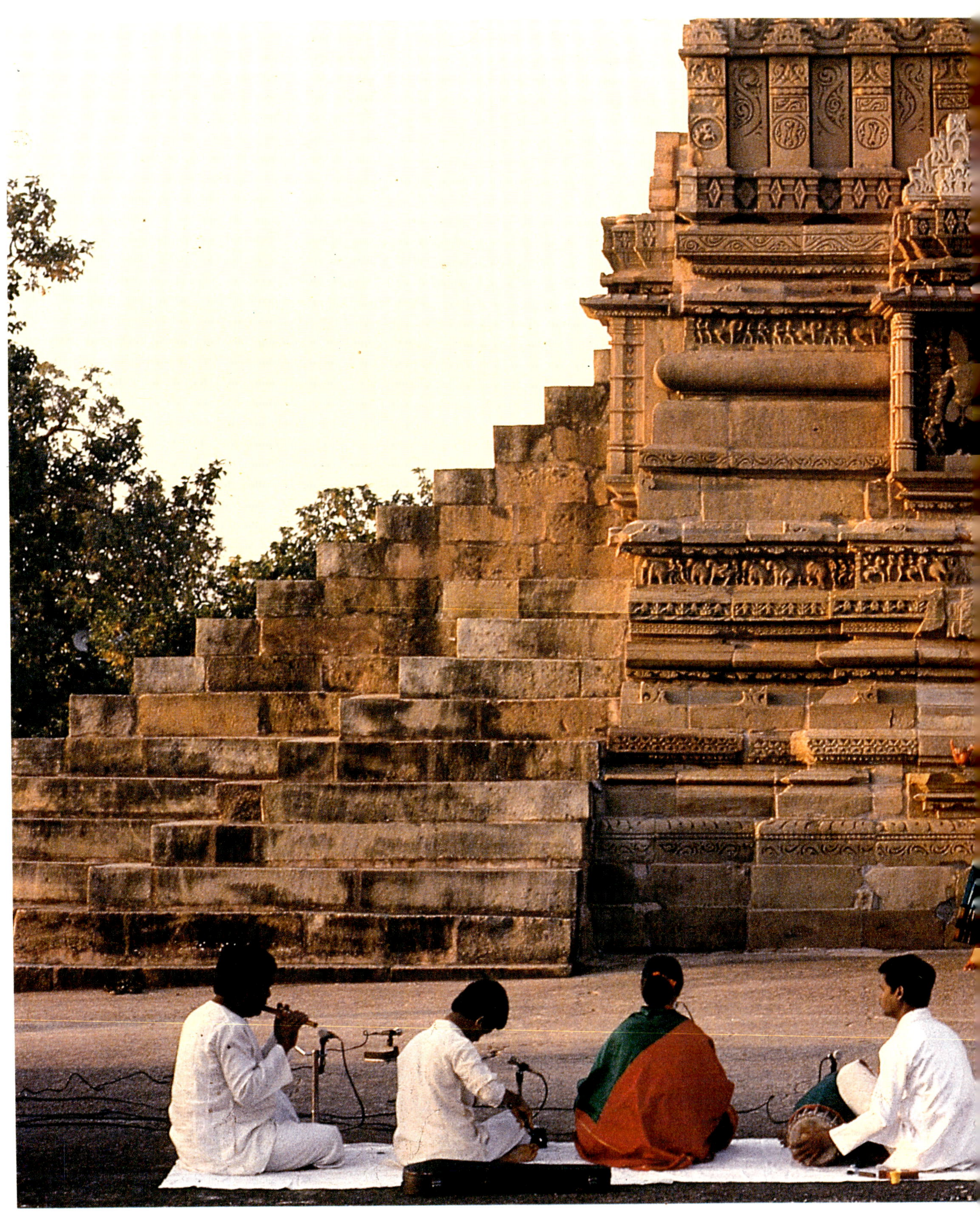

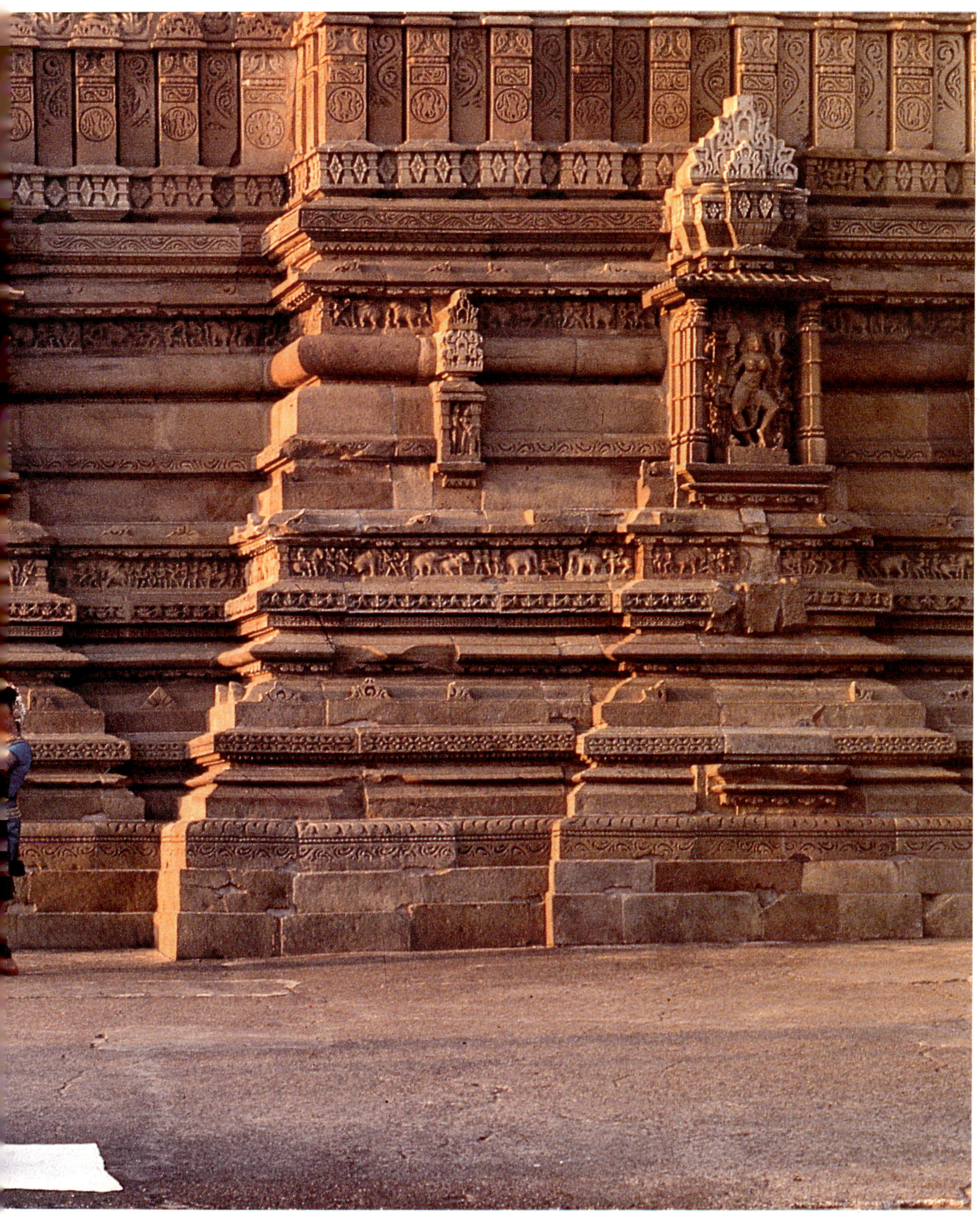

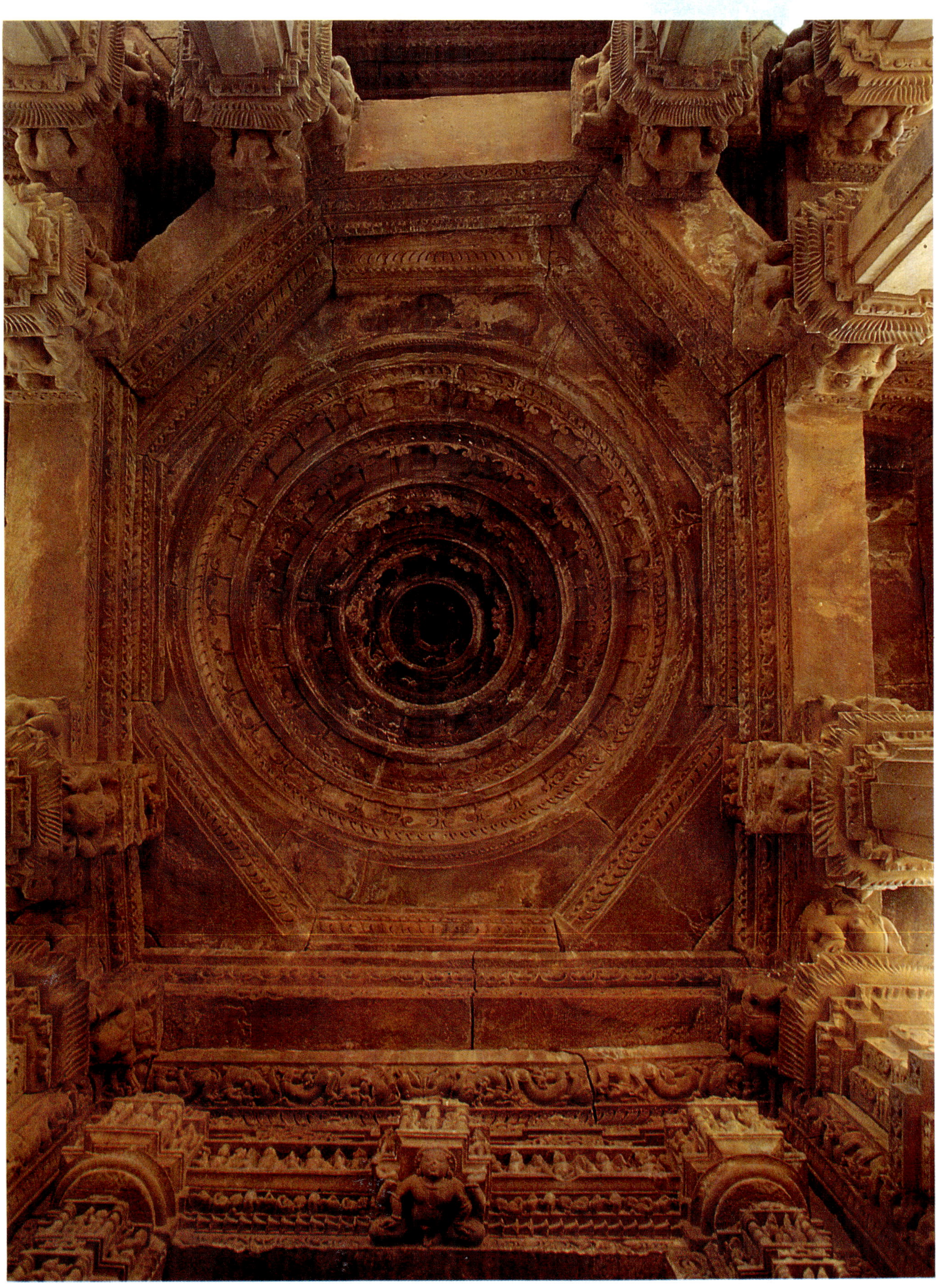

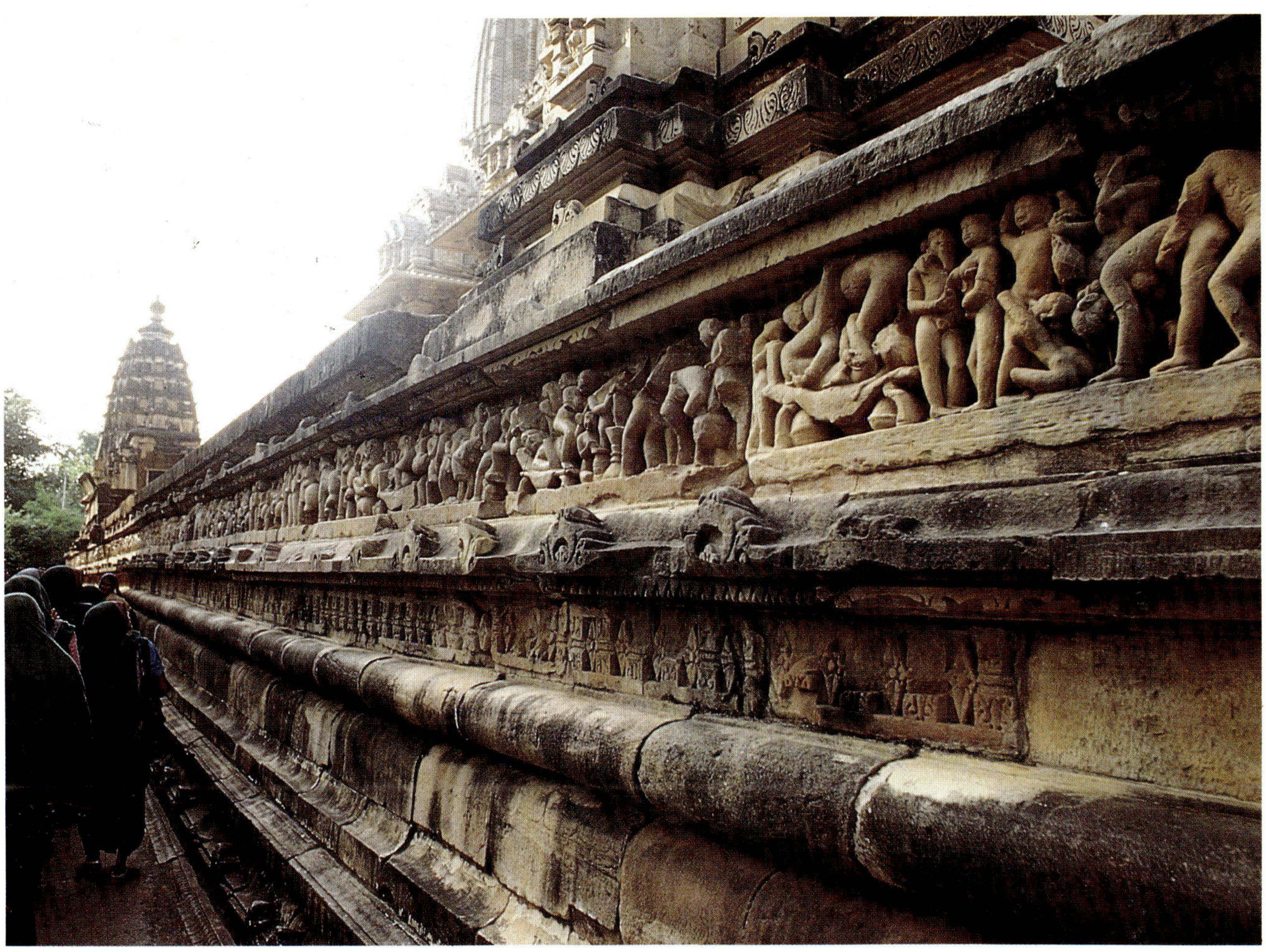

Friezes adorned the raised wall of Lakshmana Temple's platform give a unique perspective to the visitors during the ritual of clockwise circumbulation. *Pages 48-49* : Sudharani Raghupathy paying homage to Shiva. Bharatanatyam dance recital enchants the Sun God who spreads the golden rays in praise of her remarkable performance. *Page 50* : The ceiling of most of the Khajuraho temples has an exquisite depiction of sculptural and architectural excellence.

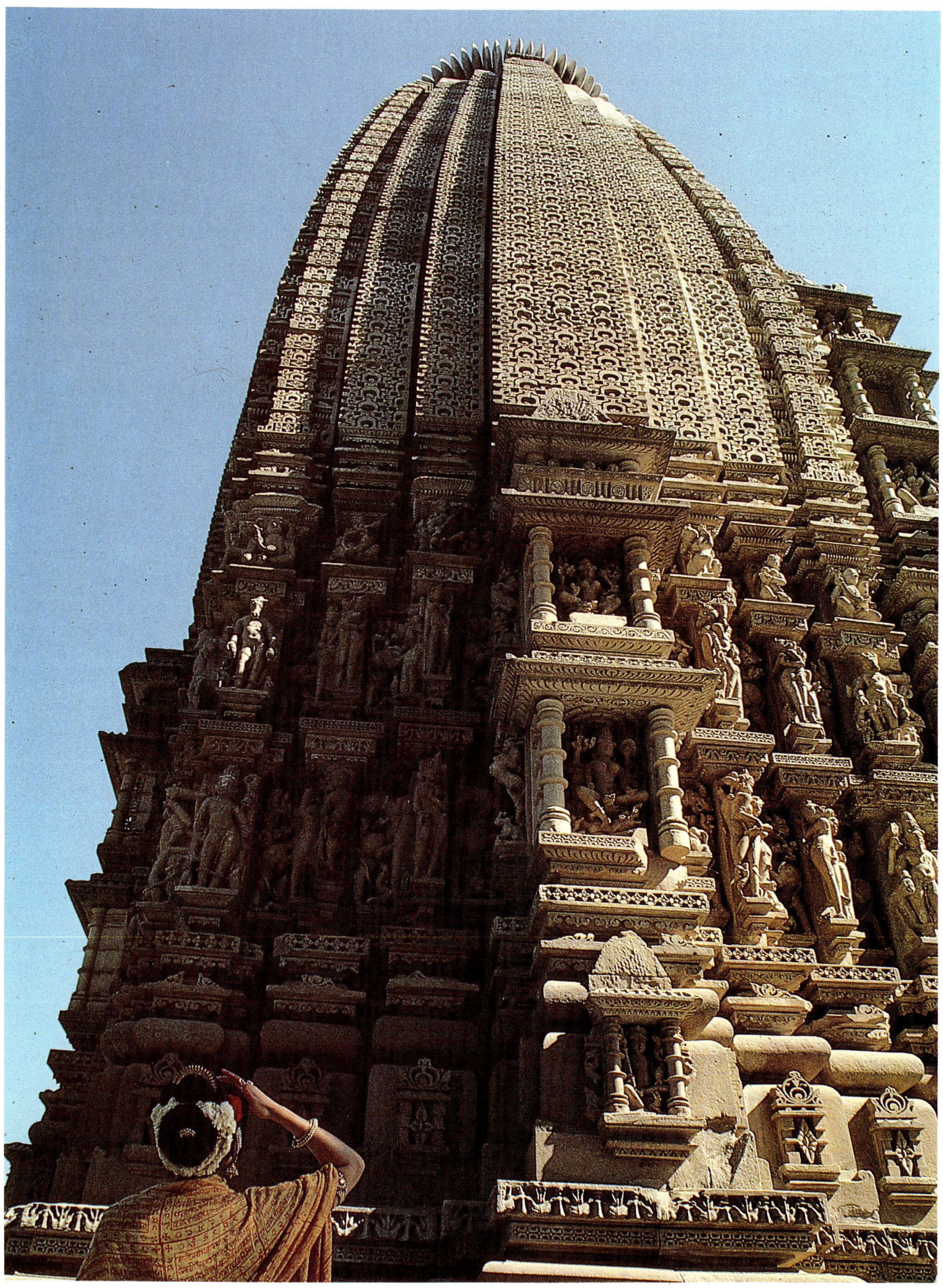

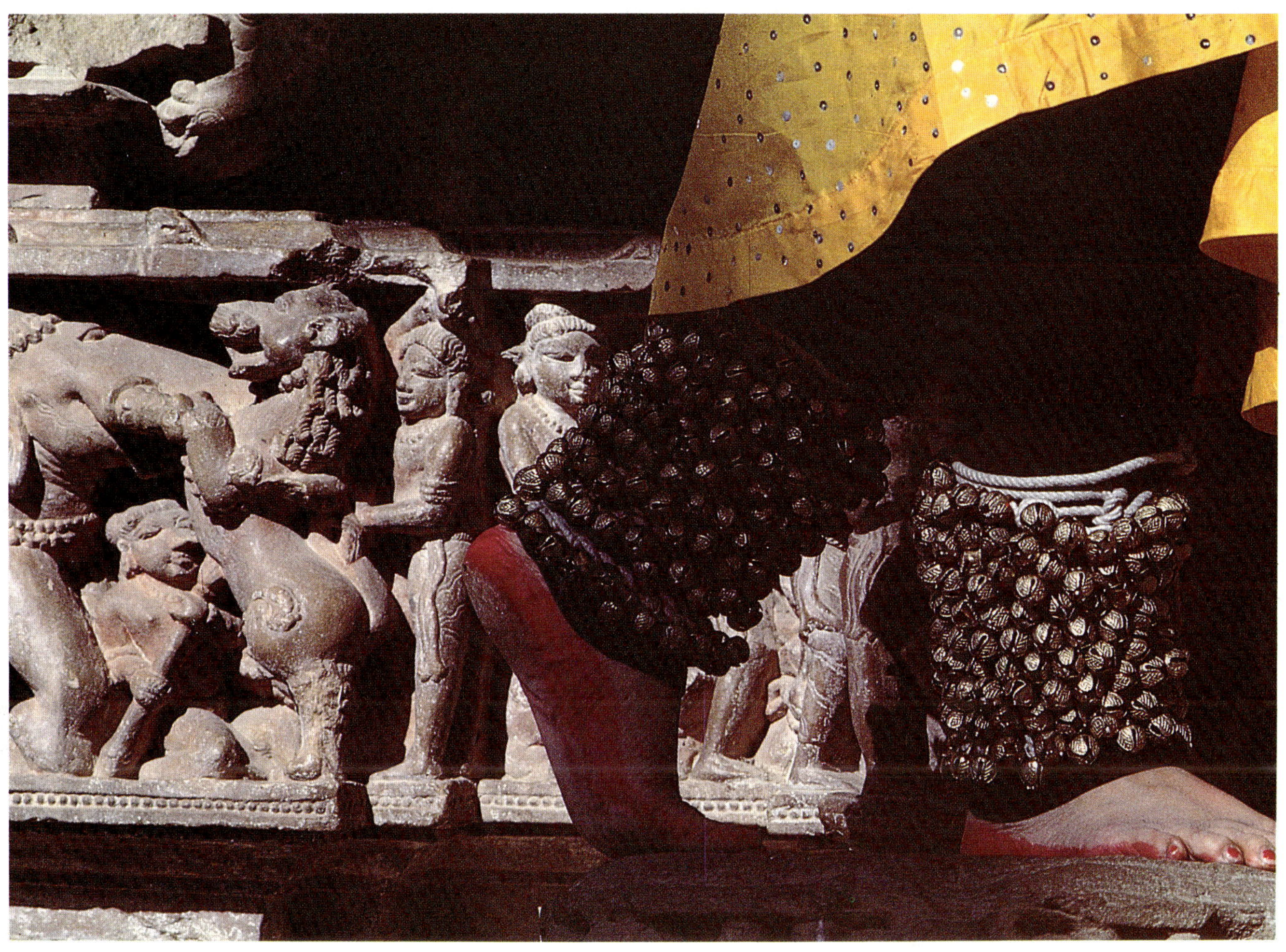

Adinath Temple : 11th Century A.D., dedicated to the Jain Tirthankar, Adinath. The sculptural decor of its exterior wall depicts elegant celestial beauties and Hindu deities.

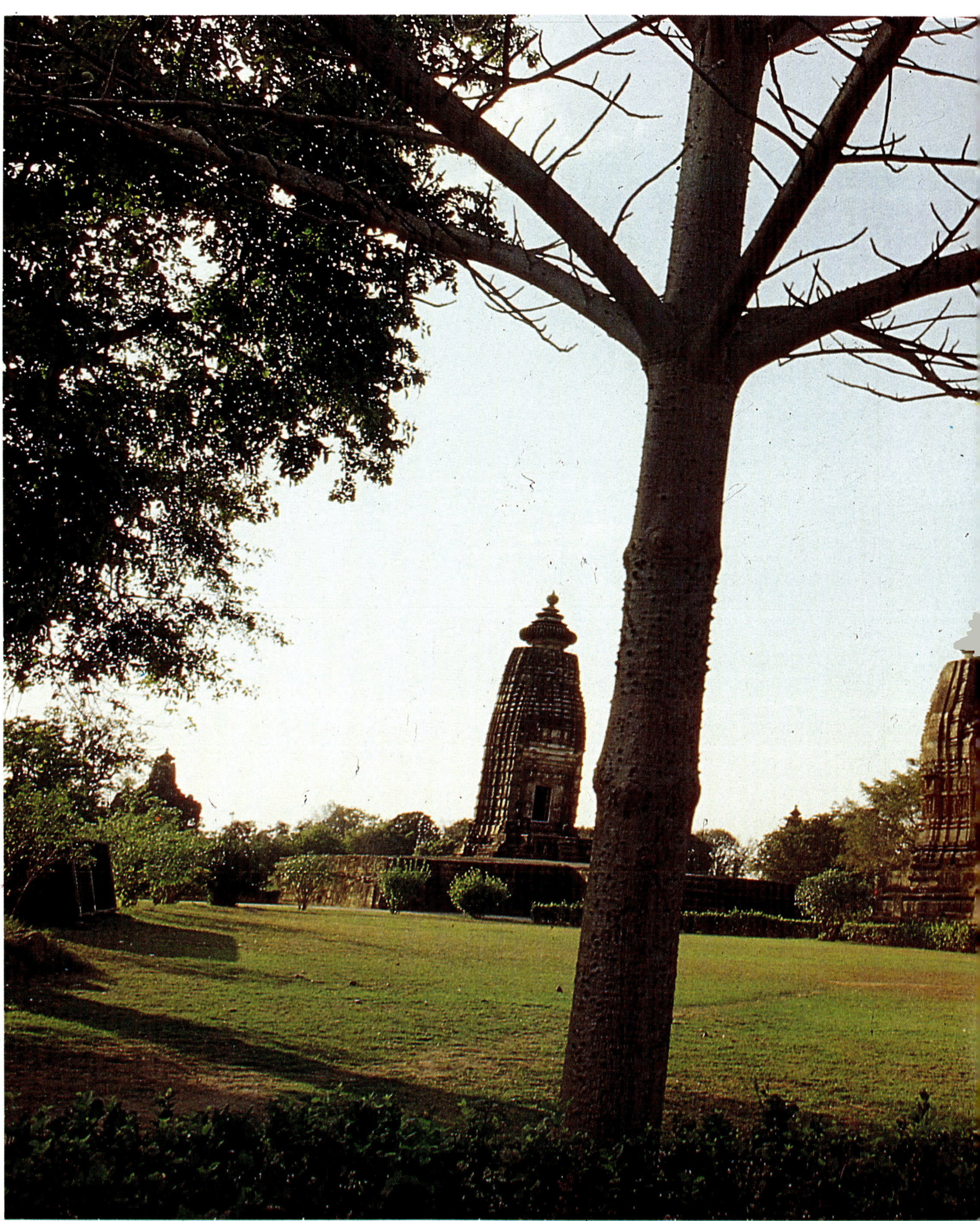

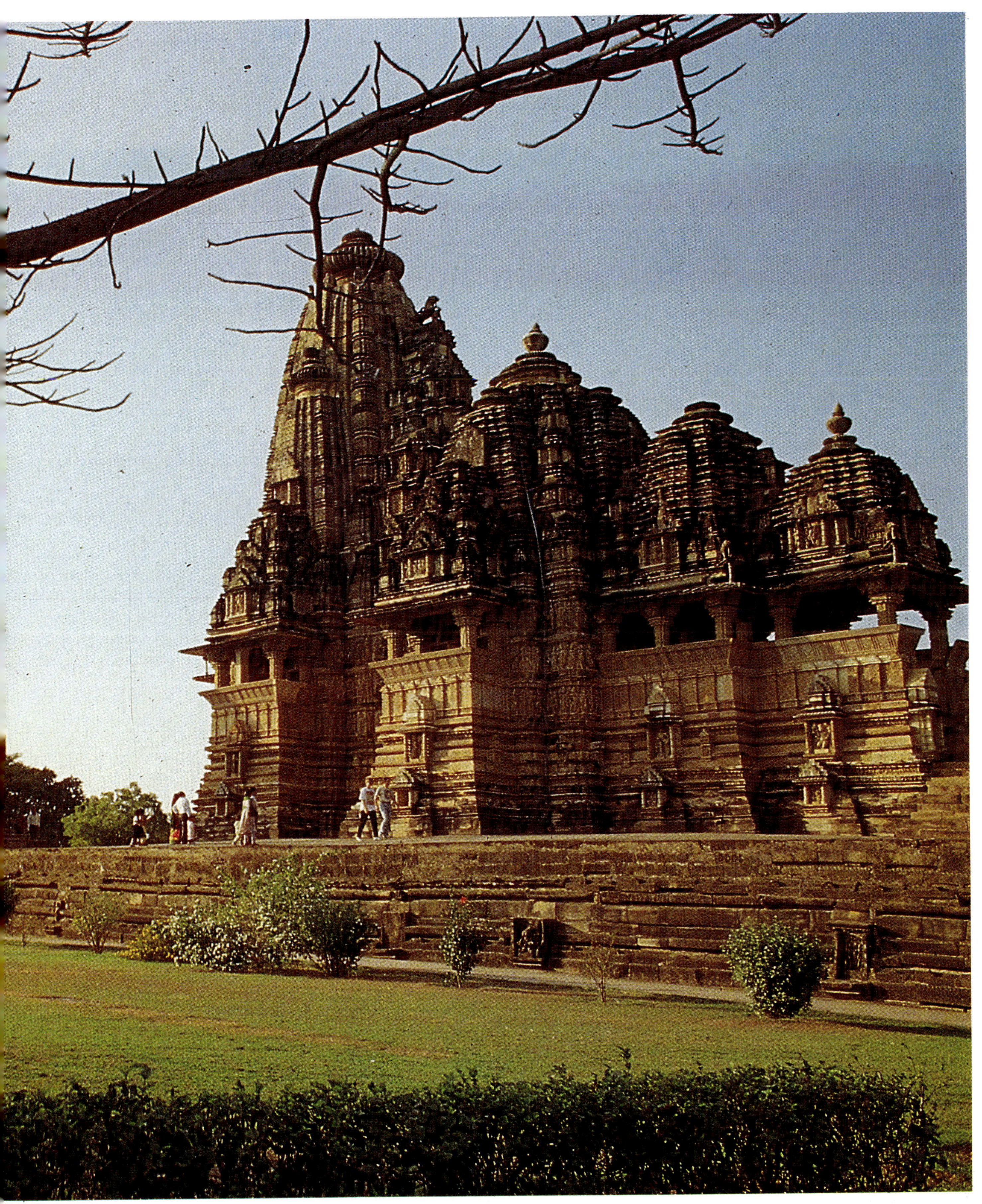

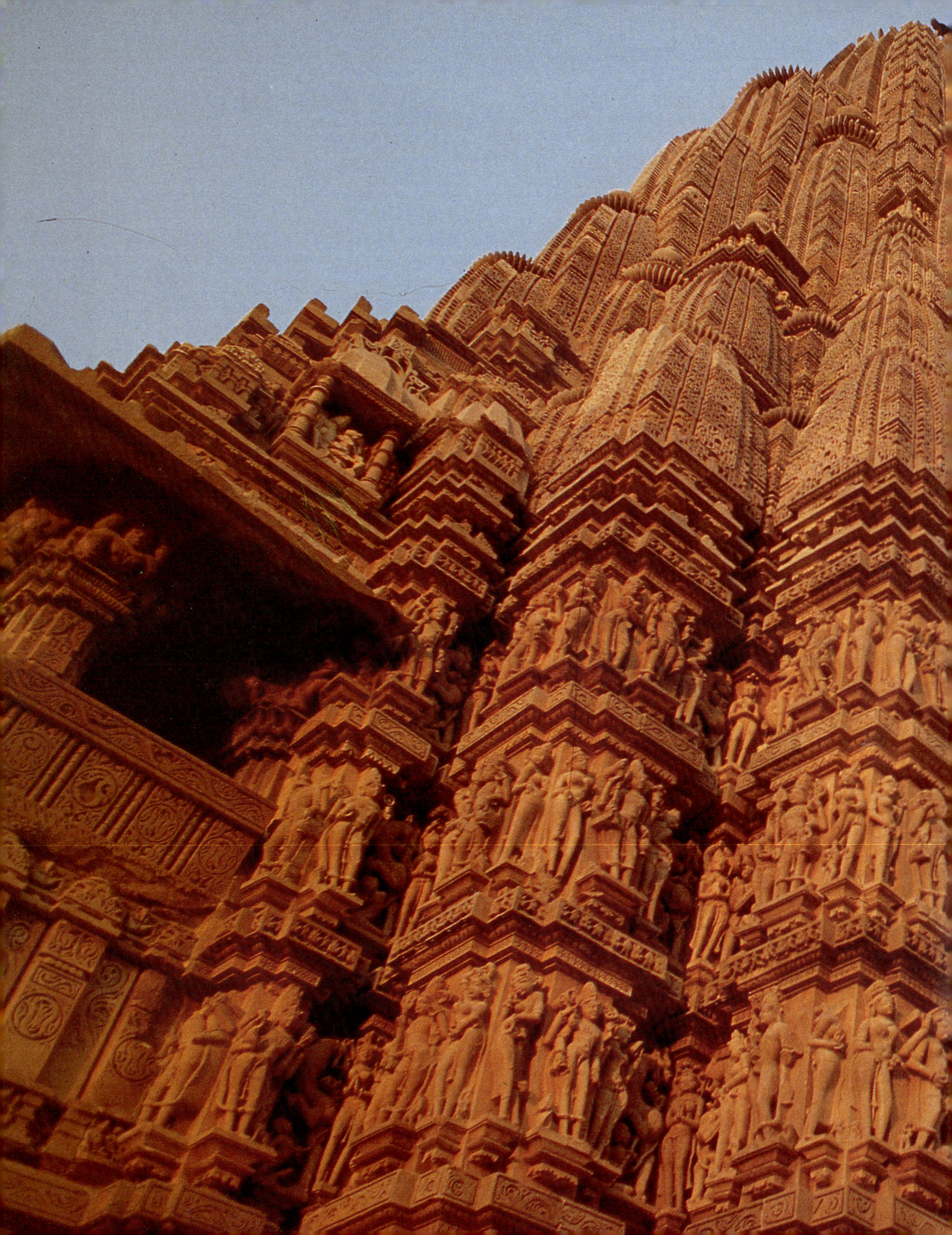

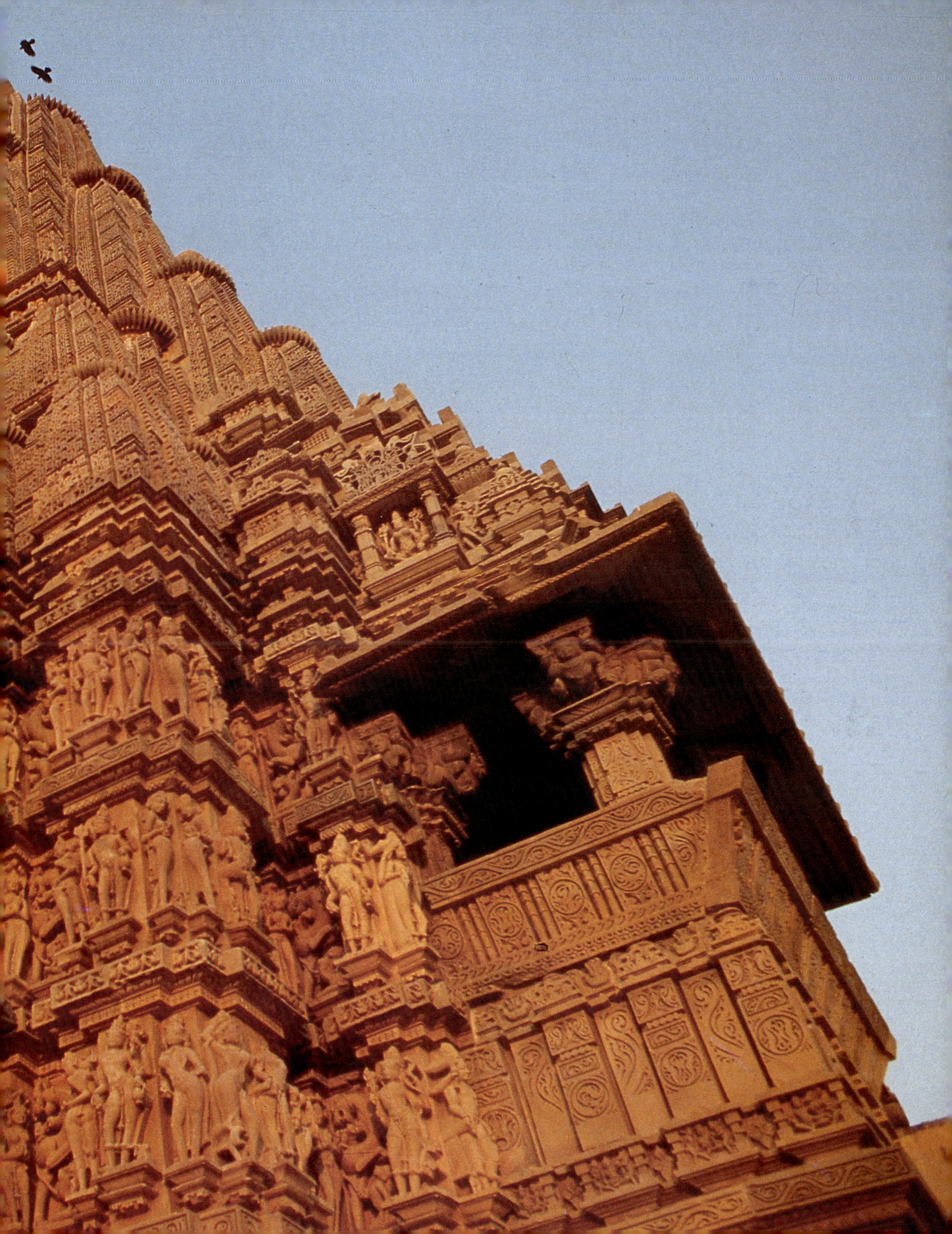

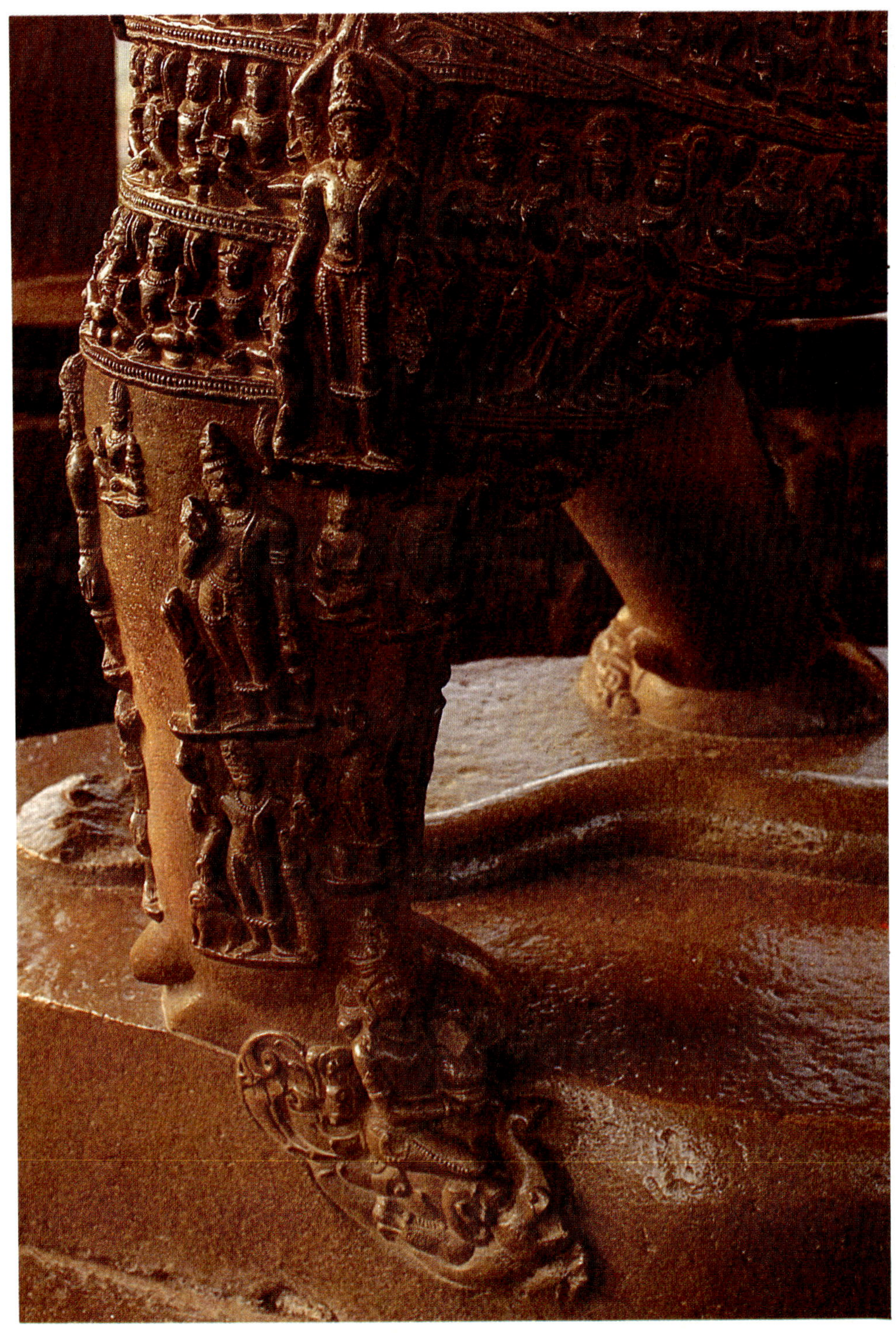

The Varah Temple enshrines a huge image of the boar incarnation of Lord Vishnu carved out of single piece of yellow sandstone. Measuring 8.5 feet long and 5.6 feet high, the body of sculpture has encarved 674 figures of the Hindu Pantheon, such as Brahma - the creator, Vishnu - the preserver, Shiva - the destroyer, Saraswati - the goddess of learning, Ganga - the mother river, the Navagraha - the nine planets.

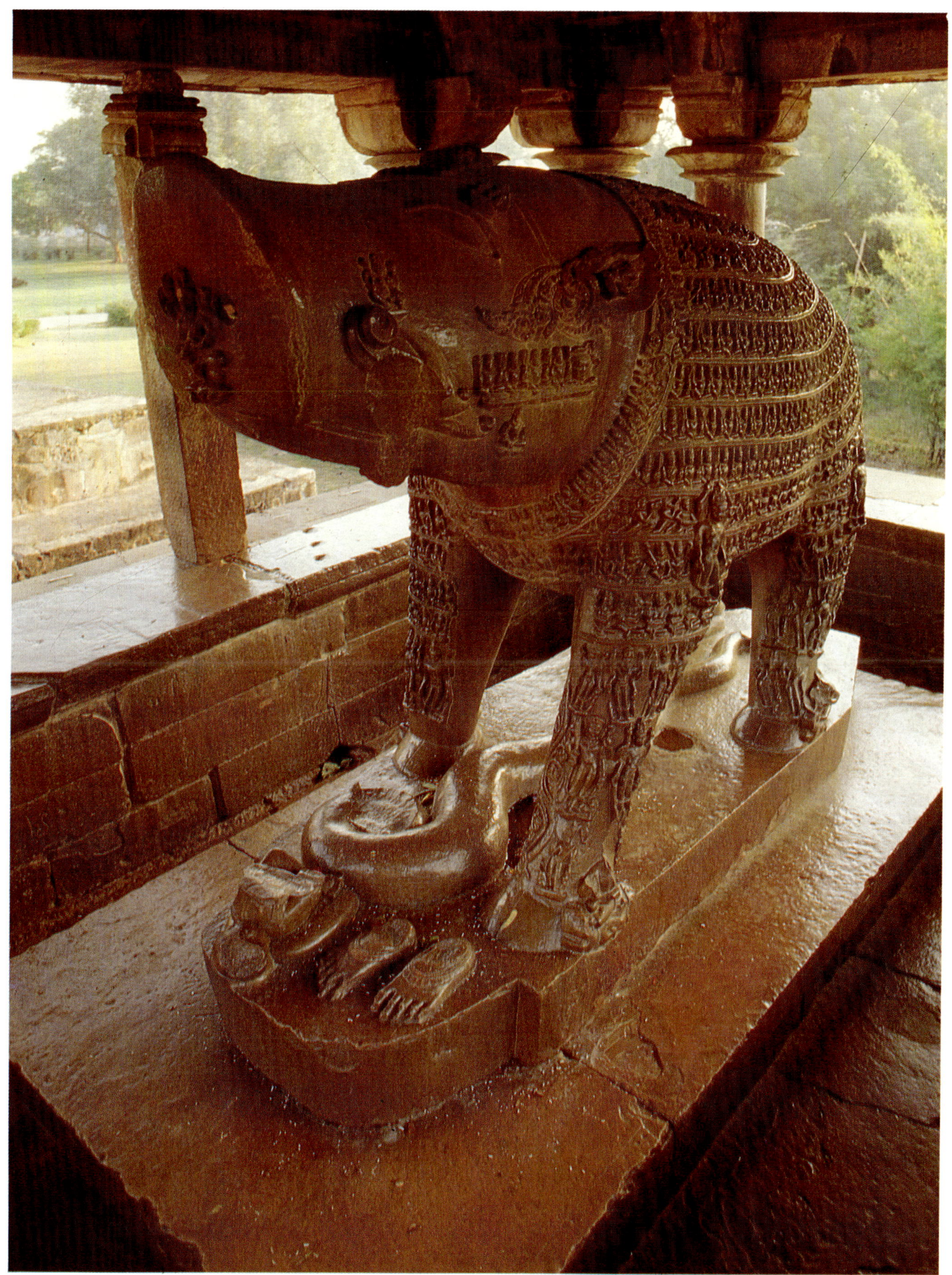

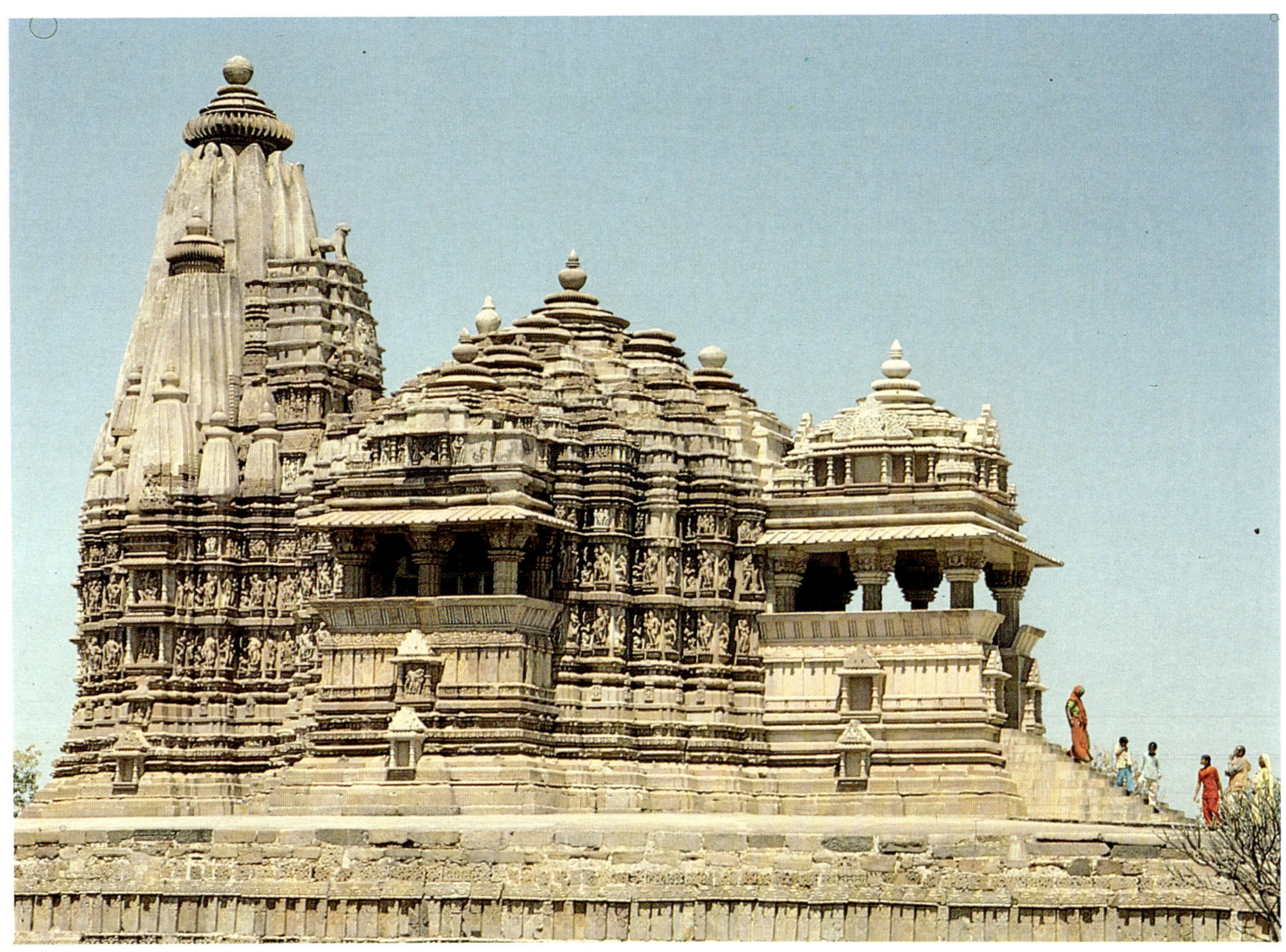

Chitragupta Temple was probably built around AD 1000. Dedicated to Surya, The Sun God, it has an impressive image of the deity in the sanctum. The temple is an exception as it is without an ambulatory passage around the *garbha griha.* The exterior walls are adorned with the images of nymphs, erotic couples and gods. *Page 61* : In front of Kandariya Mahadeo Temple, a Manipuri drummer paying homage to the Lord. The rhythm of dance movements and the music thrills the spectators. *Pages 62-63* : Witnessing a dance performance in the temple precincts is a unique experience. The rhythm created by the beauty of the dancer, music and the dance movements is .divine. With the backdrop of Kandariya Mahadeo temple, Madhavi Mudgal concentrating on her innerself as to find the God within. Hindu mythology emphasises on concentration and meditation to purge the innerself of evils, so that the God makes it His abode.

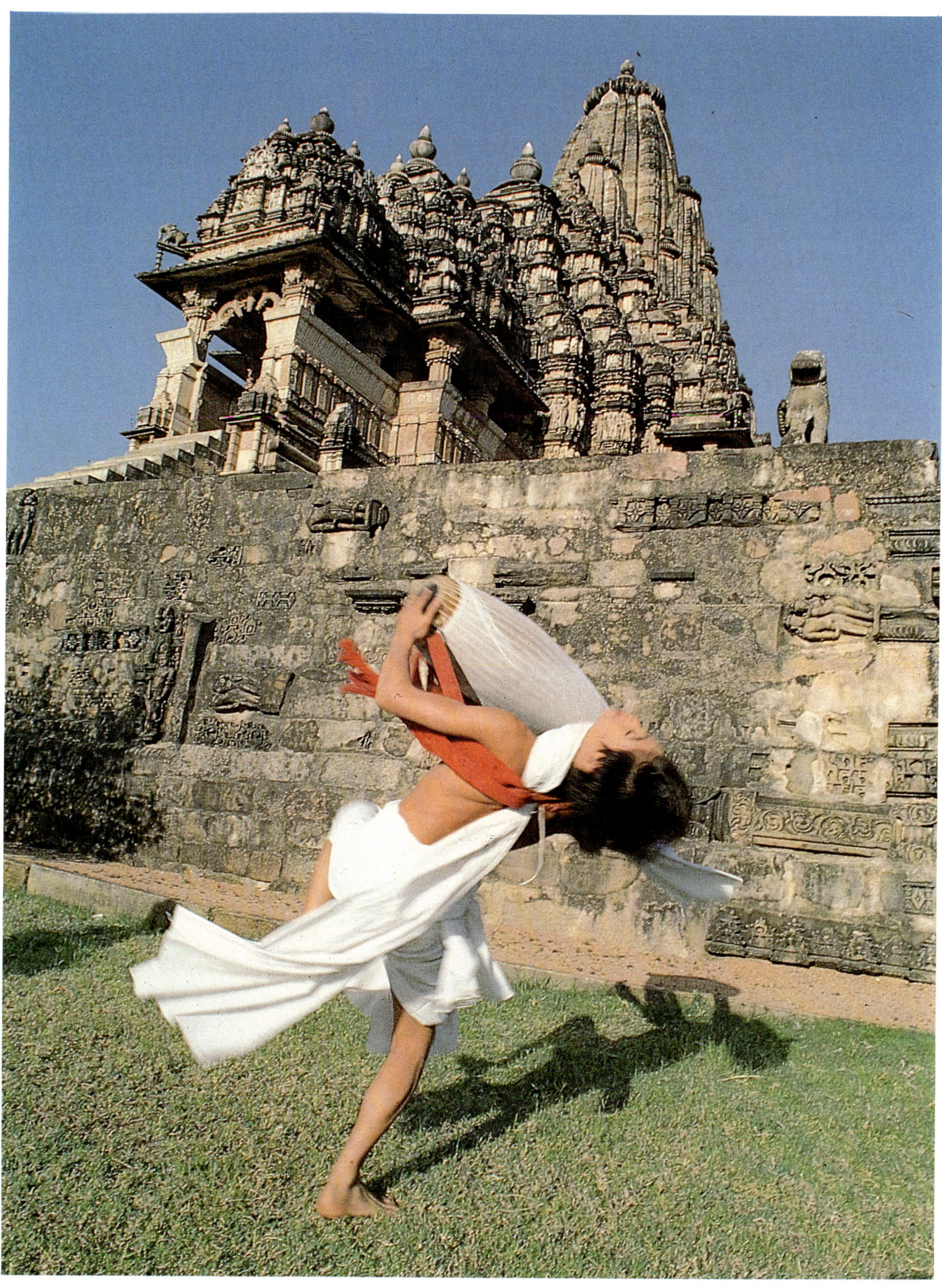

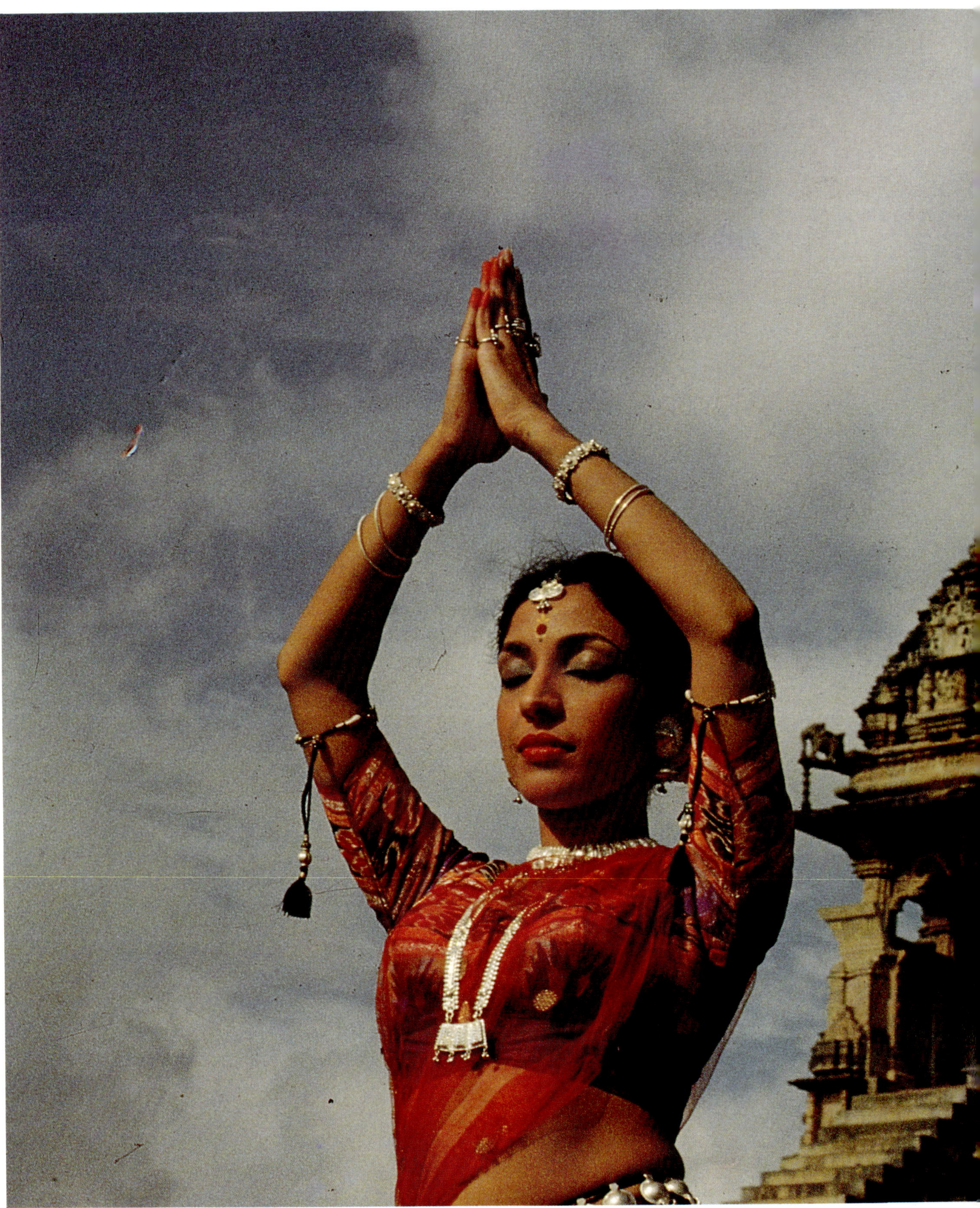

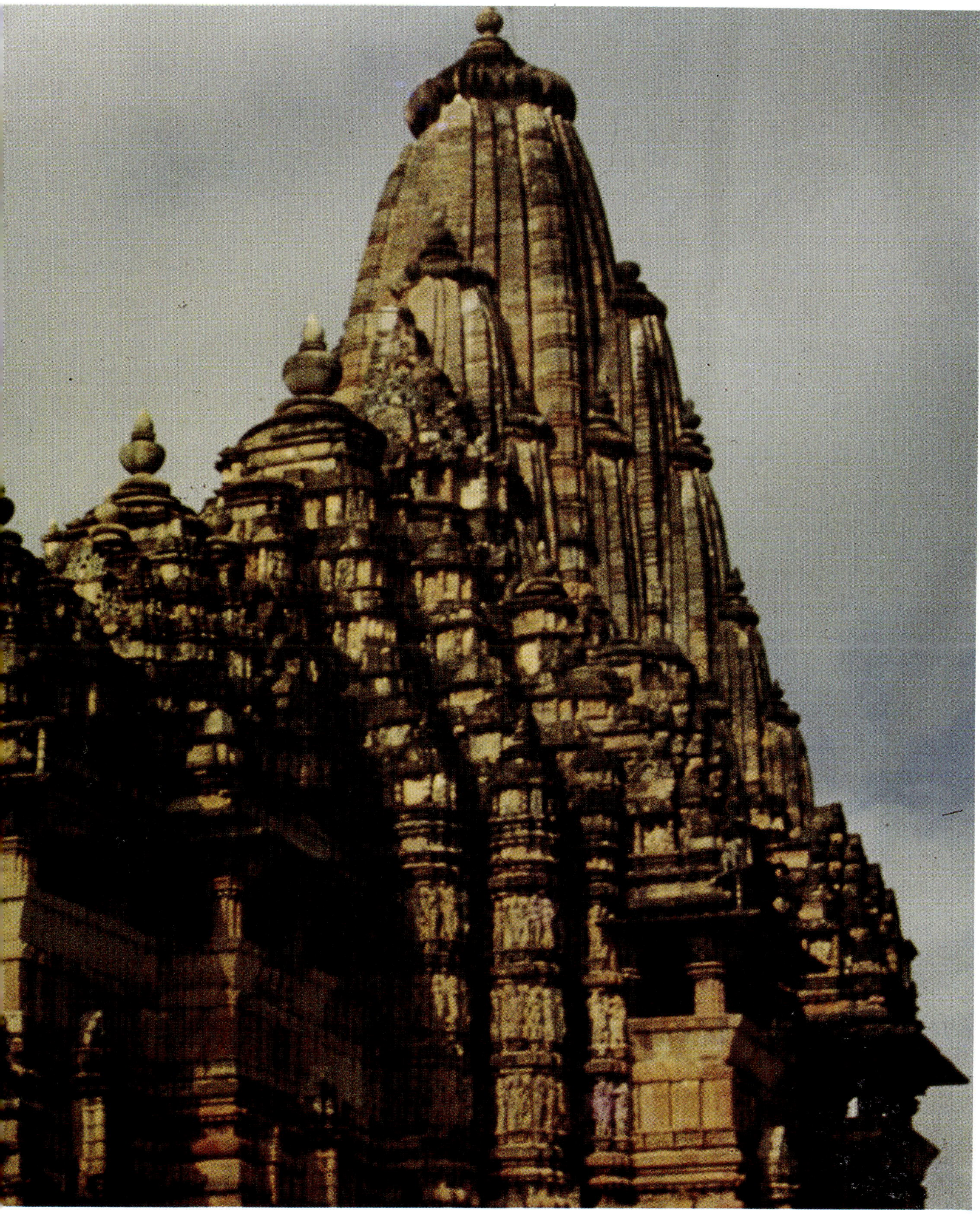

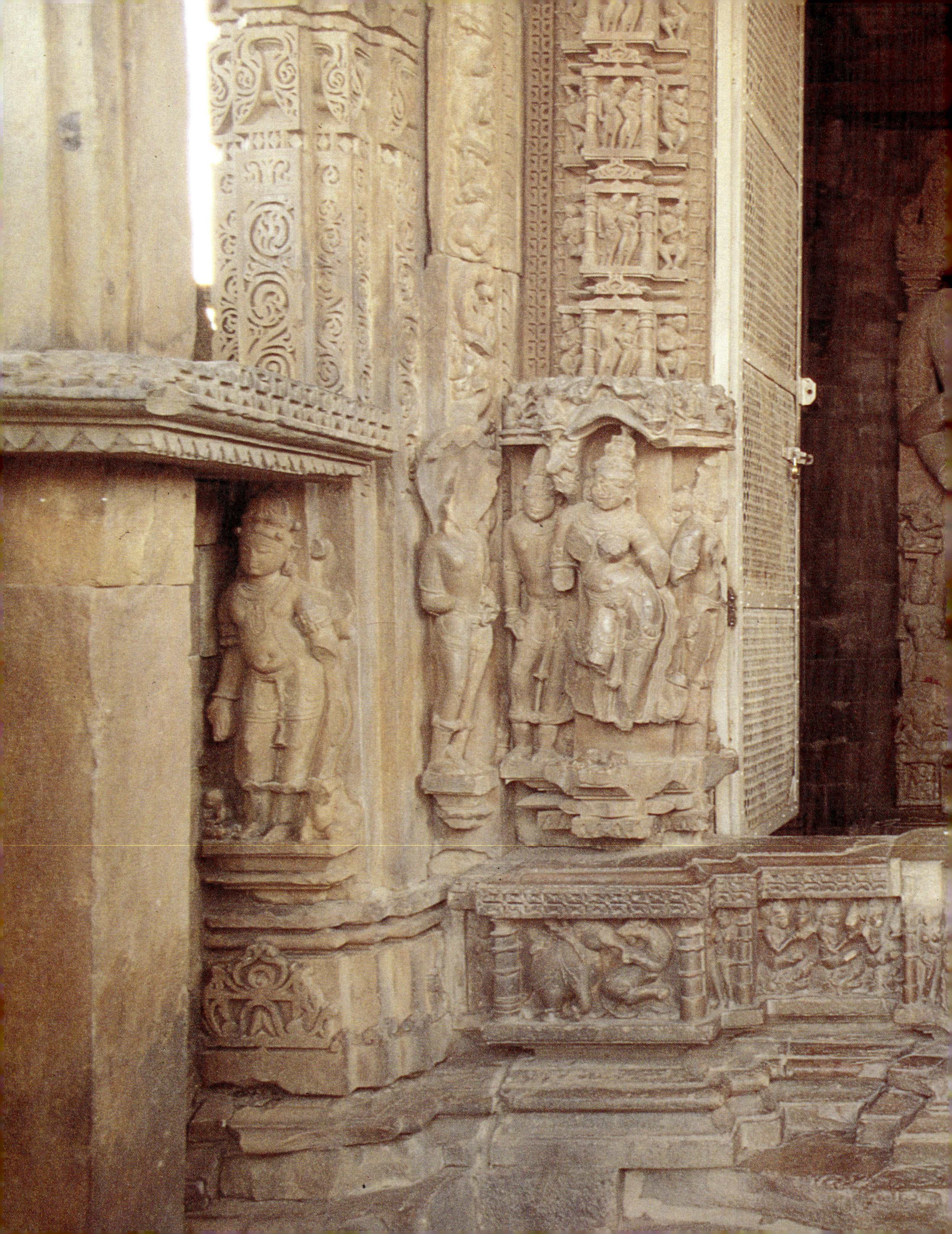

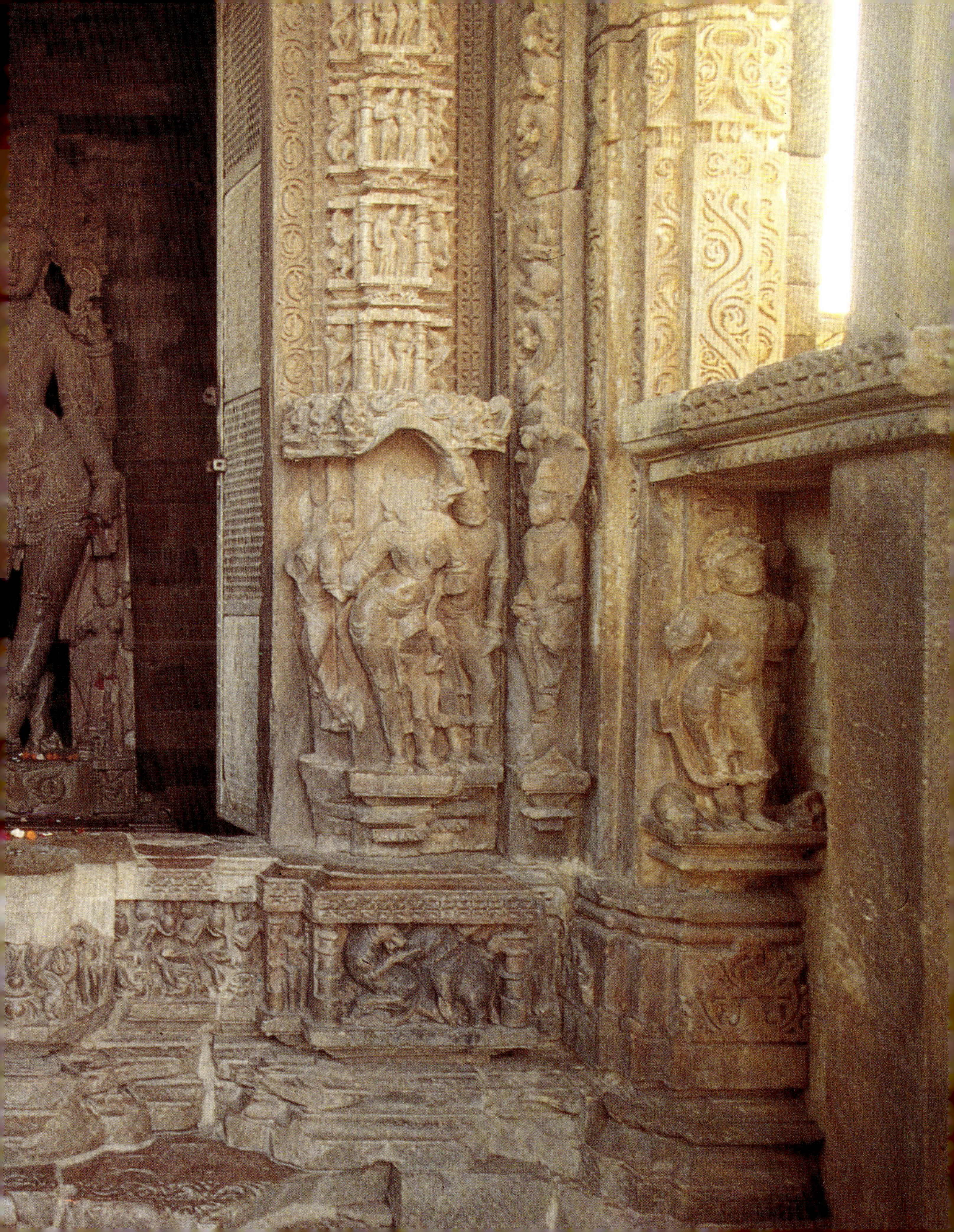

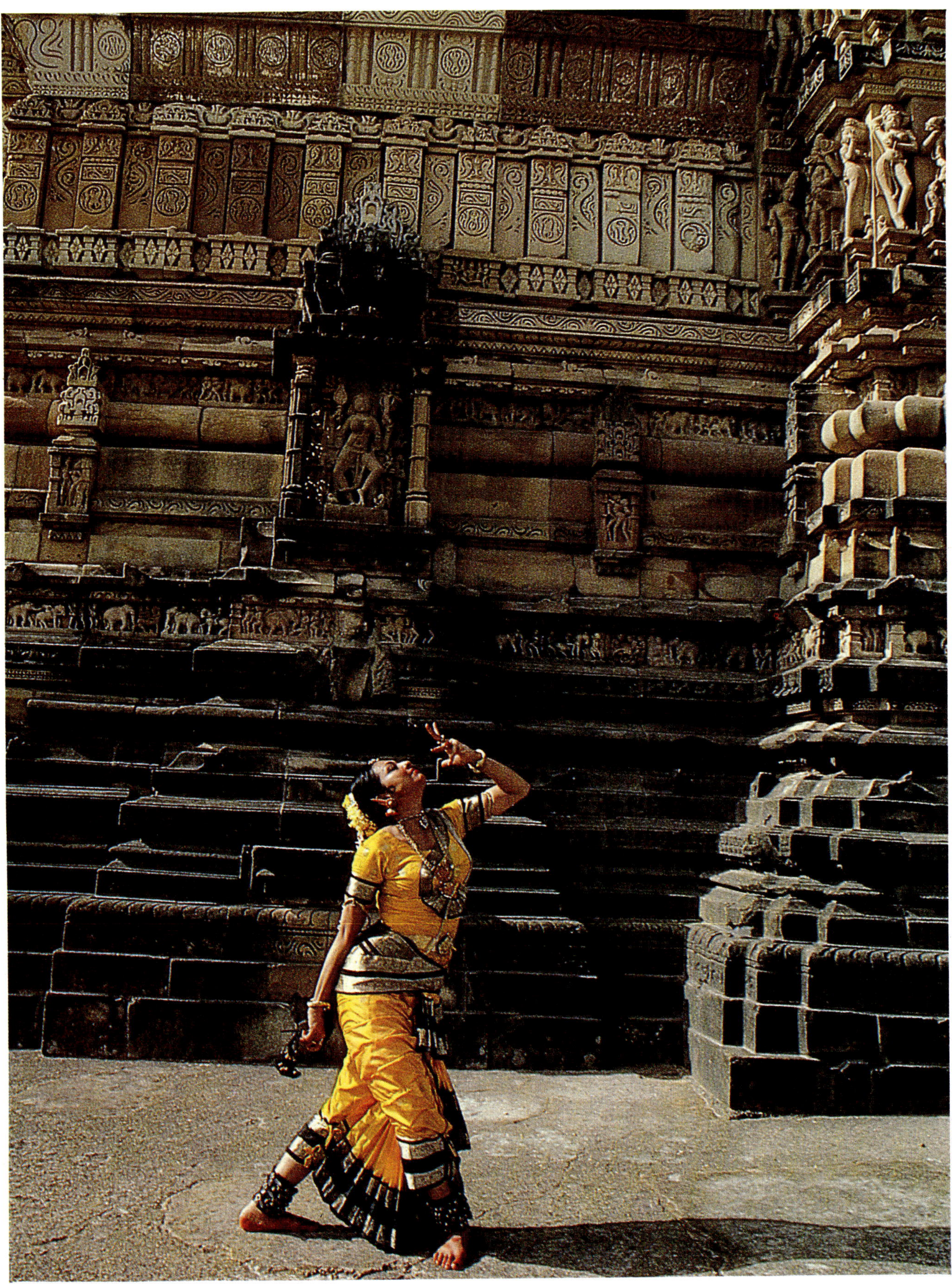

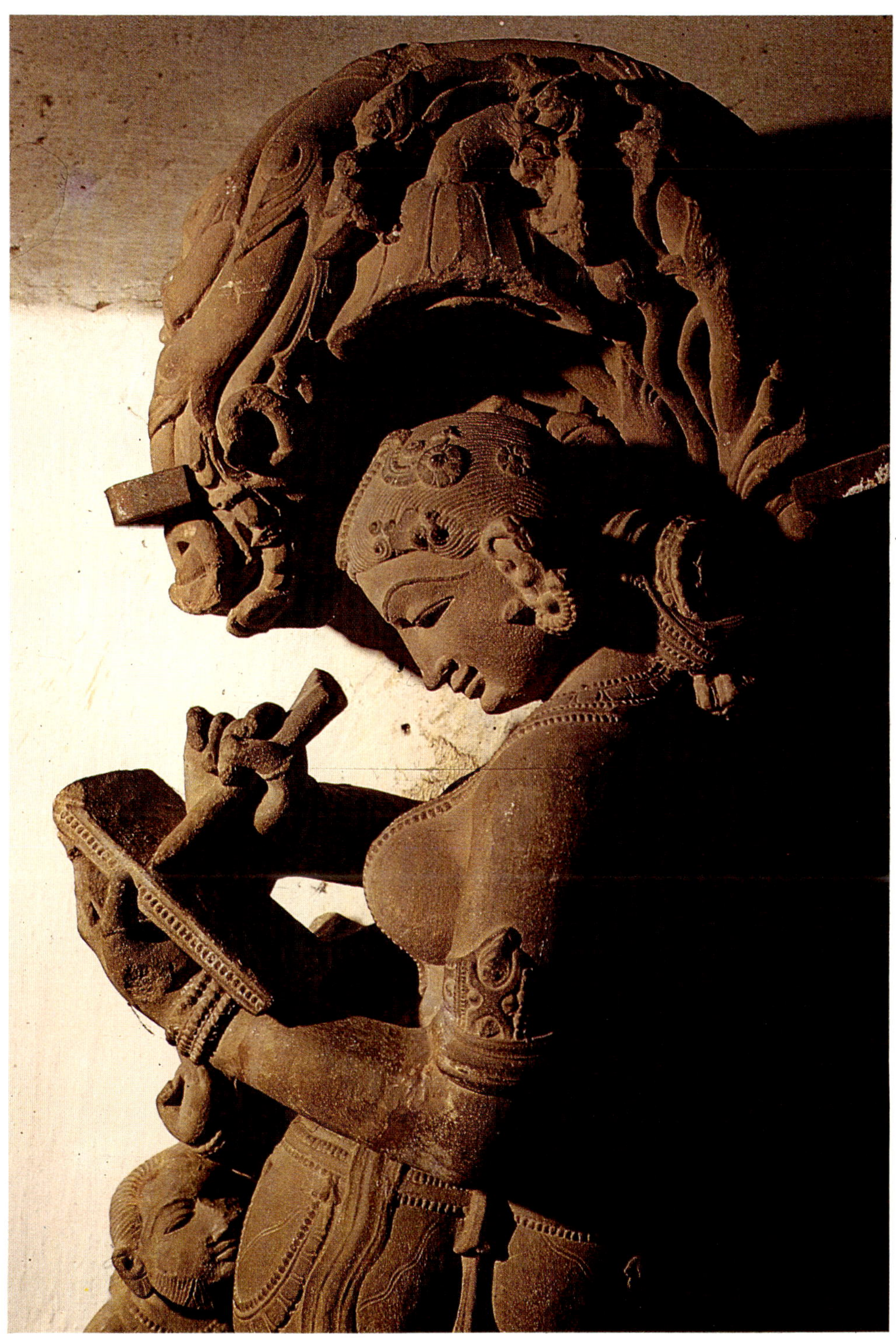

Apsara, the celestial nymph, writing a love missive, most probably to her venerable or her beloved. *Page 66* : Yamini Krishnamurthy is overwhelmed presenting a dance tribute to the Gods. The juxtaposition of her Bharatanatyam dance posture over the carvings adorned temple walls is heavenly. *Pages 64-65*: Inner sanctum of Chaturbhuj Temple has an exquisite image of four-armed Vishnu.

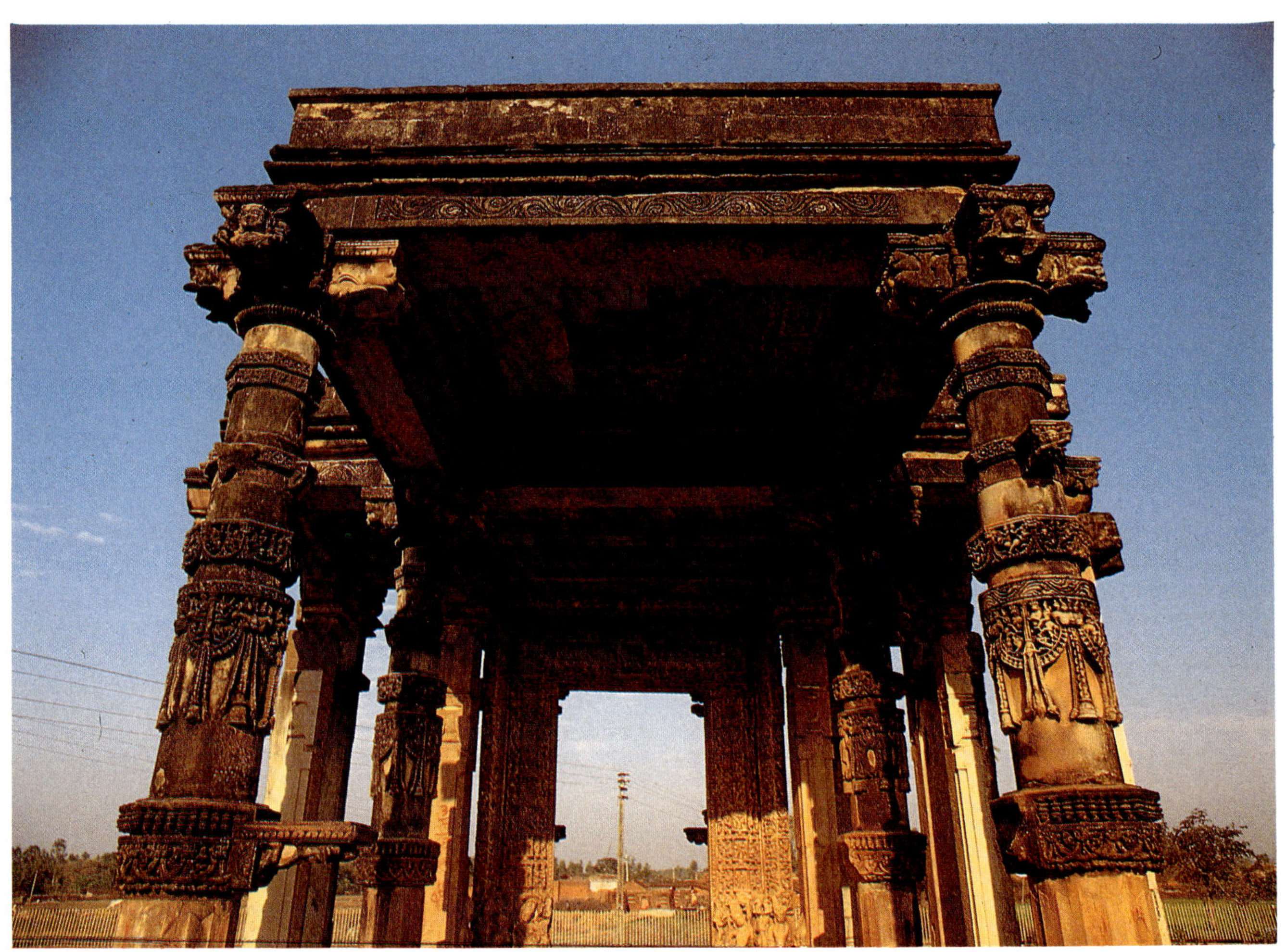

Ghantai Temple (end of 10th Century A.D.) one of the Jain temples situated a little far from the other ones in Khajuraho. Only a few pillars adorned with bell and chain motifs, ornate ceiling with the carved doorway panel depicting sixteen dreams of Jaina Mahavira's mother.

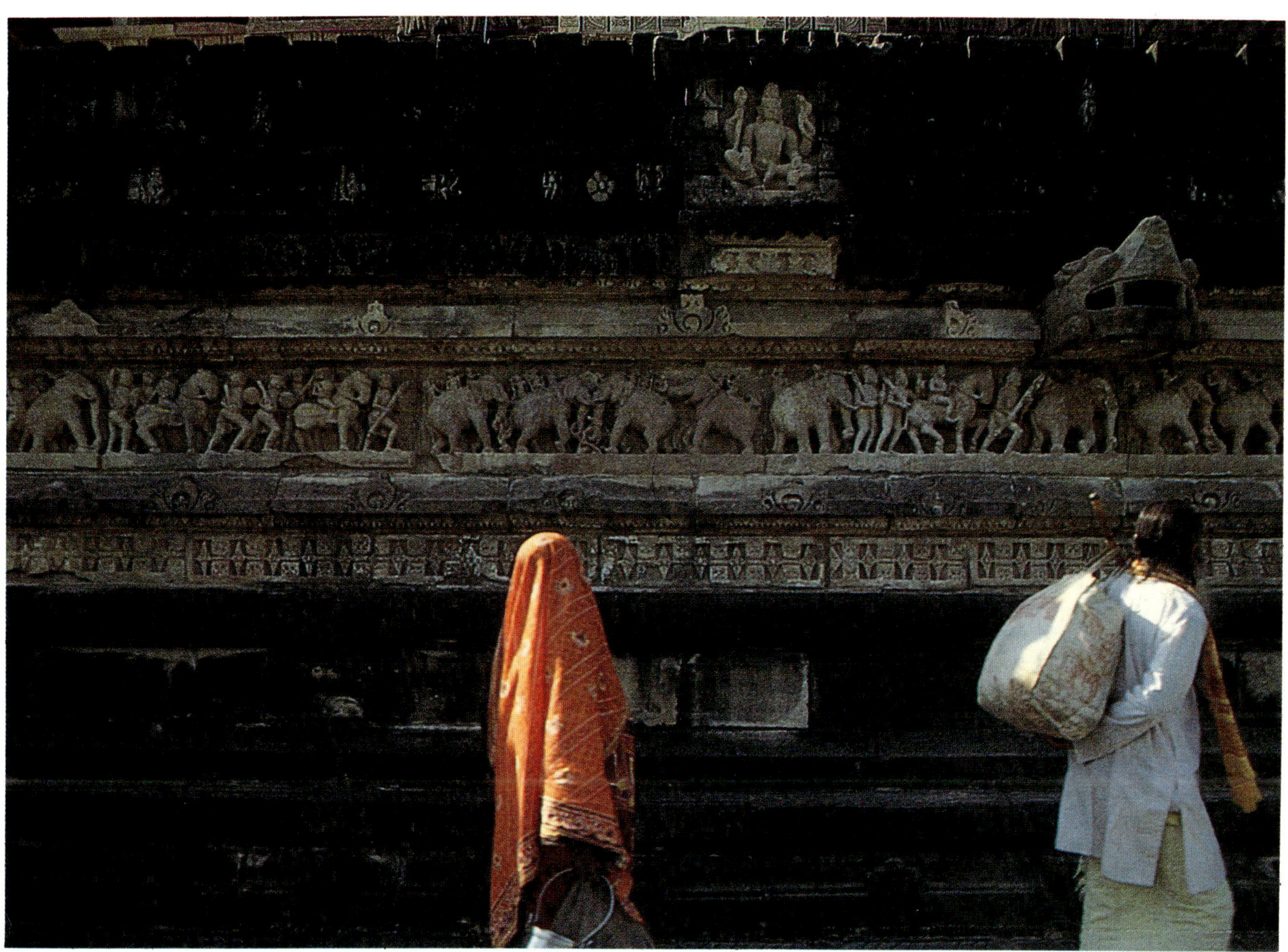

A couple from a village trying to read the language of art engraved on the stones. The friezes on the wall of raised platforms of Lakshamana temple gives this opportunity as the devotee performs 'Pradakshina', clockwise circumbulation, of the temple, an important ritual of worship.

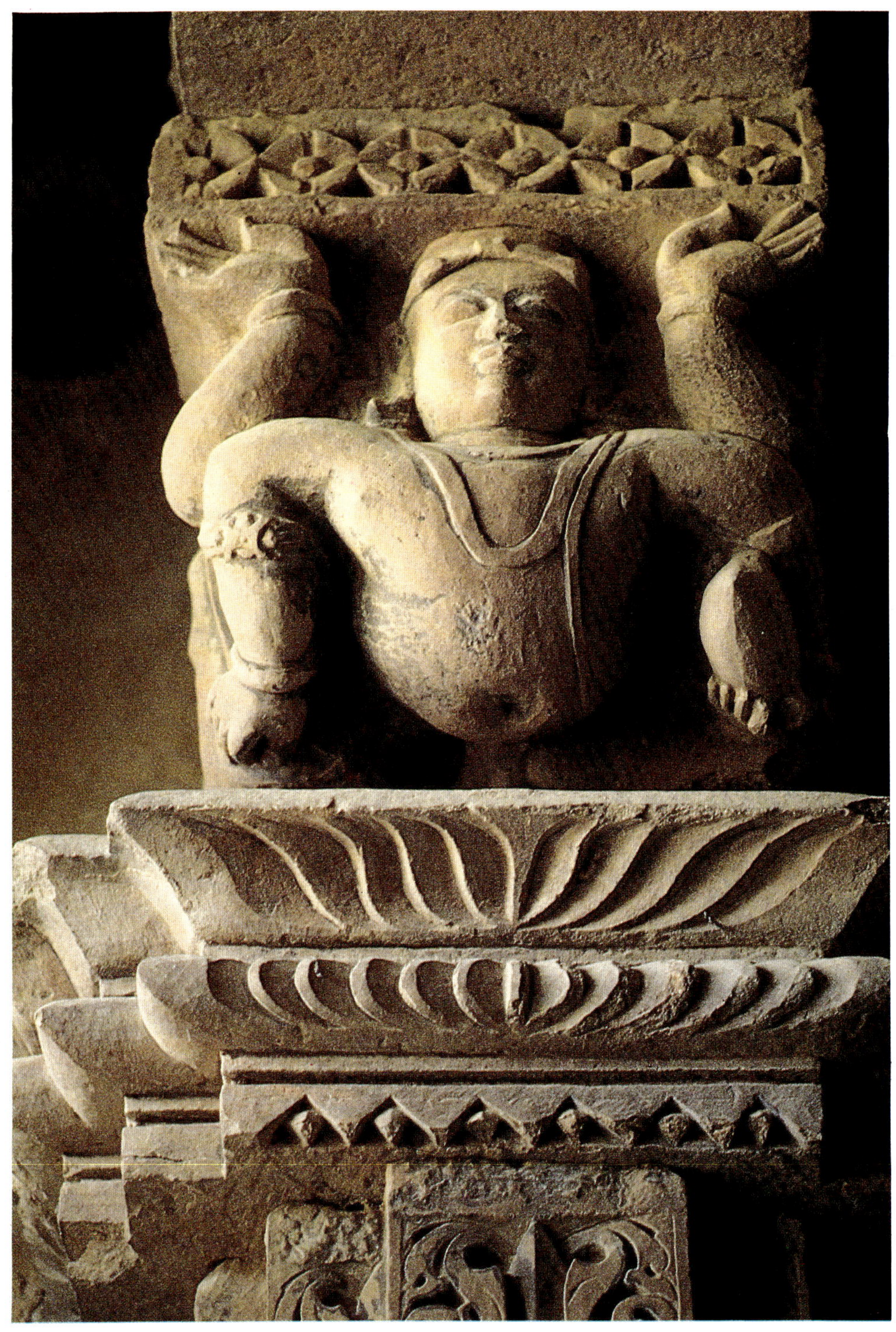

The pillars of the temples have exquisite carvings along with depiction of a celestial body 'Keechak' which carries the weight of temple walls and spires. Did the architects invoke the divinity for the safety of the structure? *Page 71* : The dancer couple Raja and Radha Reddy depicting a chapter from Kamasutra, the ancient text by Sage Vatsayana, 4th century A.D., which describes the art of love and sex. The dancers appear to reflect the erotic sculpture in live form.

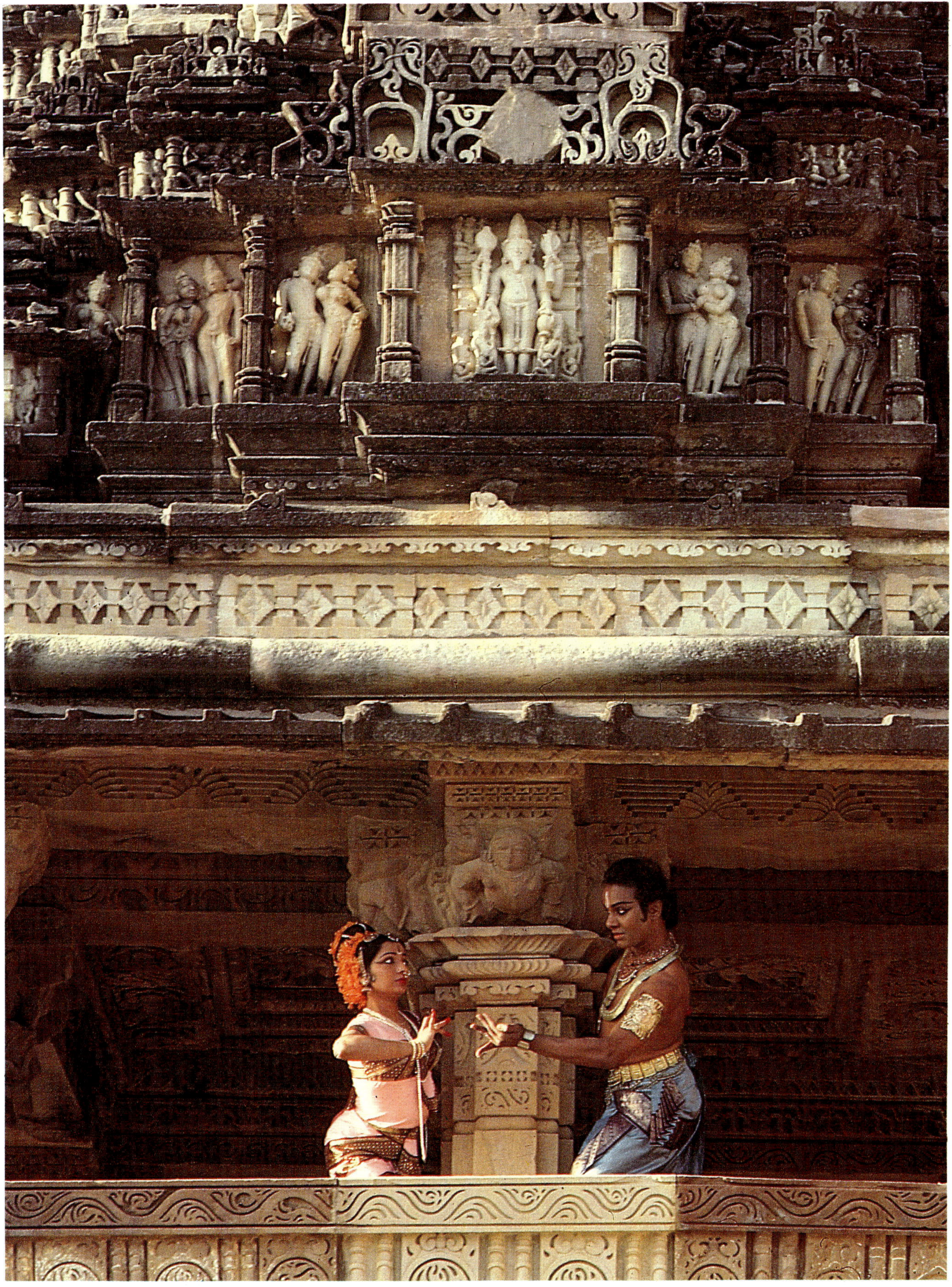

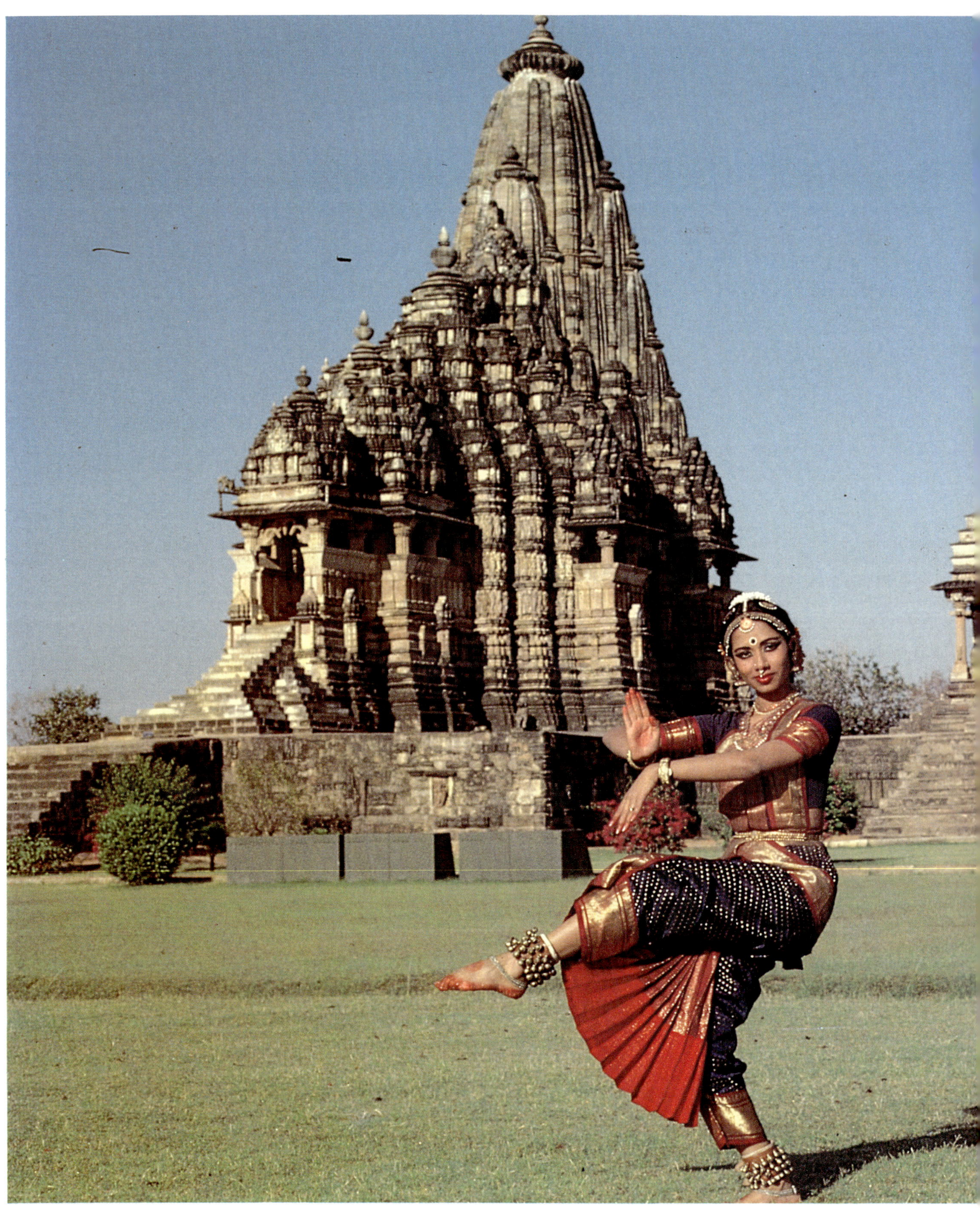

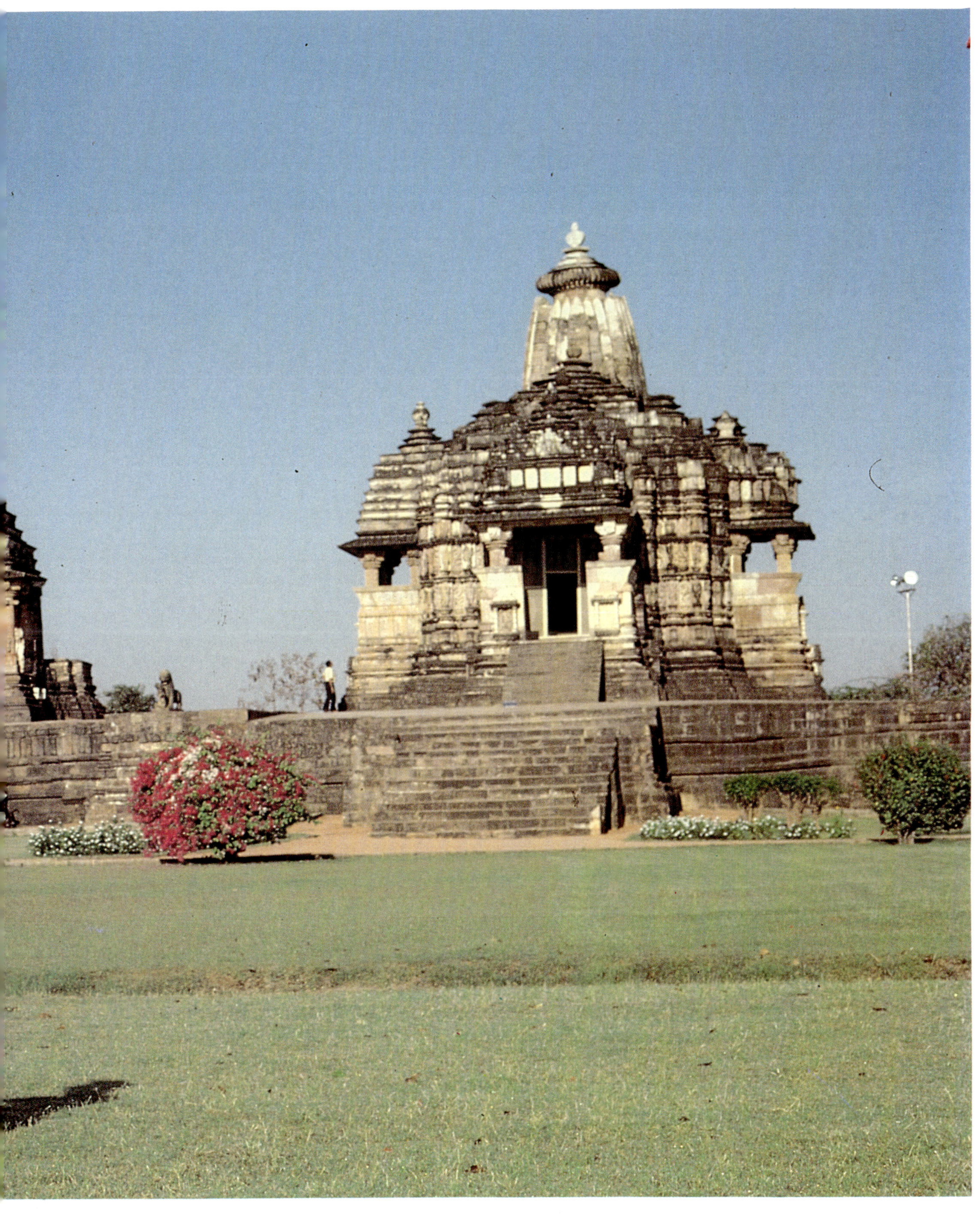

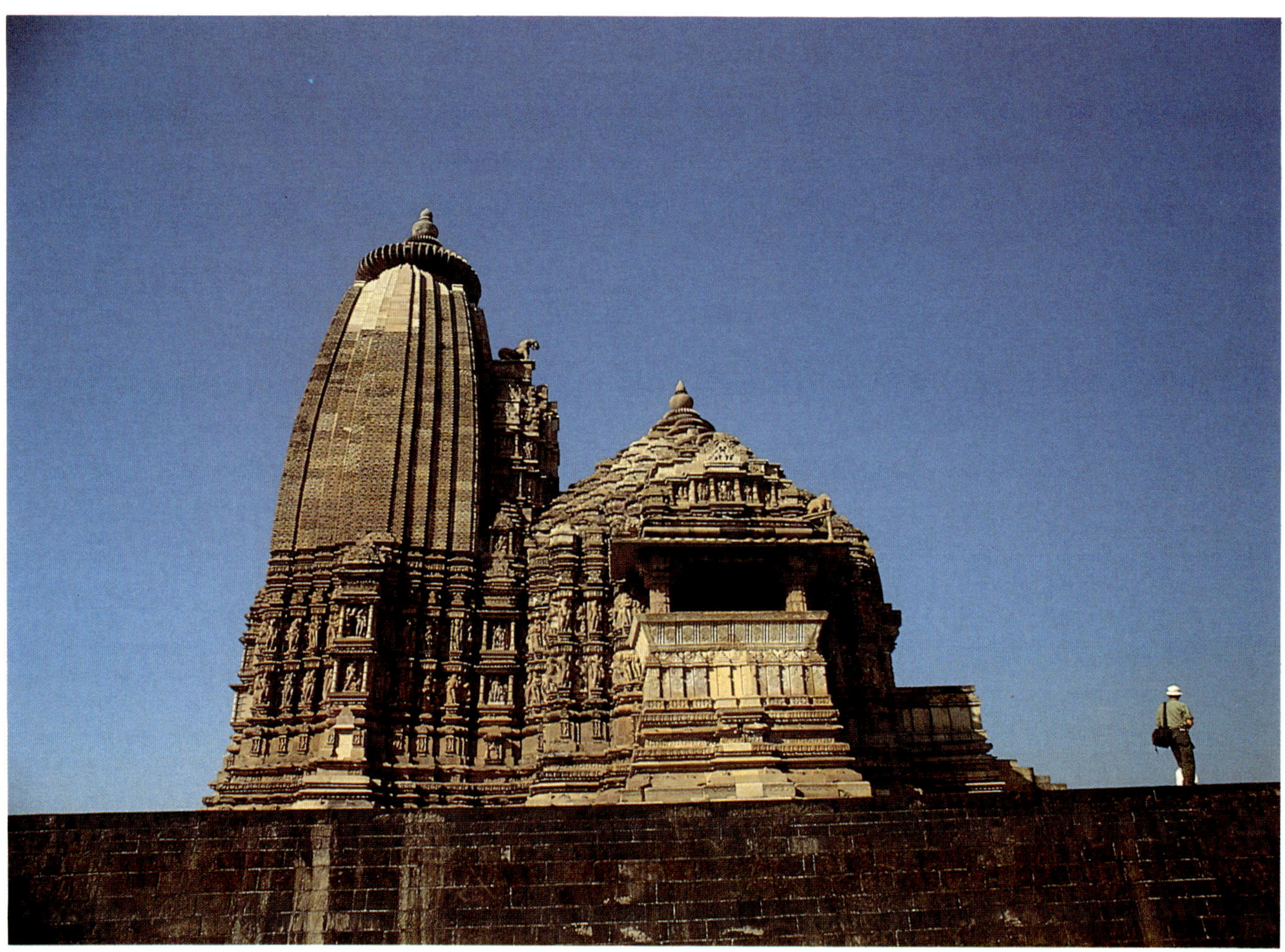

Vamana Temple (A.D. 1050-1075) : dedicated to Vamana, the dwarf incarnation of Vishnu. The carved images of the holy trinity Brahma, Vishnu and Shiva with their consorts are placed in the upper row of main niches of the sanctum. A carved depiction of Buddha inside the sanctum mirrors intermingling of Hinduism and Buddhism and religious tolerance of the Chandela dynasty. *Page 75* : Duladeo Temple (AD 1100-25) is now dedicated to Shiva while considered to be originally dedicated to Kartikeya, commander of the divine army. According to a local legend the temple acquired its name from 'dulha' (bridegroom), to commemorate the death of a young man who died on way to his marriage. The exterior wall of the temple has been adorned with the celestial nymphs moulded with grace and elegance, and rich ornamental carvings, musicians and dancers heralding the presence of the gods. The sunset time puts a golden glow on the sculptures. *Pages 72-73* : The trinity of Kandariya Mahadeo, Devi Jagdamba and Chitragupta Temples share a common platform raised at about 3 metres height from the ground. Alarmel Valli, the renowned Bharatanatyam dancer, fills the arena with a unique rhythm. Homage to Shiva takes the spectator to a different world and different time where he feels the divine bliss.

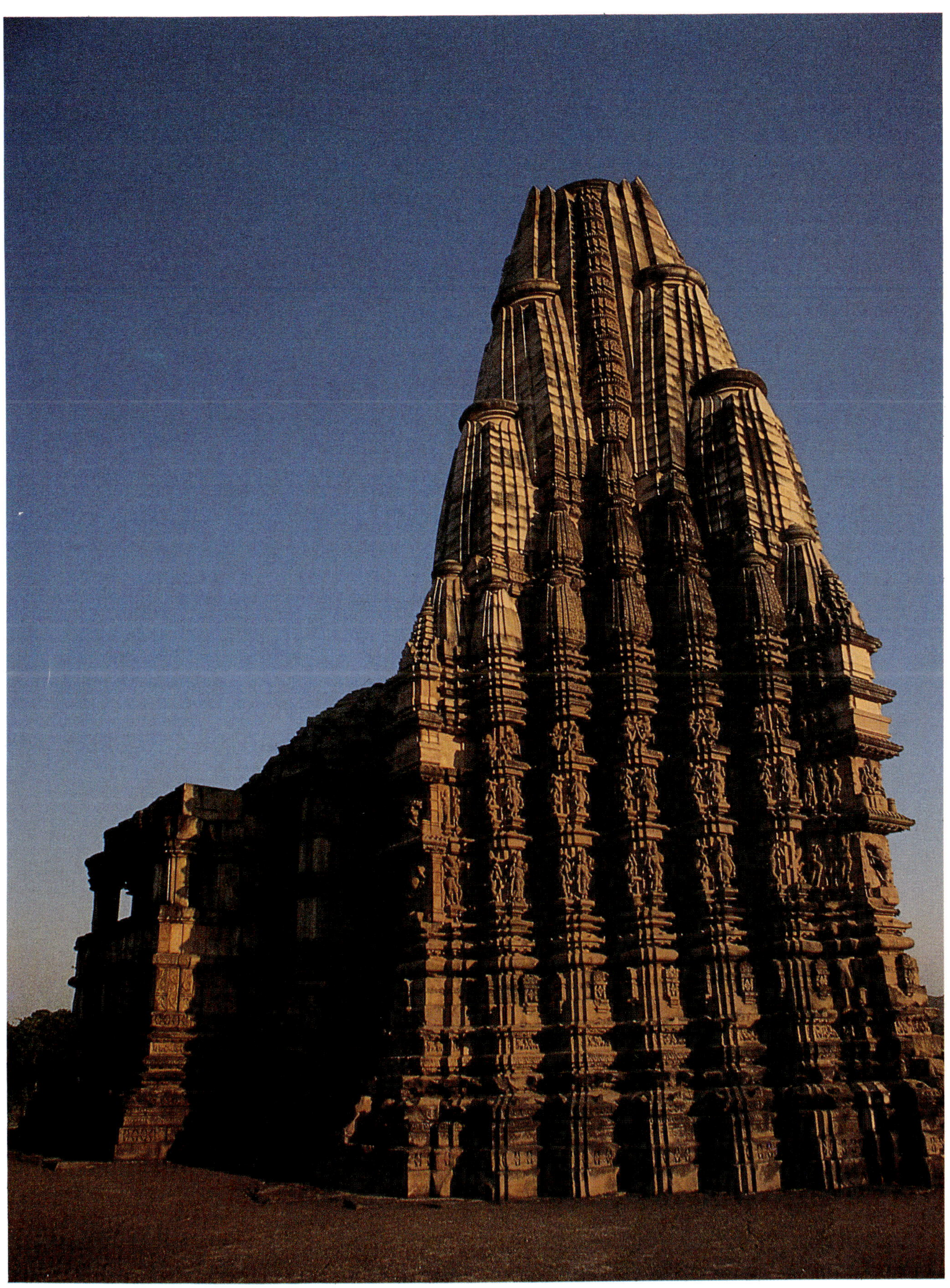

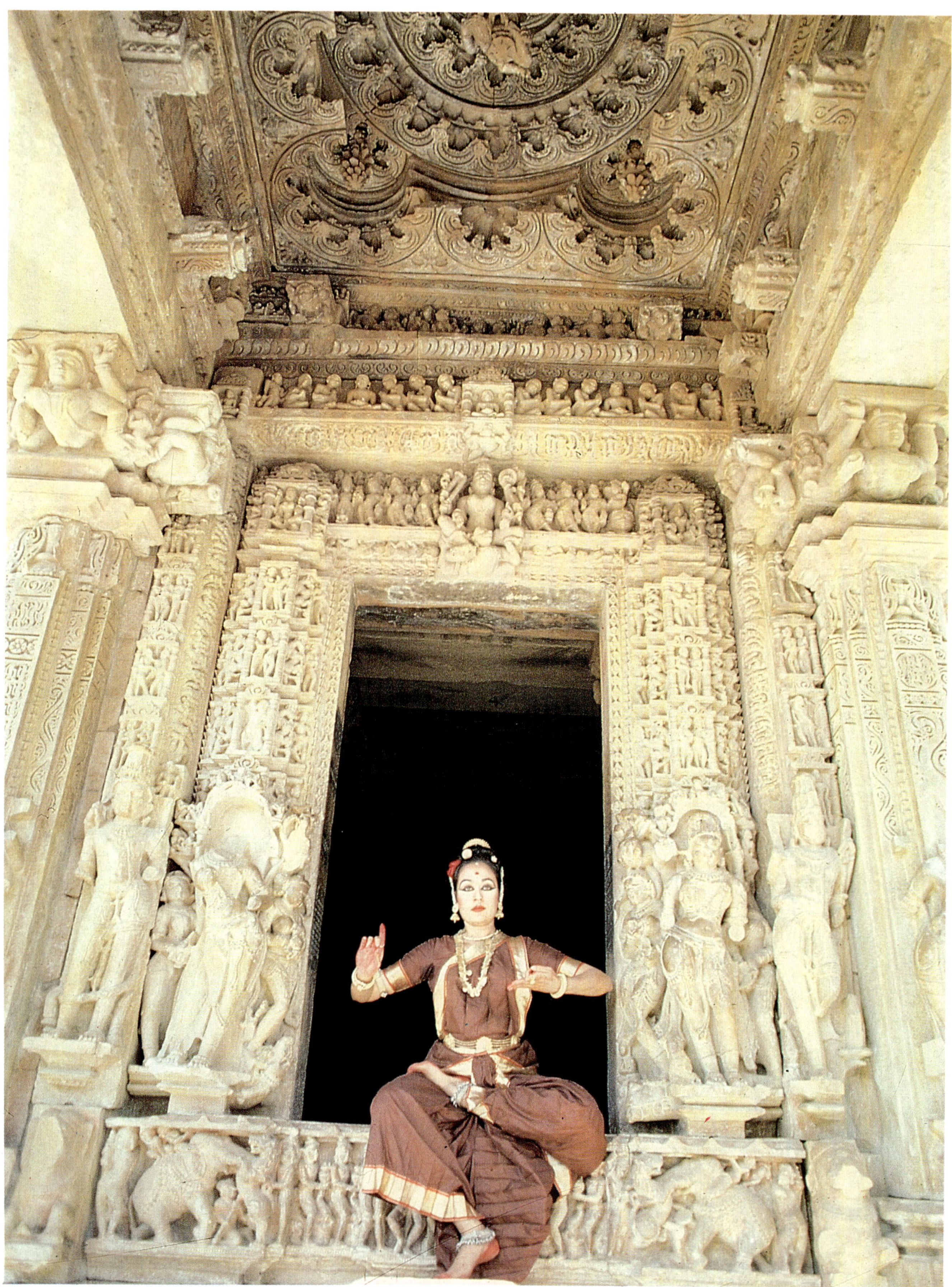

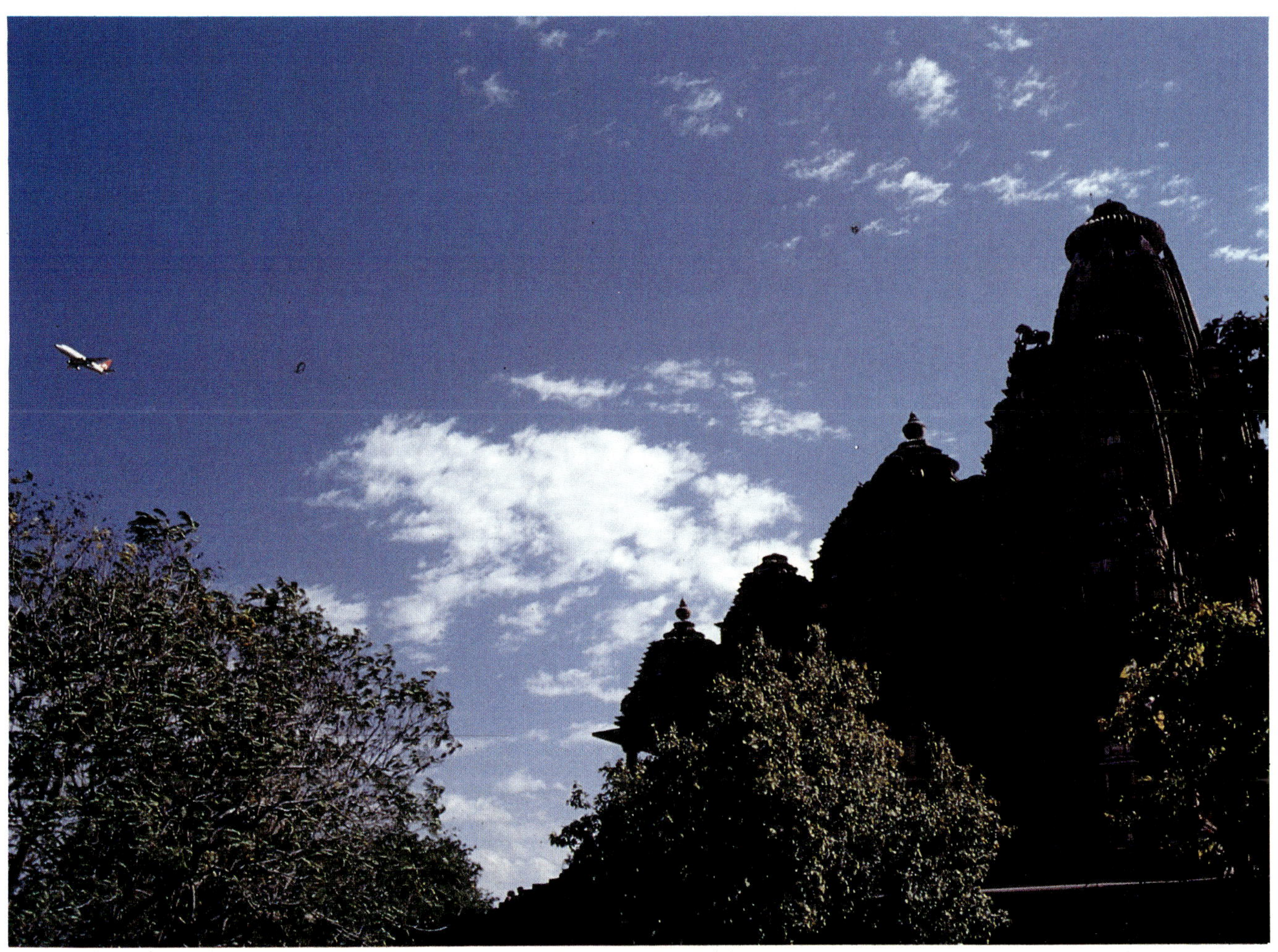

The Khajuraho village is probably the only village having a runway, where many aeroplanes bring the foreign tourists to witness the rhythm in its medieval legacy. One will certainly love to watch the masterpieces from the air but due to possible vibration hazards for the Khajuraho temples, aeroplanes are not allowed to fly at lower altitude. *Page 76* : Sonal Mansingh meditating at the door of the Jain Temple. Her Bharatanatyam dance postures tuned with the divine art carved in the Khajuraho temples create a unique rhythm.

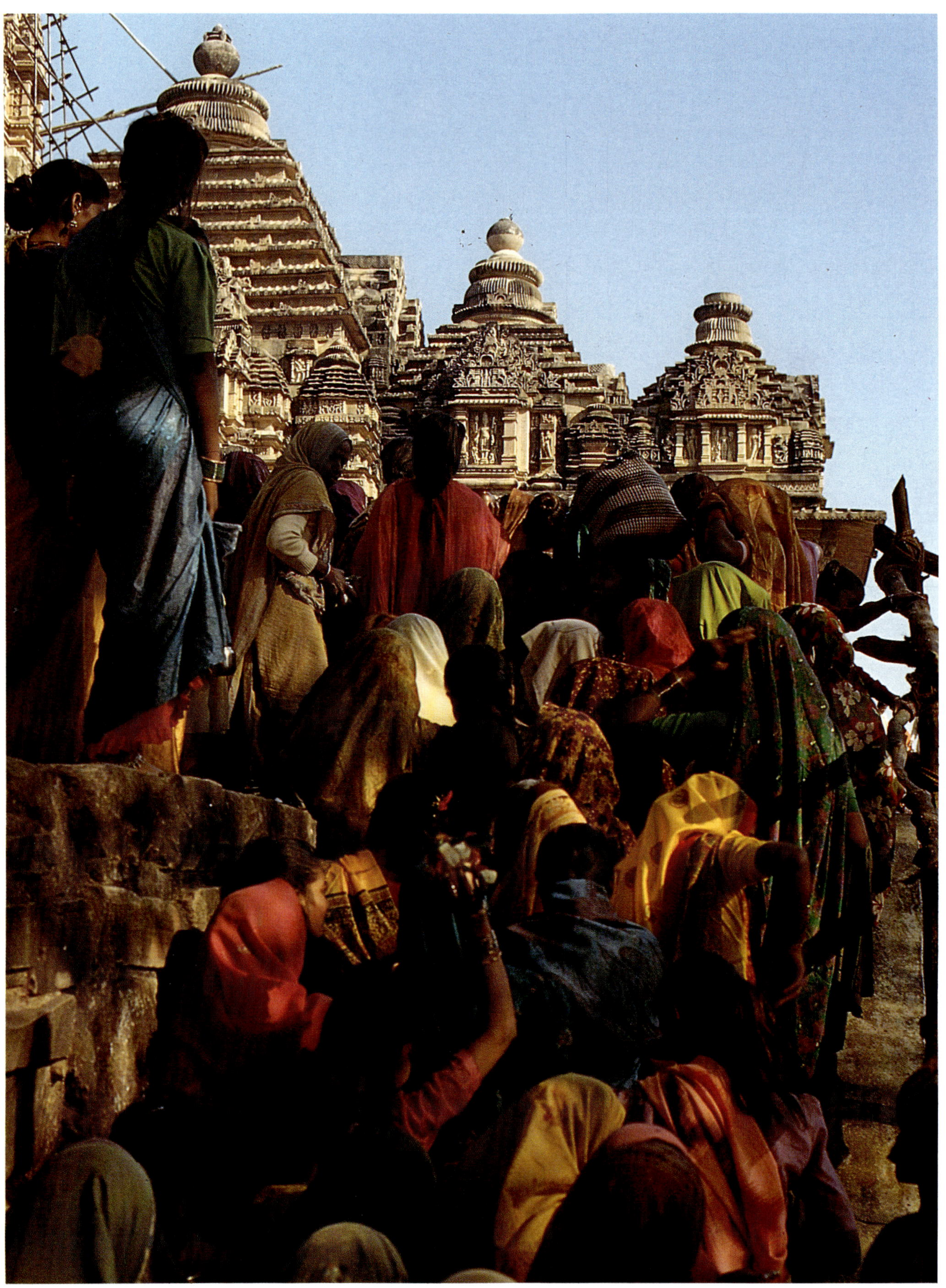

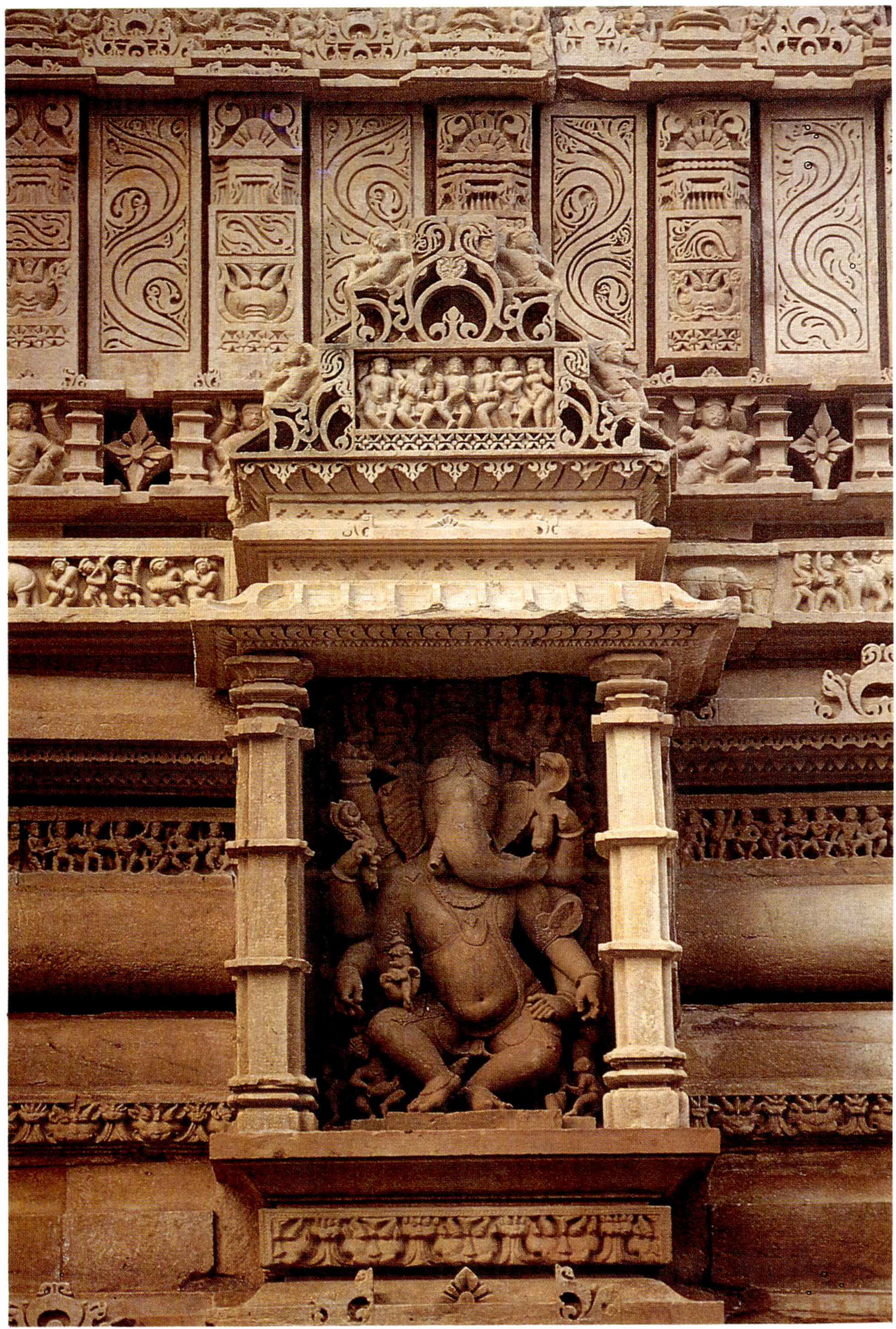

Ganesha, the Shiva's son, with an elephant head and typical belly. He is regarded as a remover of obstacles and hence propitiated before invoking other gods. Khajuraho temple walls have a few famous sculptures depicting Ganesha as a mendicant or as cosmic dancer. *Page 78* : Women throng outside the Matangeshwar temple to pay homage to Shiva.

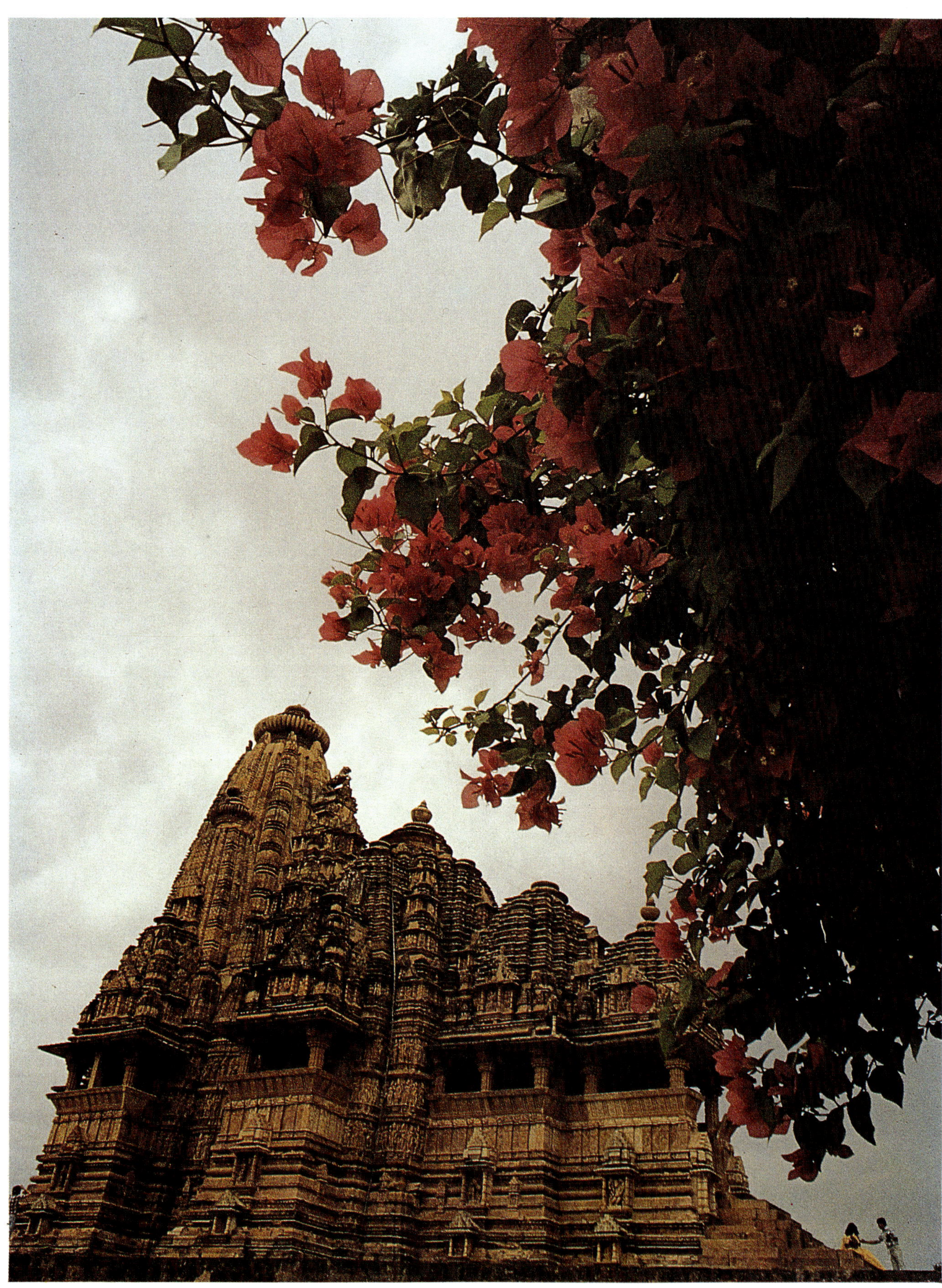

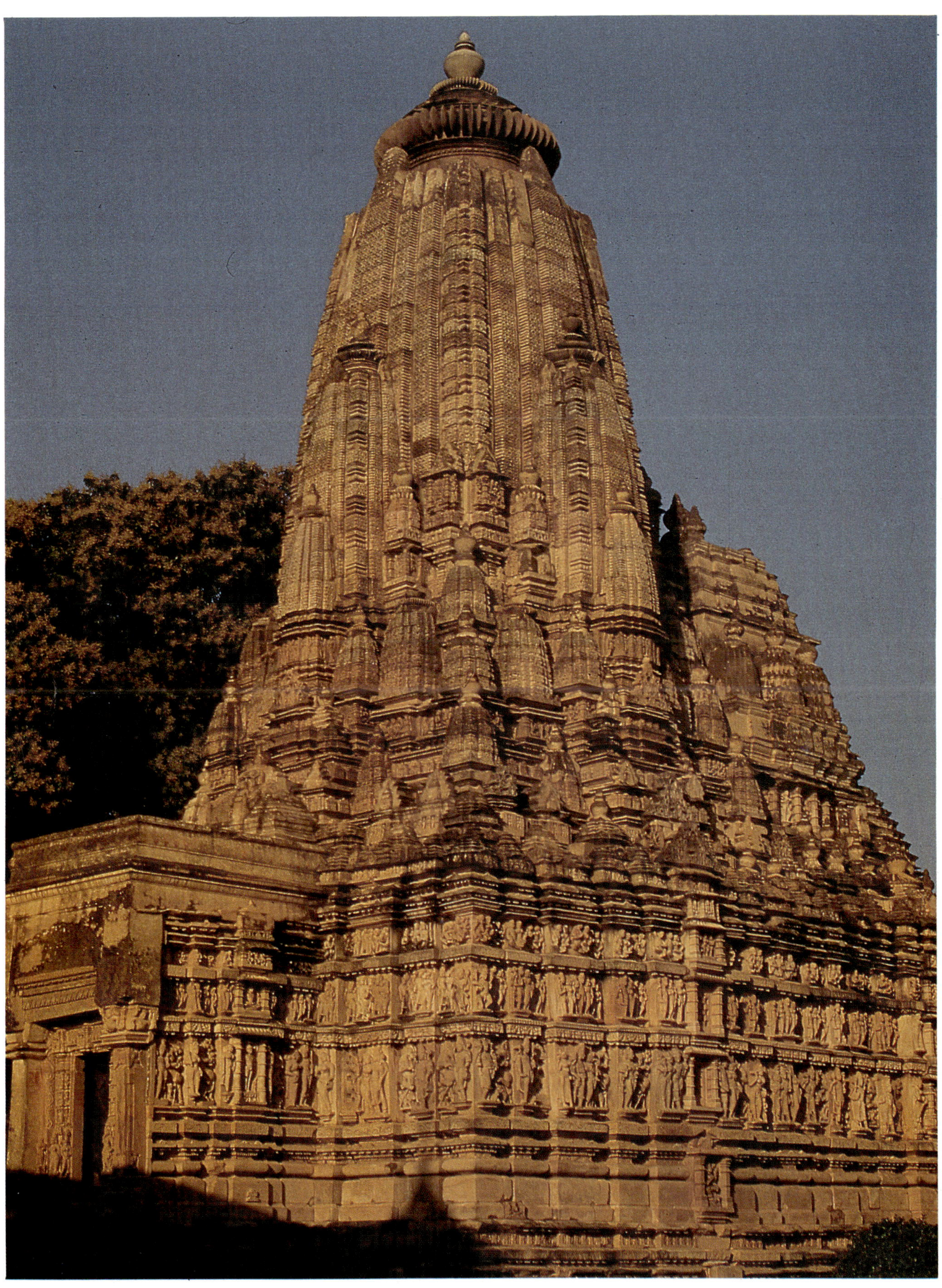

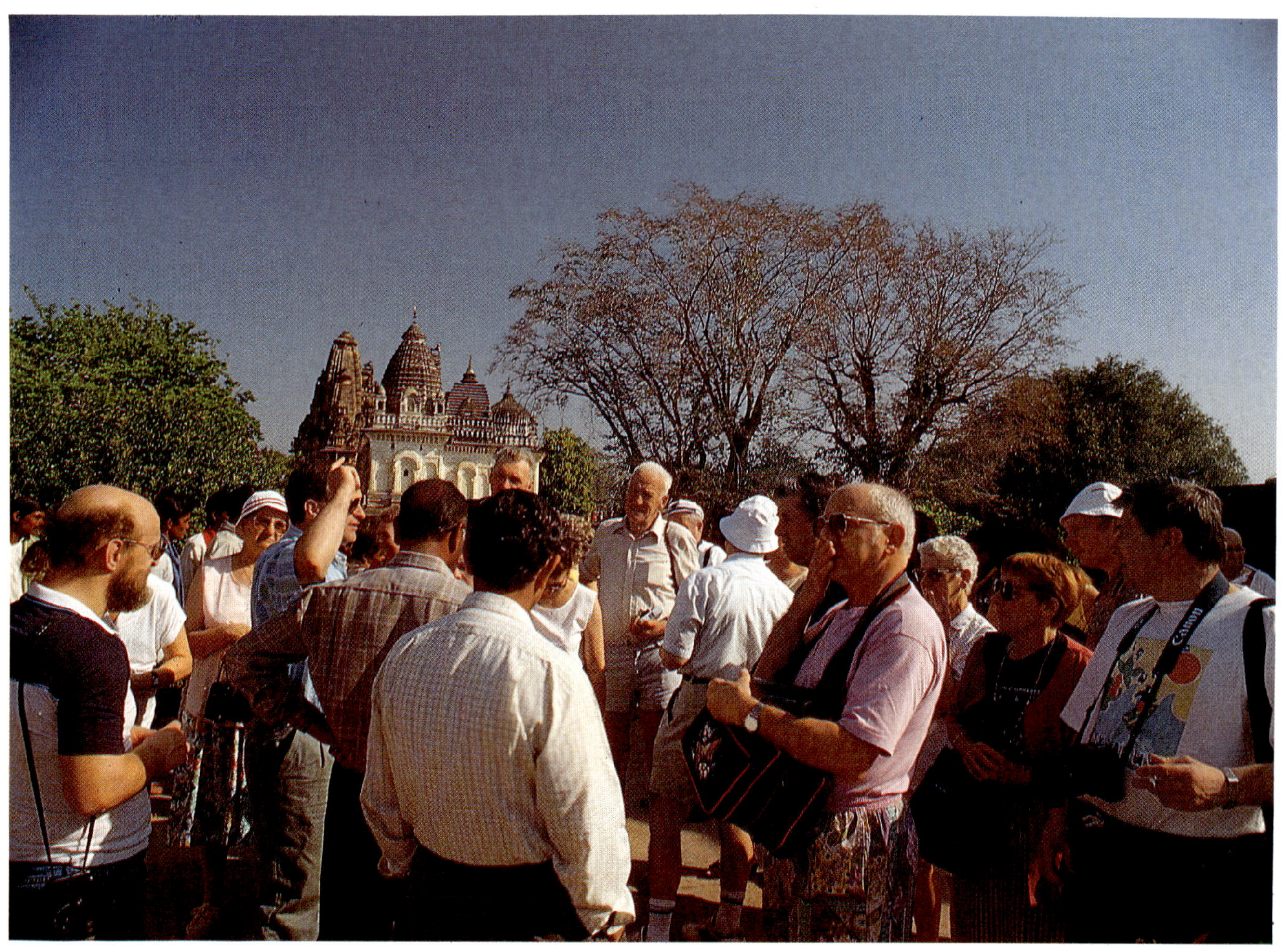

Although the erotic sculpture art attracts the foreigners as also the rural folk from Indian villages they find it difficult to decide the motive behind the unparallel sculptural art of the medieval India. *Page 83* : Torana is a significant architectural embellishment at the entrance of a temple. Kandariya Mahadeo temple has a single-stone carved torana staging the celestial Gandharvas and Kinnars on the heads of mythical crocodiles. *Page 81* : Pasarvanath Temple.

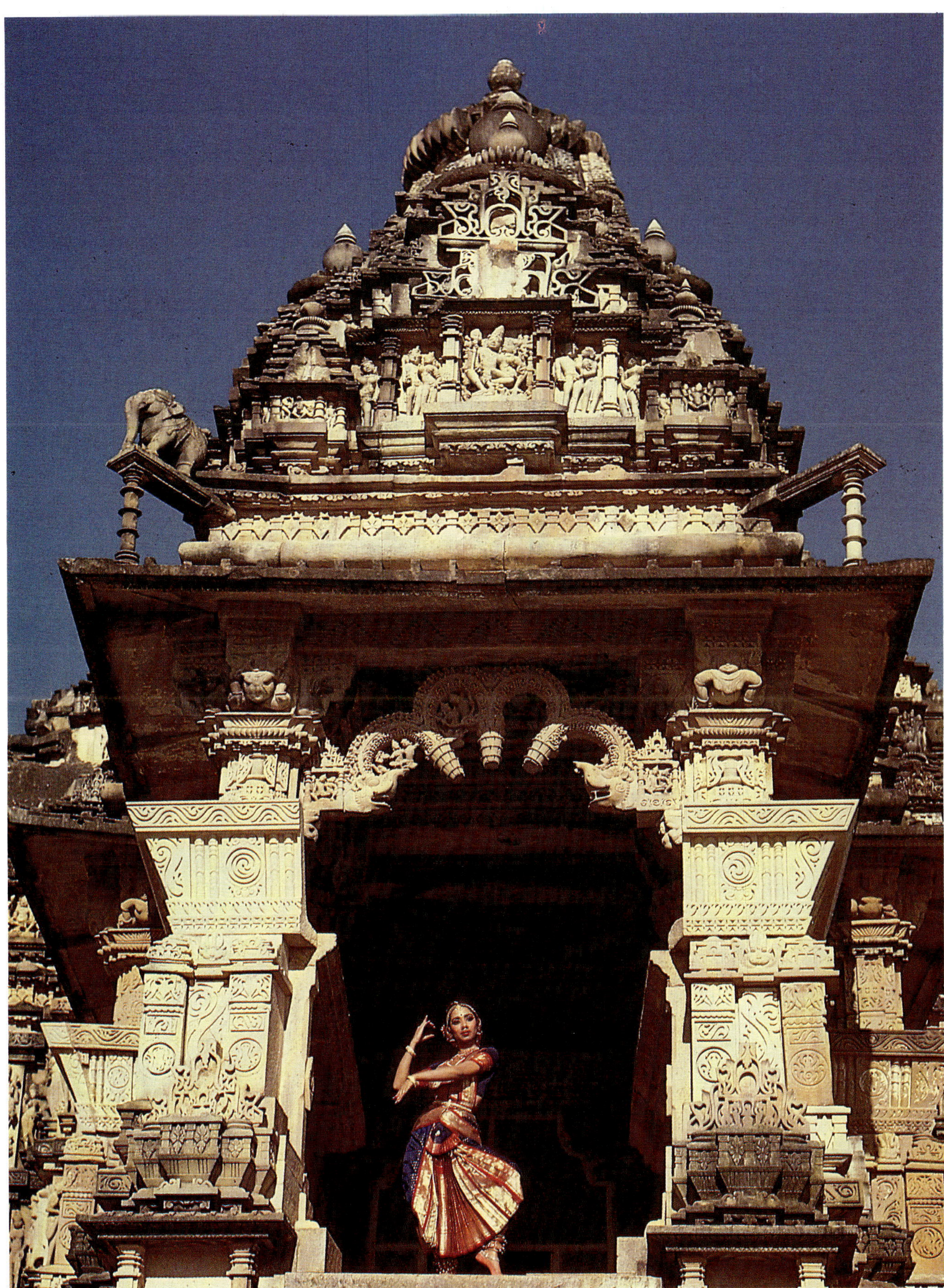

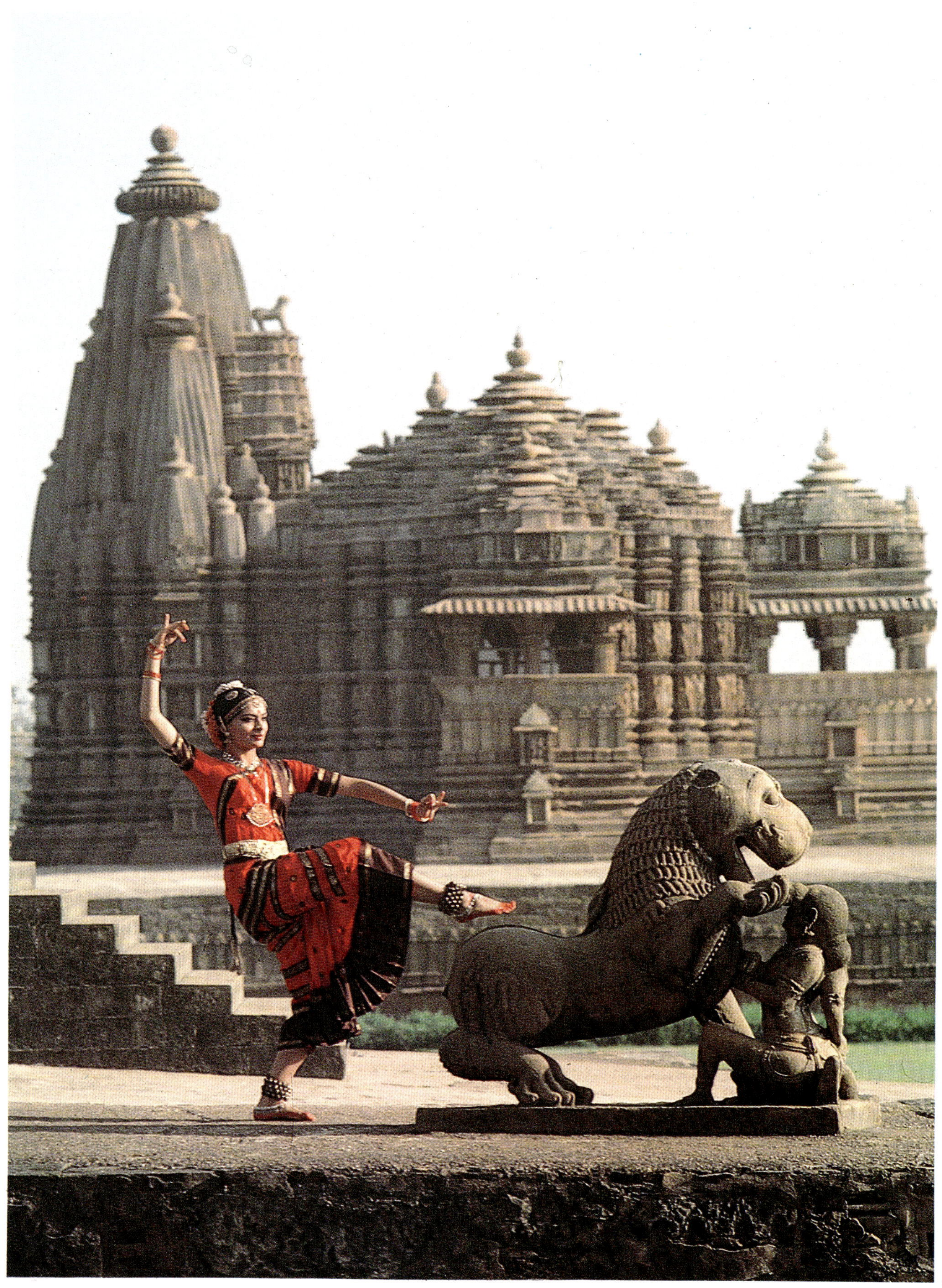

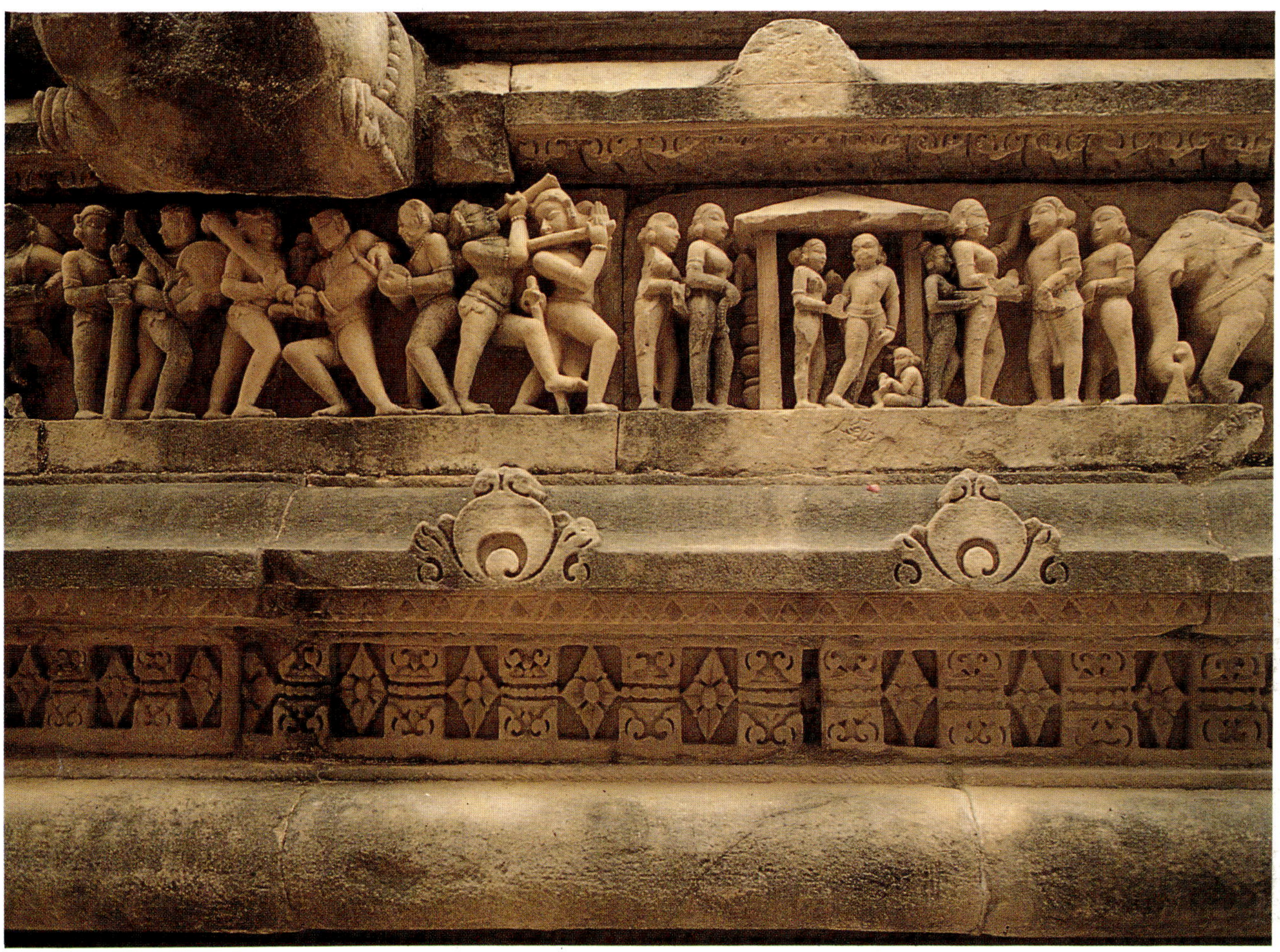

Lakshmana temple : platform frieze showing marriage ceremonies and festivities.
page 84 : Malavika Sarukkai, in a Bharatanatyam dance posture, pays homage to the Lord Shiva. The image of a warrior grappling with a lion is a typical emblem or monogram of the Chandela dynasty whose progenitor was known to have fought barehanded with lions in his youth. The backdrop of Chitragupta Temple adds a unique rhythm to the scene.

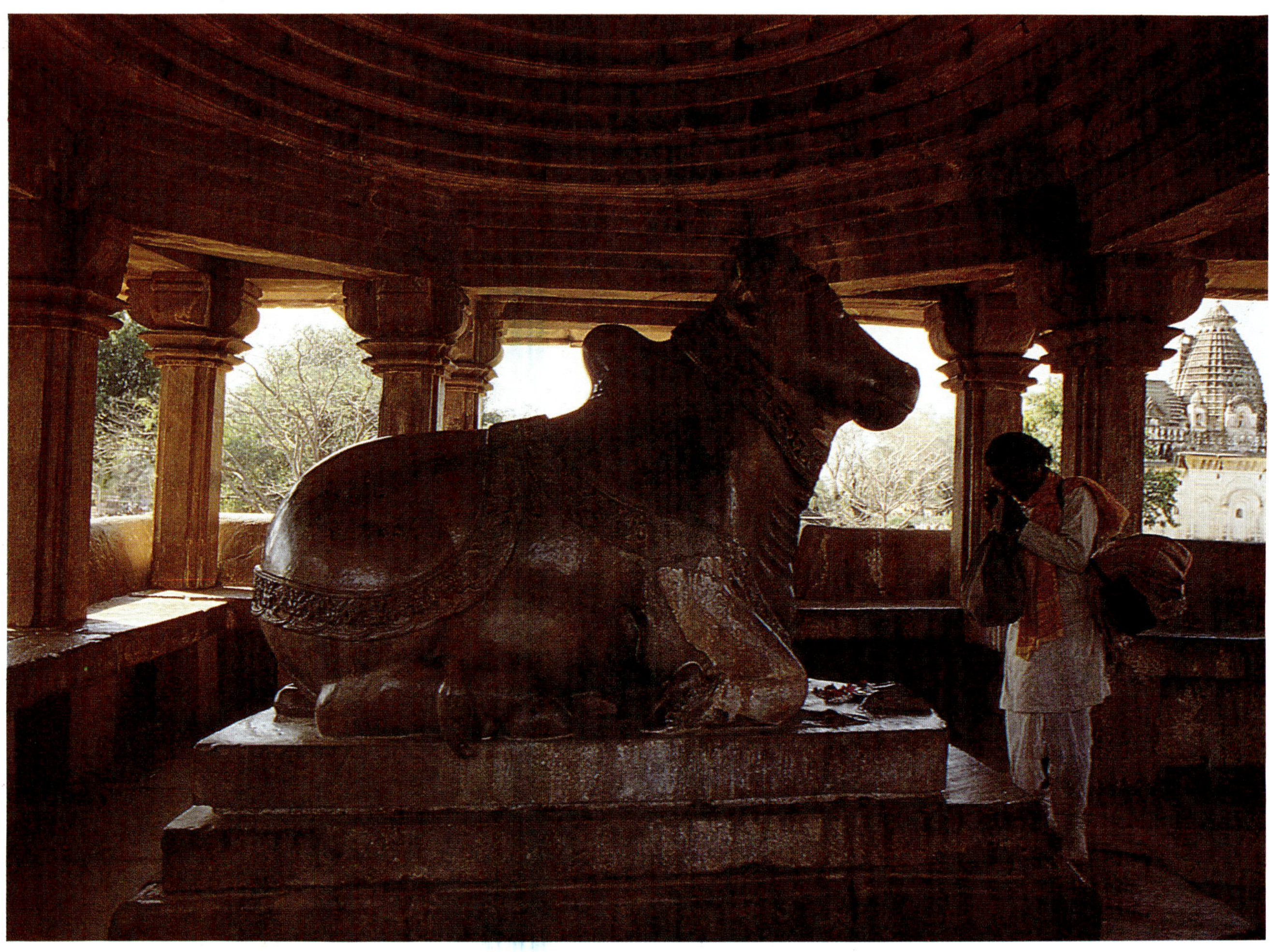

Nandi Temple : a separate pavilion forming a part of Vishvanath complex. One of the rare temples open to the west, its *mandapa* houses a colossal image of Shiva's vehicle, 'Nandi' the bull. Situated to the east of Vishvanath Temple, Nandi faces to its entrance, on the same platform. Its huge pyramid-shaped roof is supported by a series of pillars resting on a low wall. The symbol of bull has link with the fertility cult of Indus Valley civilisation. *Page 87* : Protima Bedi paying homage to gods and goddesses through the Odissi dance posture. The backdrop of Khajuraho temples adds richness to the beauty of her movements.

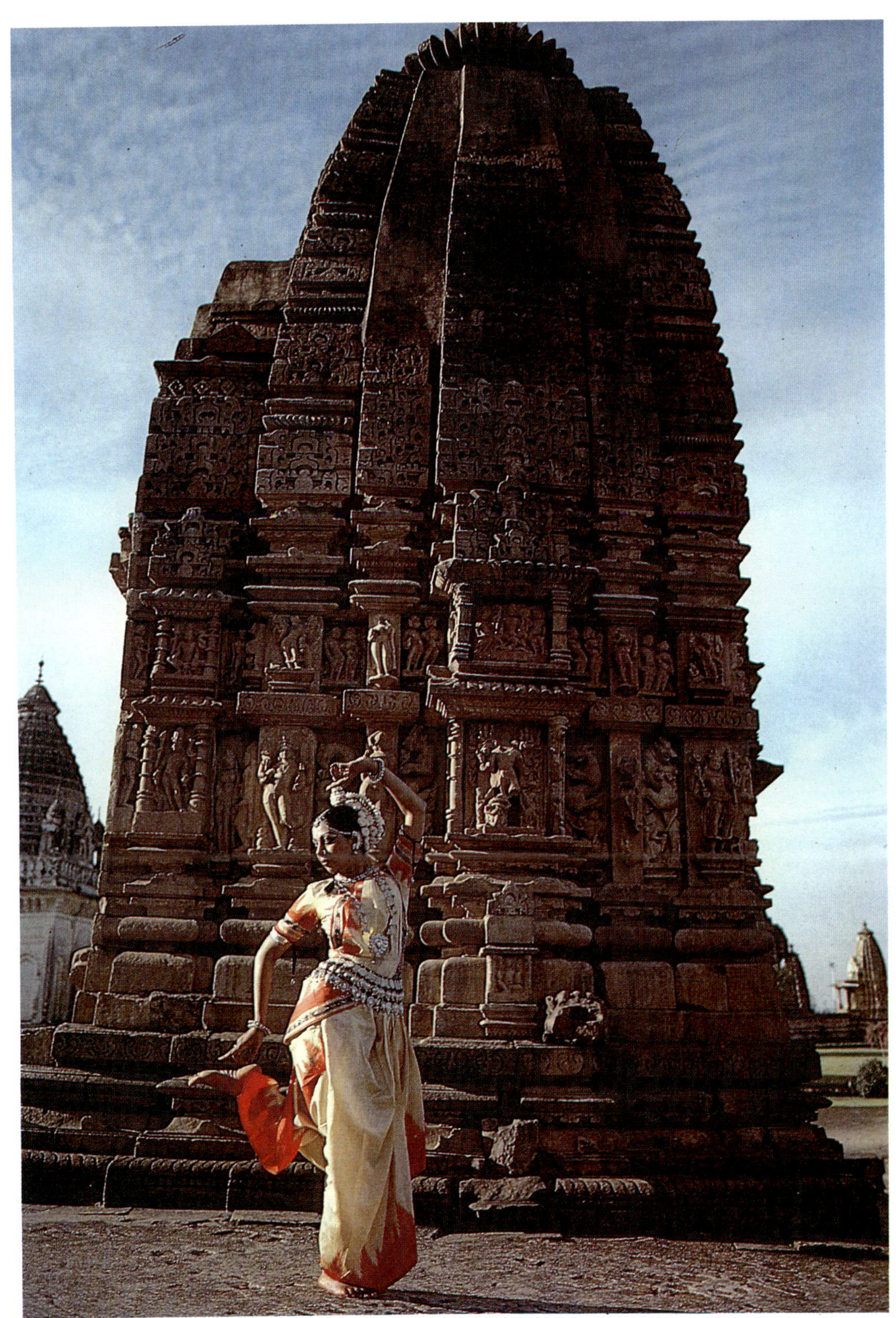

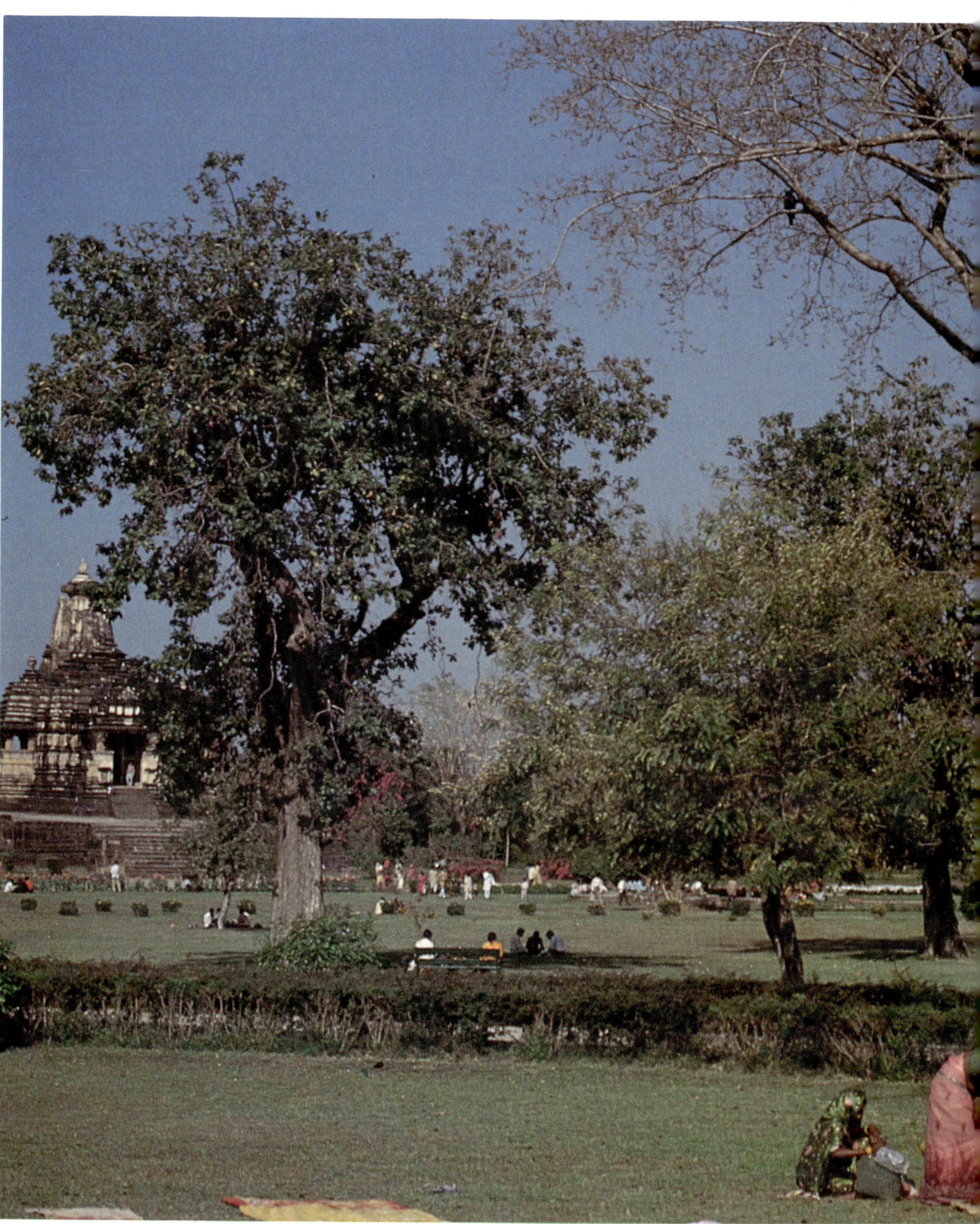

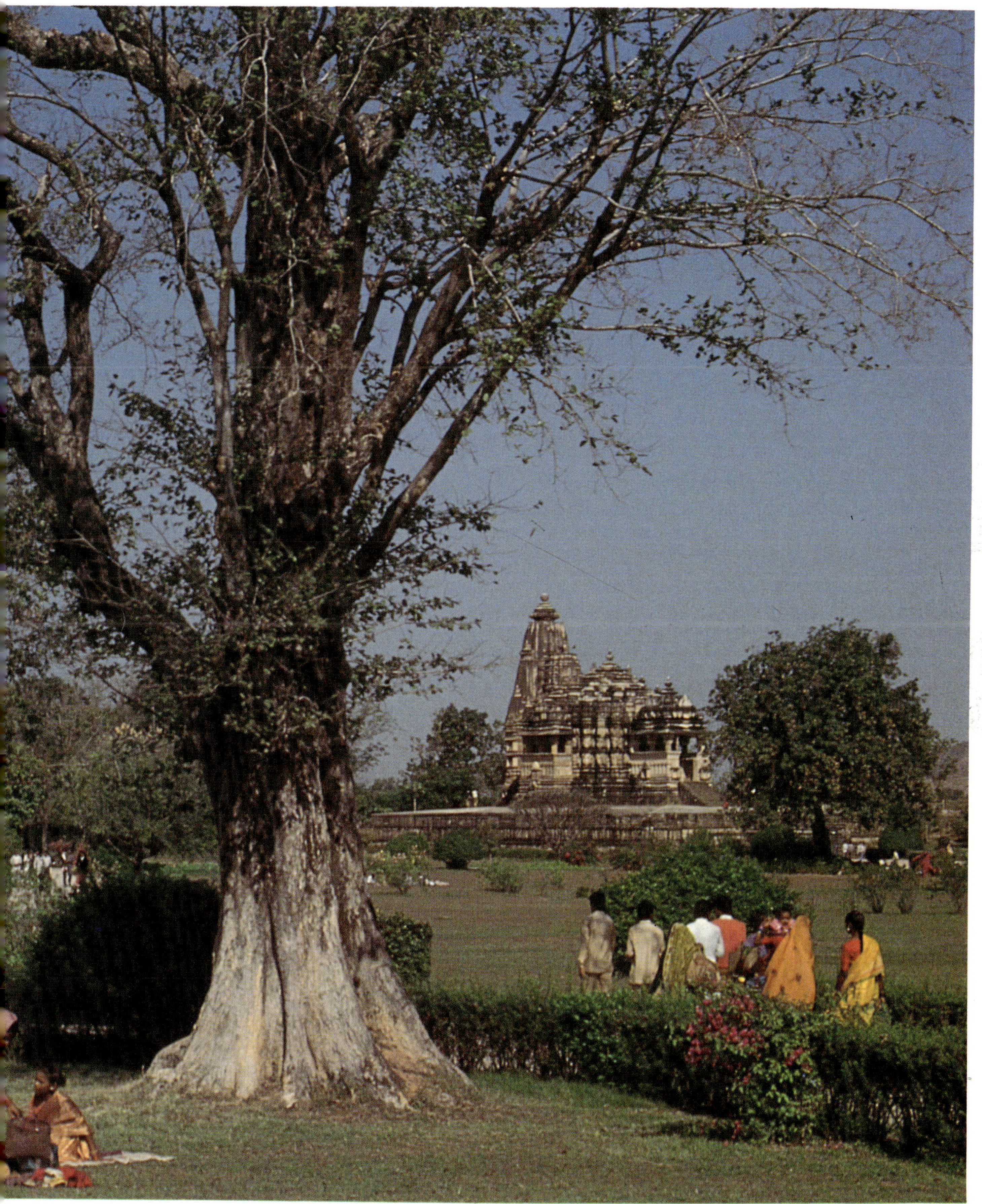

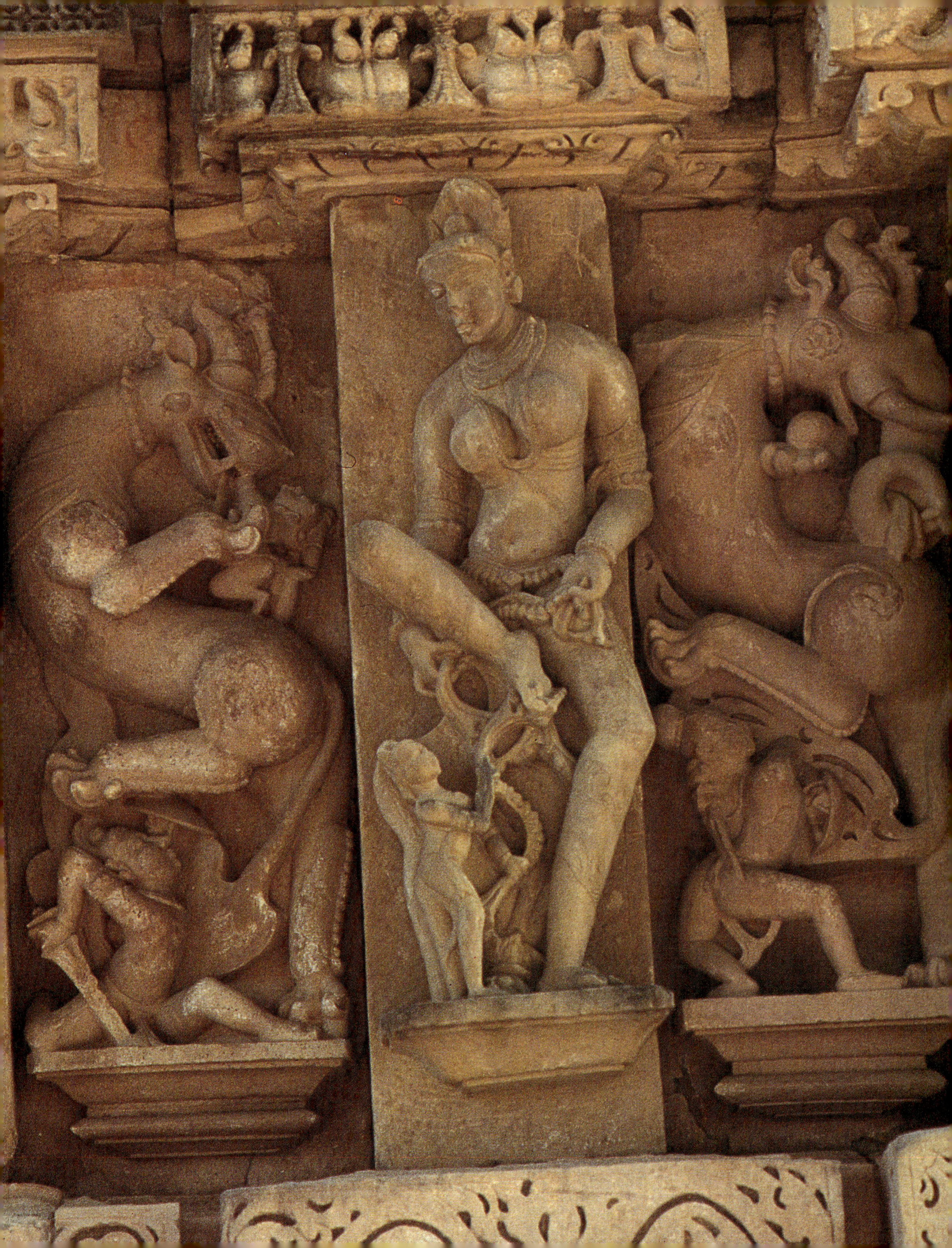

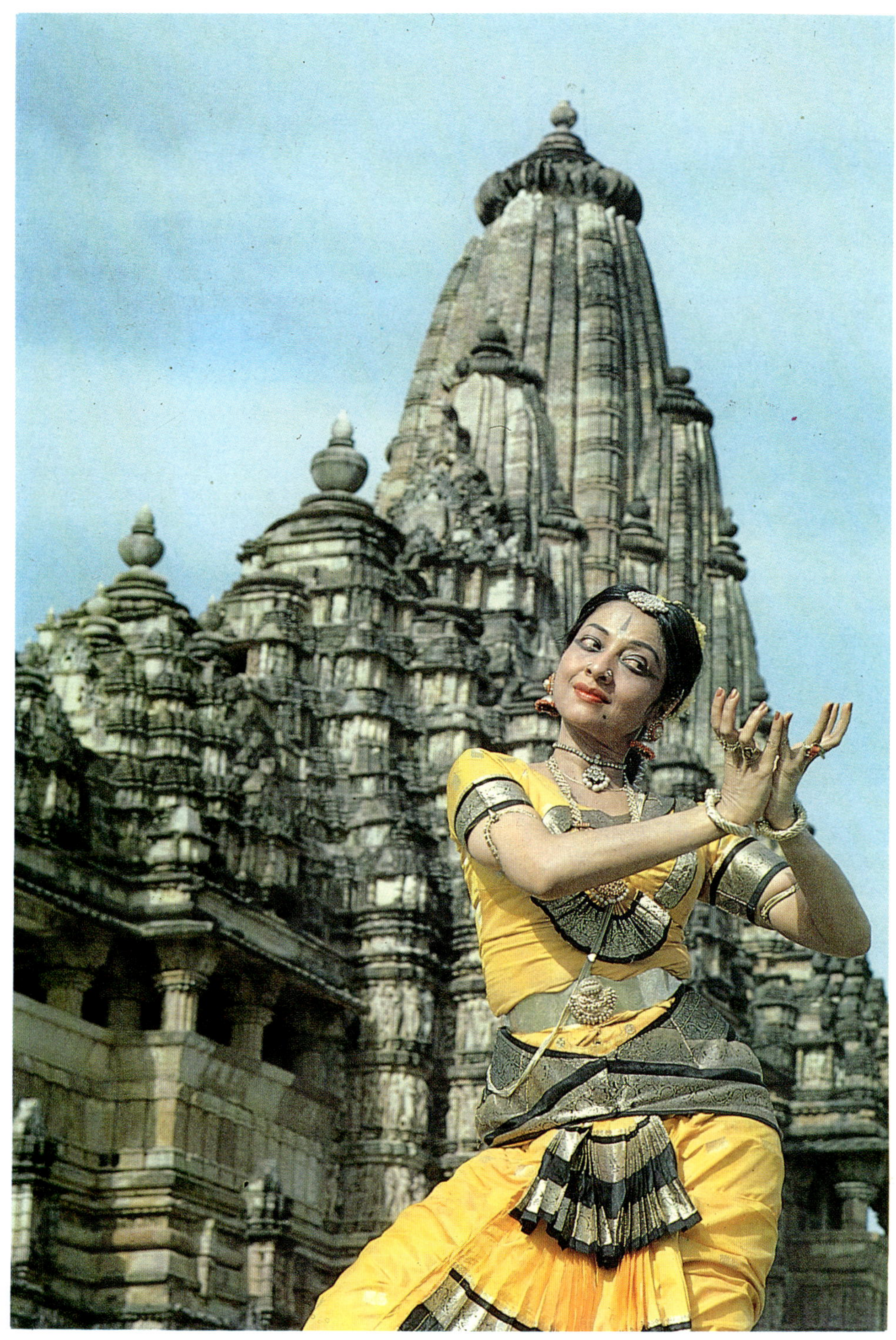

Yamini Krishnamurthy paying homage to Shiva through her Bharatanatyam dance. The backdrop of Kandariya Mahadeo creates a unique rhythm, the ultimate bliss of union with the divinity. *Page 90* : An Apsara putting on her ankle-bells while her maid helps her (Parsvanath Temple).

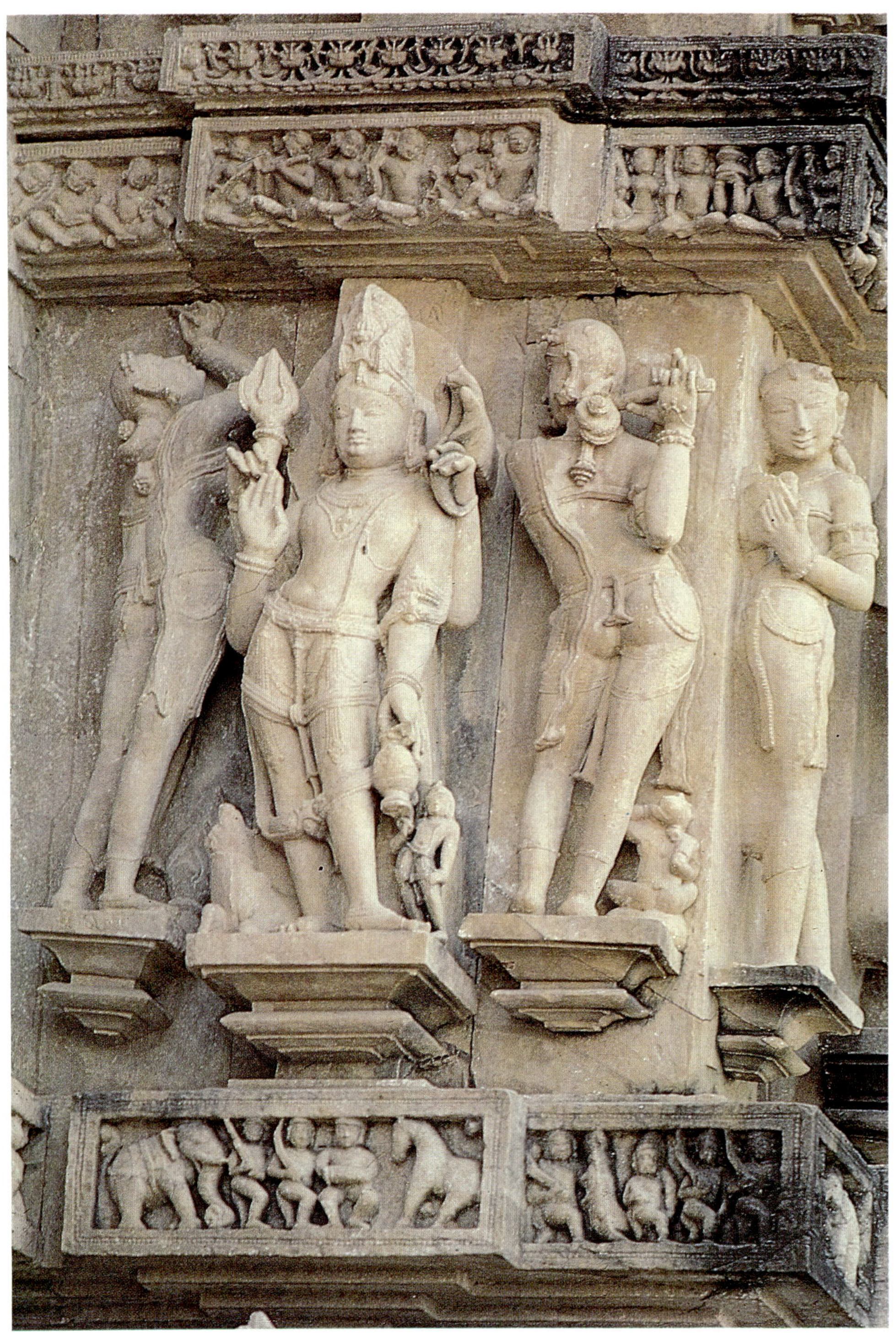

The Apsara turns her back on the visitor as if inviting him to follow her to more eternal heights. *Page 93* : Bharati Shivaji's Bharatanatyam dance postures against the adorned walls of Khajuraho temples create a feeling as if celestial nymphs have appeared before the visitor.

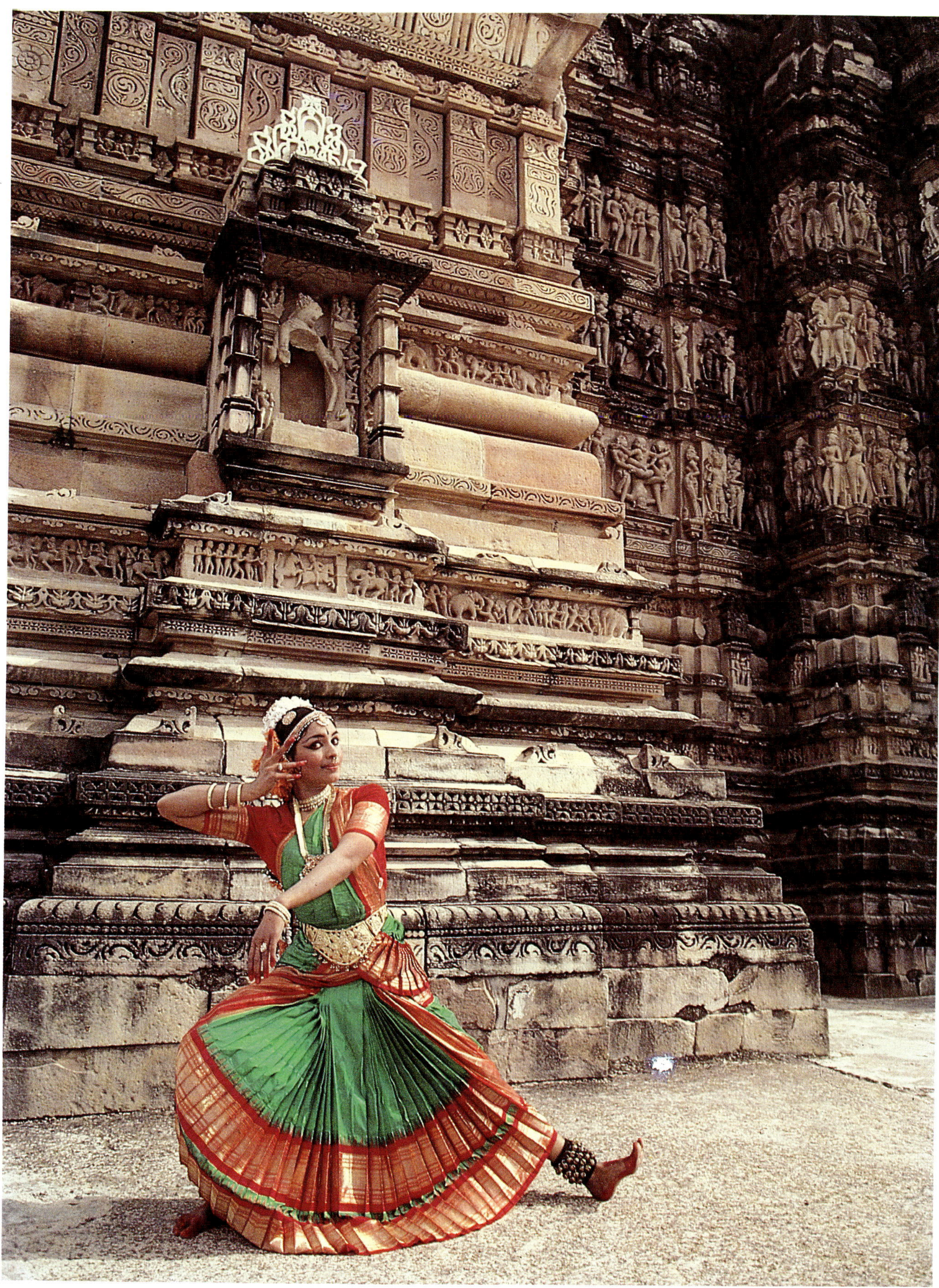

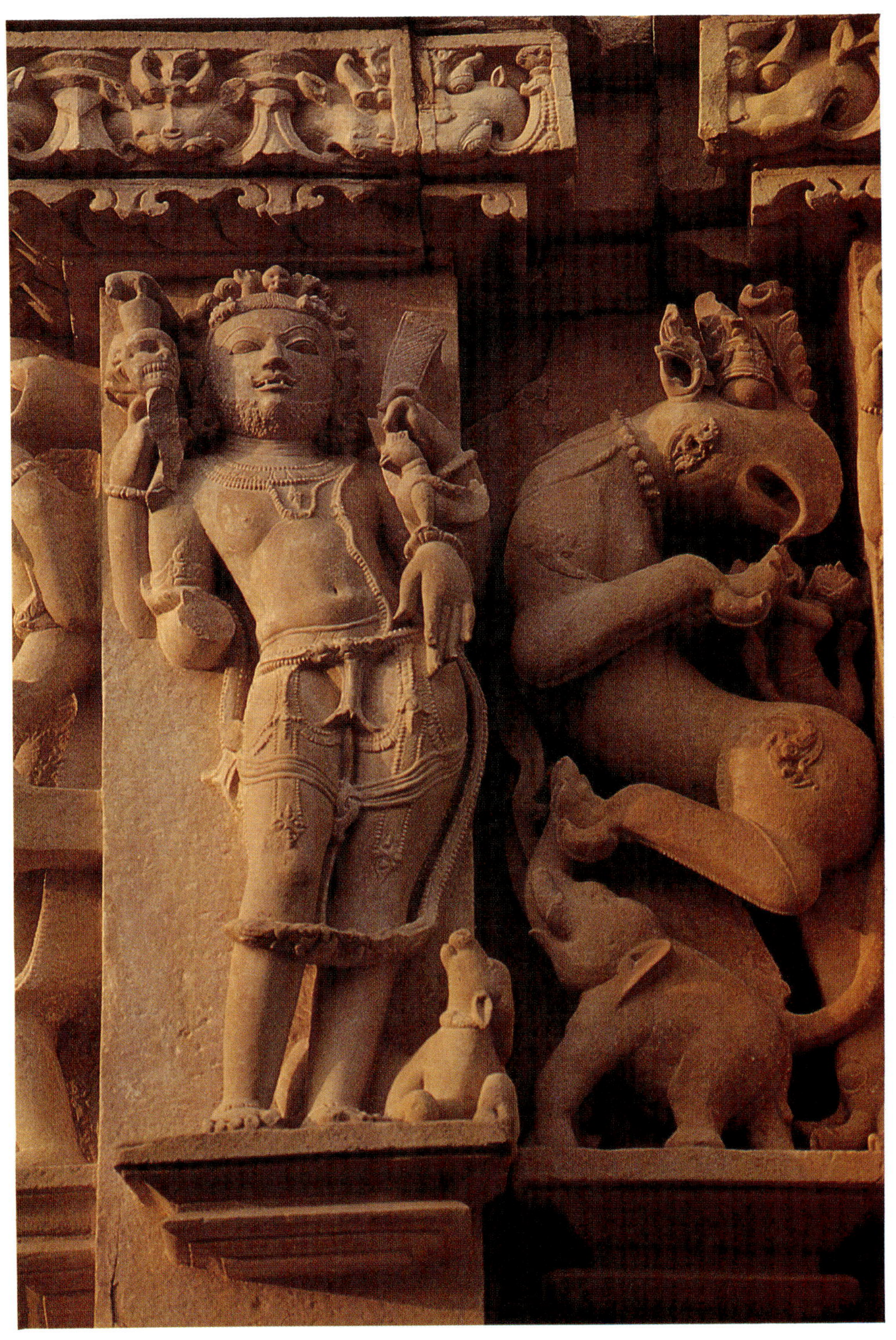

Mahakaal — God of Death, a Hindu diety, on the wall of Pasarvanath Temple.

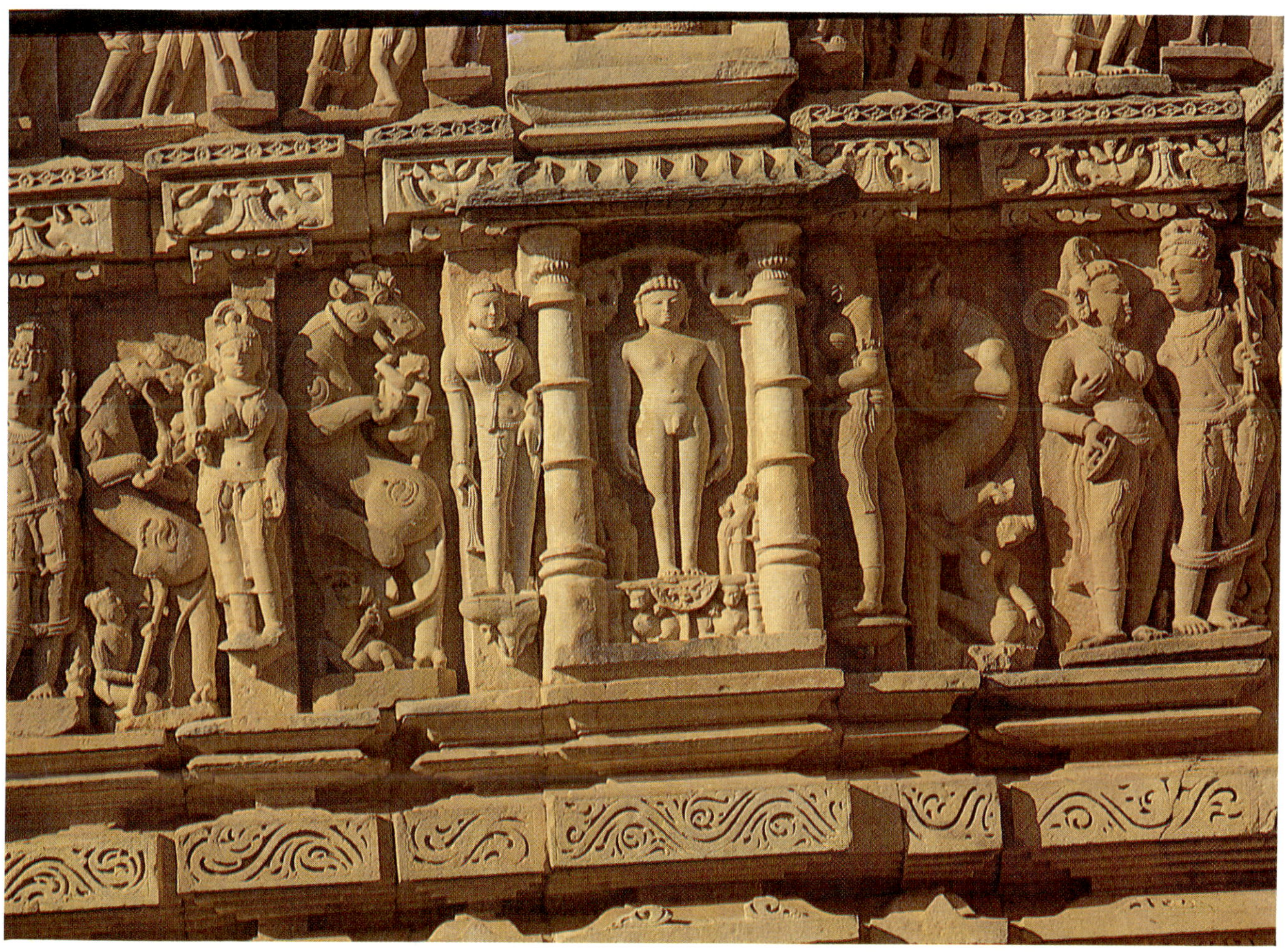

Parsvanath Temple : The panel depicting an image of Jain Tirthankar 'Parsvanath' in the centre. The temple, considered to be the best amongst the Jain temples of Khajuraho, resembles with that of a Hindu temple's architectural plan and design. Although the temple is affiliated to the Jain sect the deities of Hindu pantheon have been conspicuously portrayed. The sanctum has a statue of Parsvanath flanked by a nude male figure on the left and a nude female figure on the right.

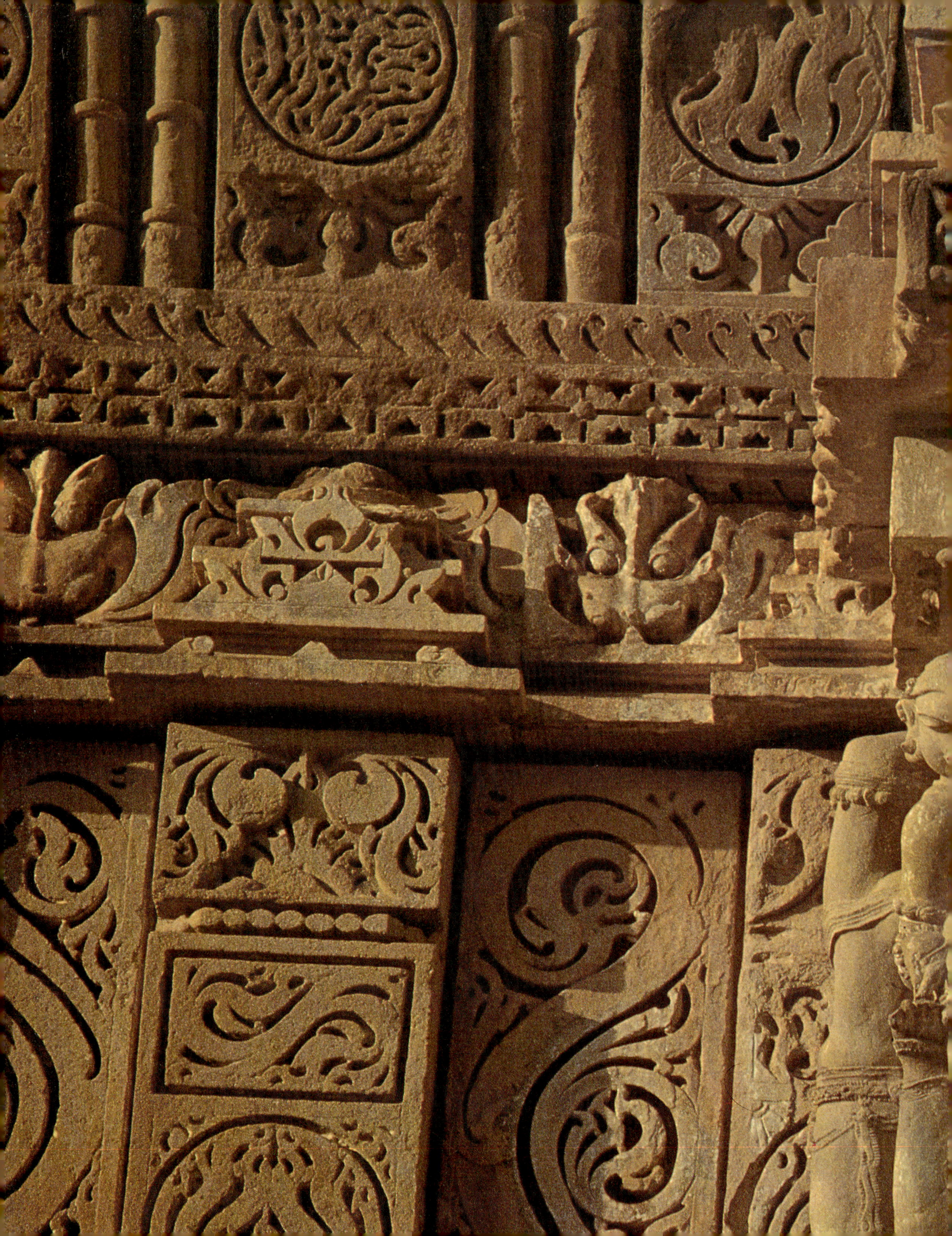

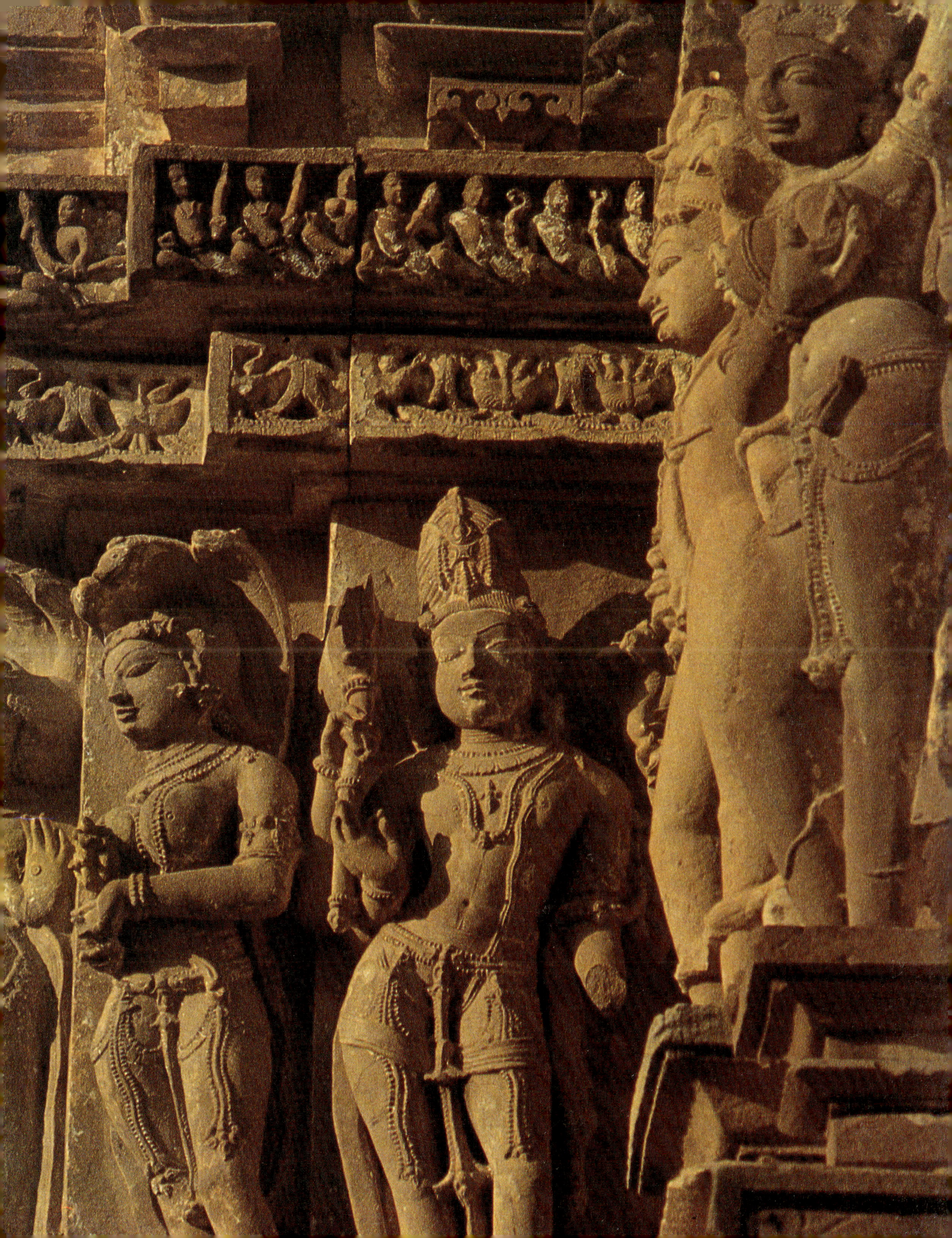

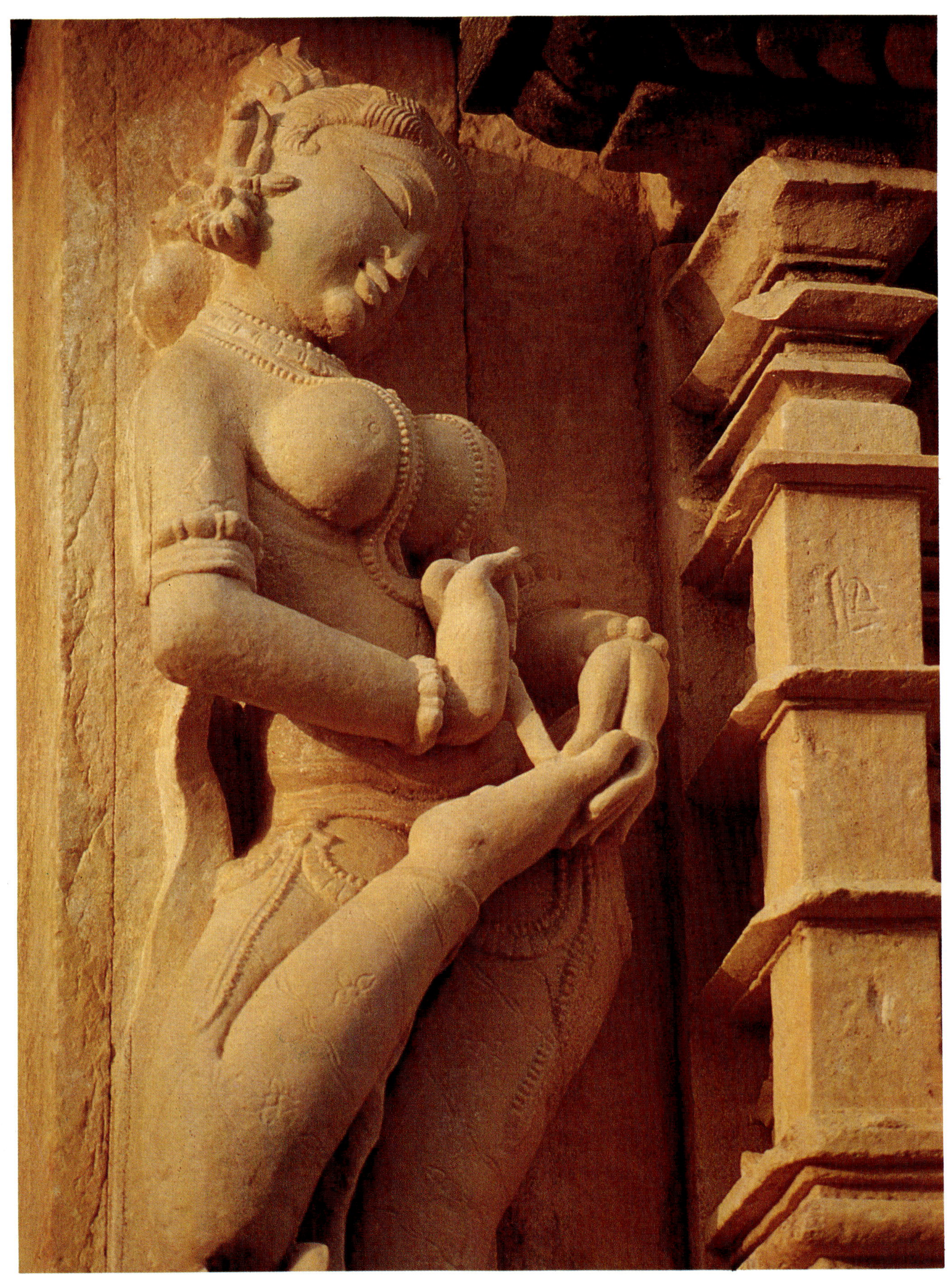

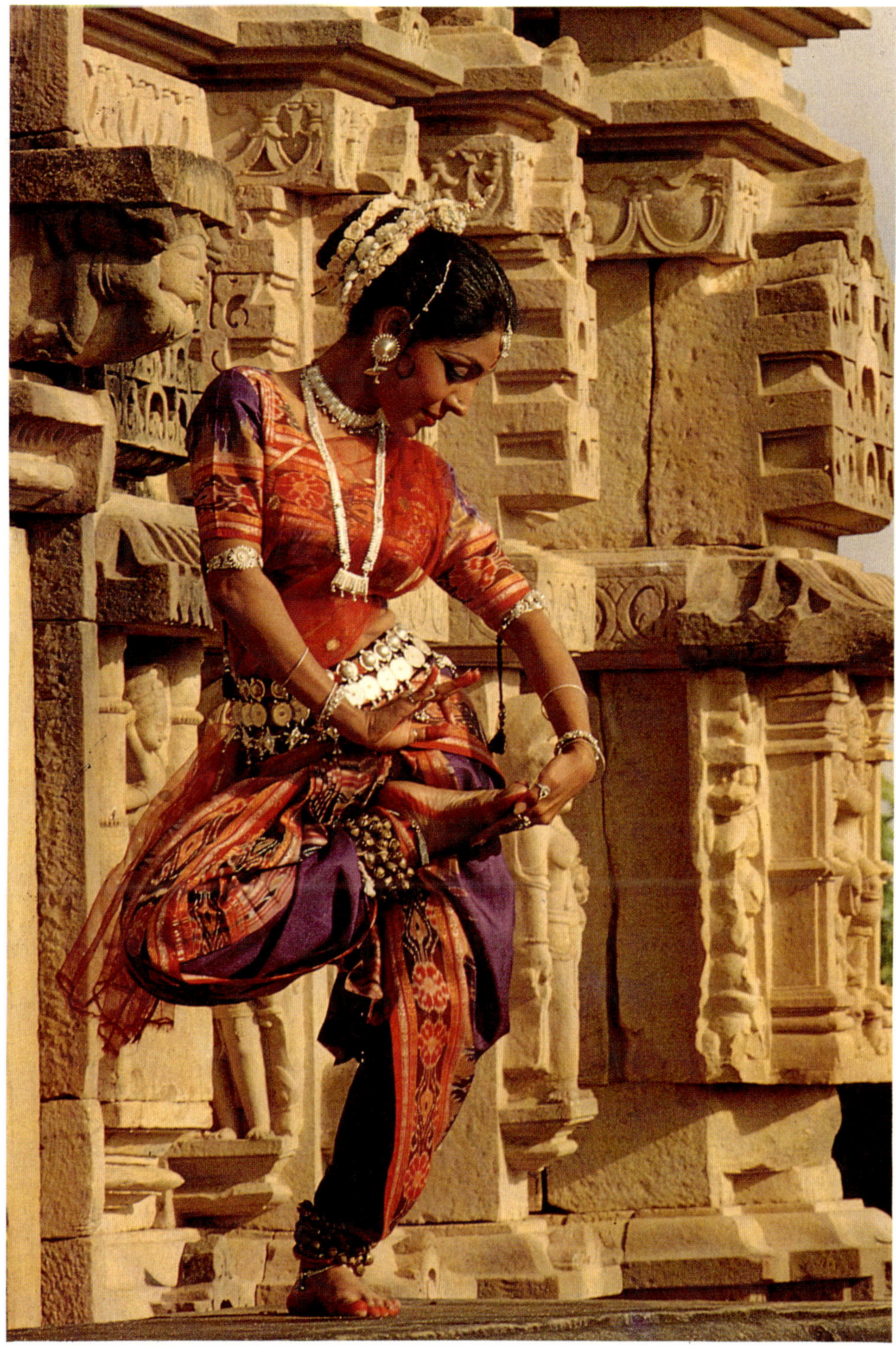

Madhavi Mudgal, the renowned Indian classical dancer, in a Odissi dance posture juxtaposed with an Apsara, the celestial nymph, painting her foot (Parsvanath Temple). In India dyeing the soles of the feet is a necessary part of her make up. The woman in love takes great care of her body in order to please her lover who, when they come together, is both her god and her prey. The perfection of her heavy breasts is filled with promise of sensual satisfaction for the man-god.

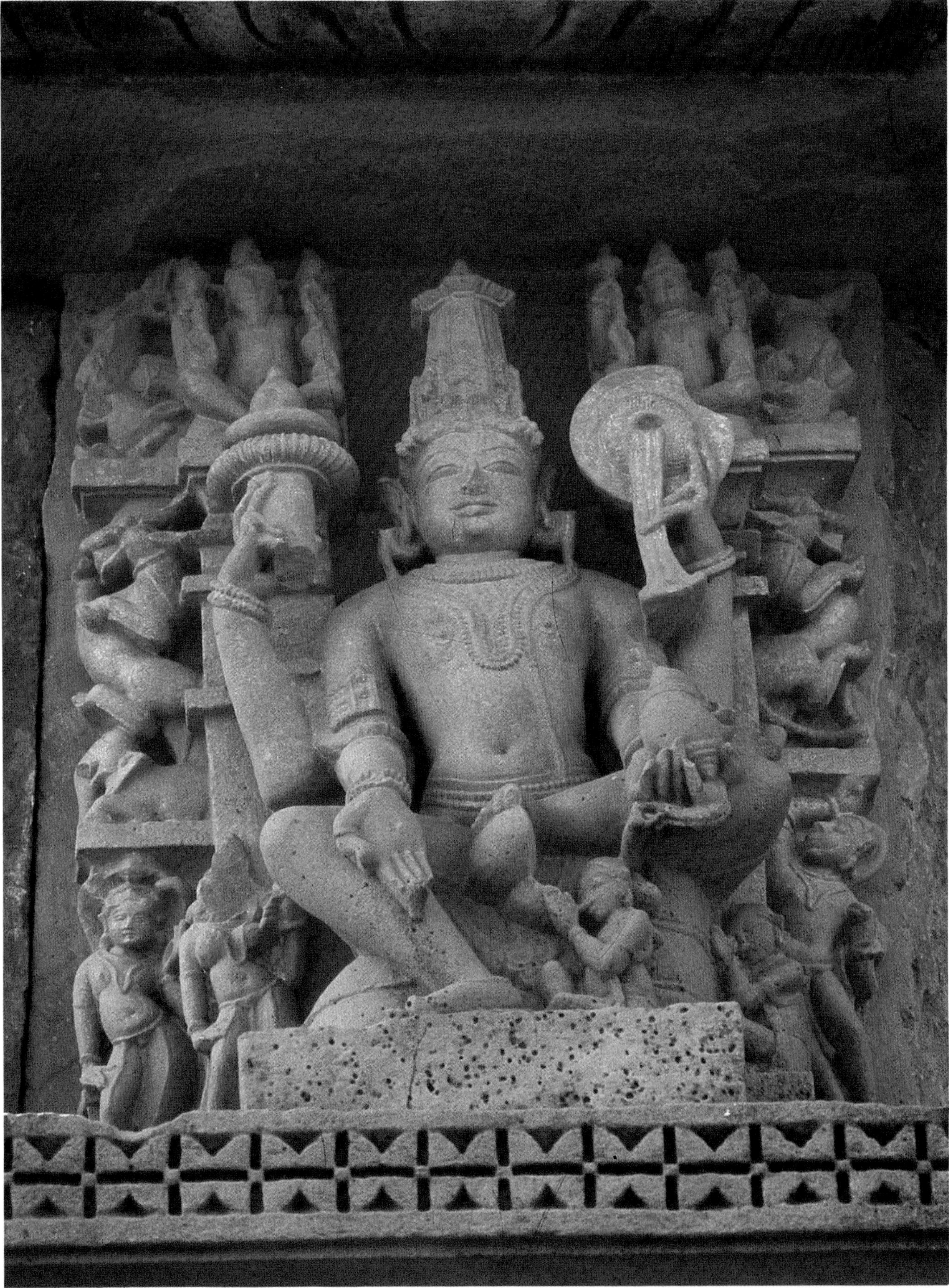

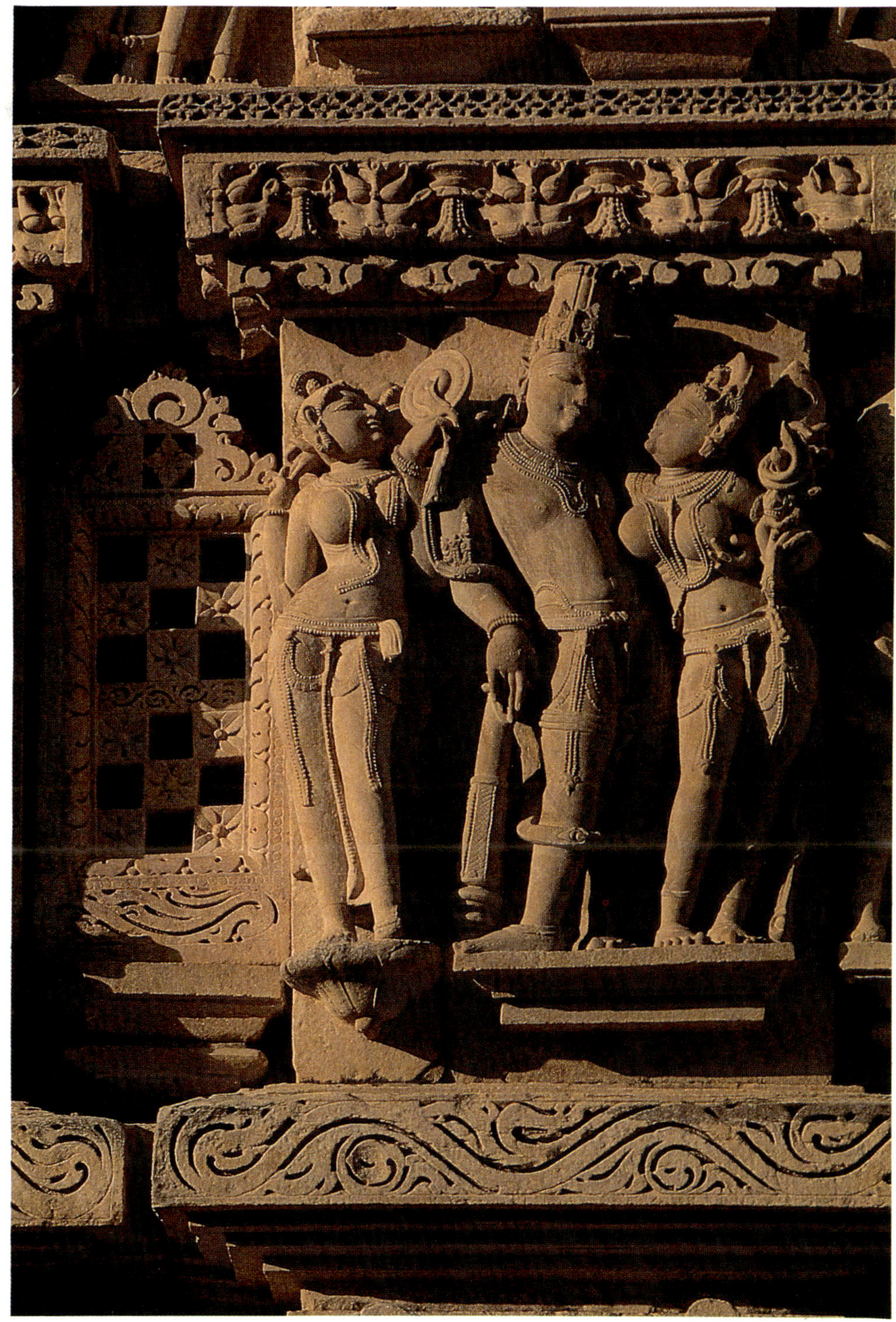

Although the Parsvanath temple is affiliated to the Jain sect, the deities of Hindu pantheon have been remarkably portrayed. The Hindu gods with their energy partners — the goddesses depict astonishing delicacy and divine expressions which symbolise unity and wholeness.

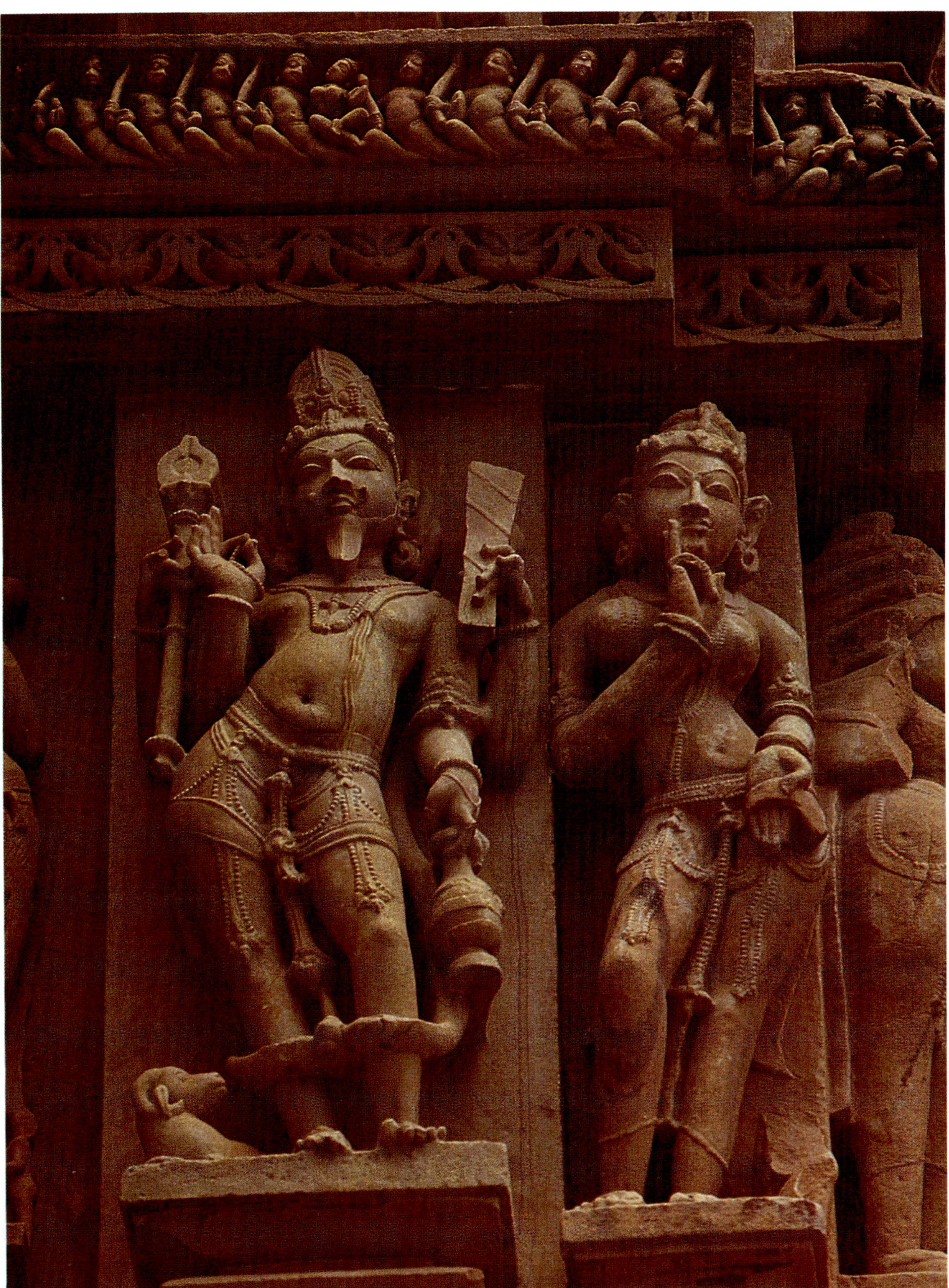

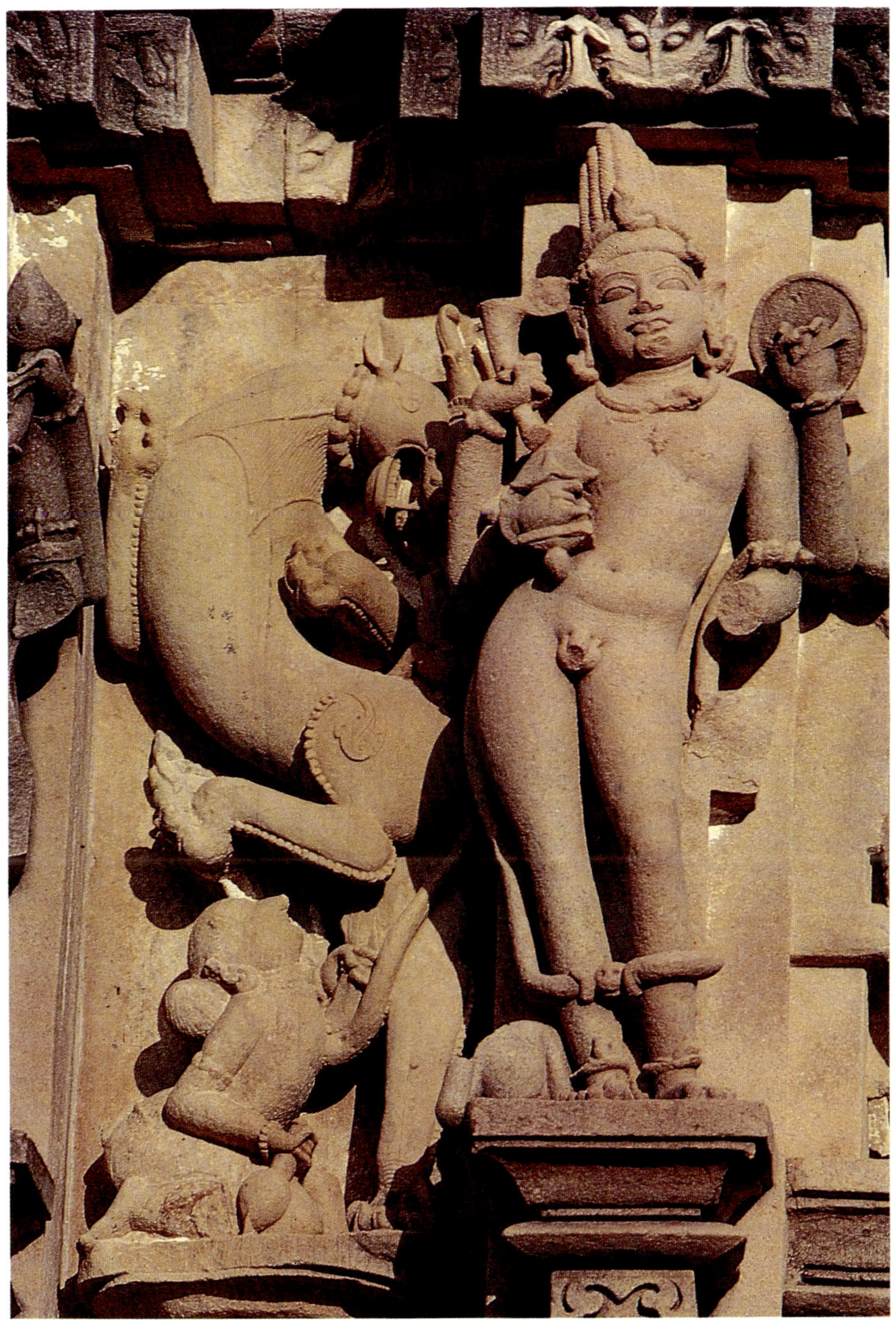

An incarnation of Shiva, flanked by the mythical 'Shardul' which represents the animal within man. It depicts constant battle between knowledge and ignorance. *Page 102* : Beautifully portrayed Agni (Fire) a Hindu god with moustache and beard, flanked by Sura Sundari, with a latter in a thoughtful mood (Lakshmana temple).

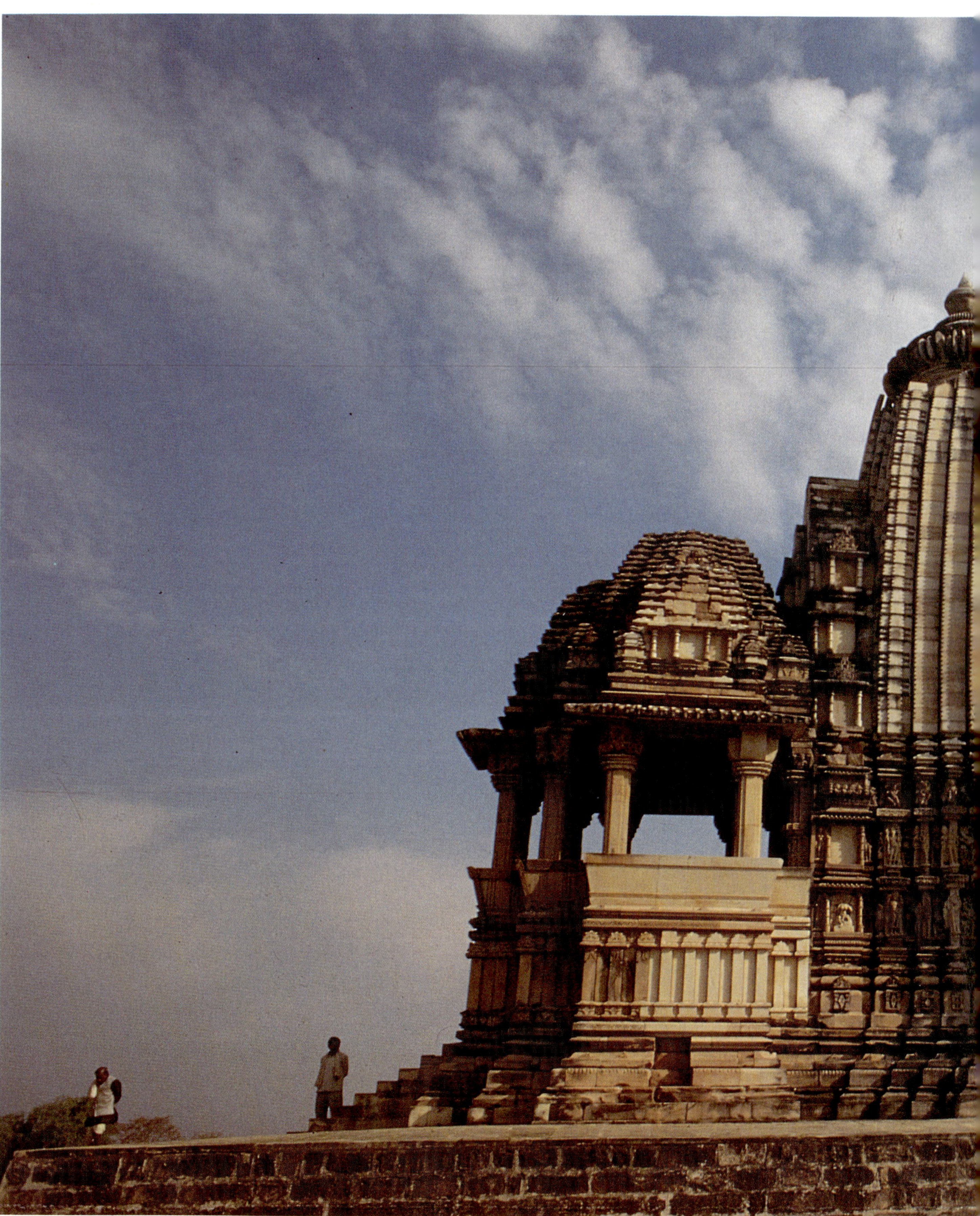

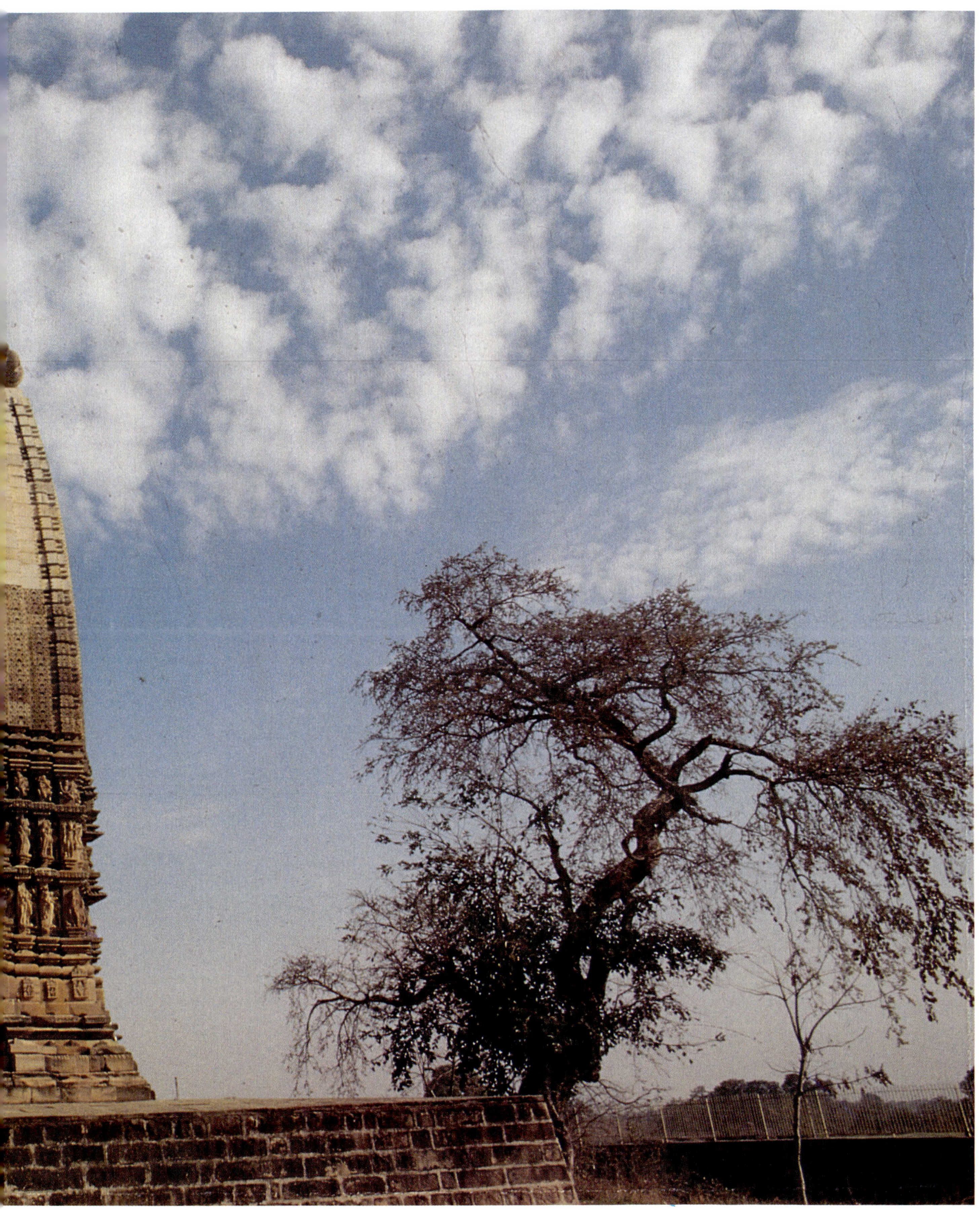

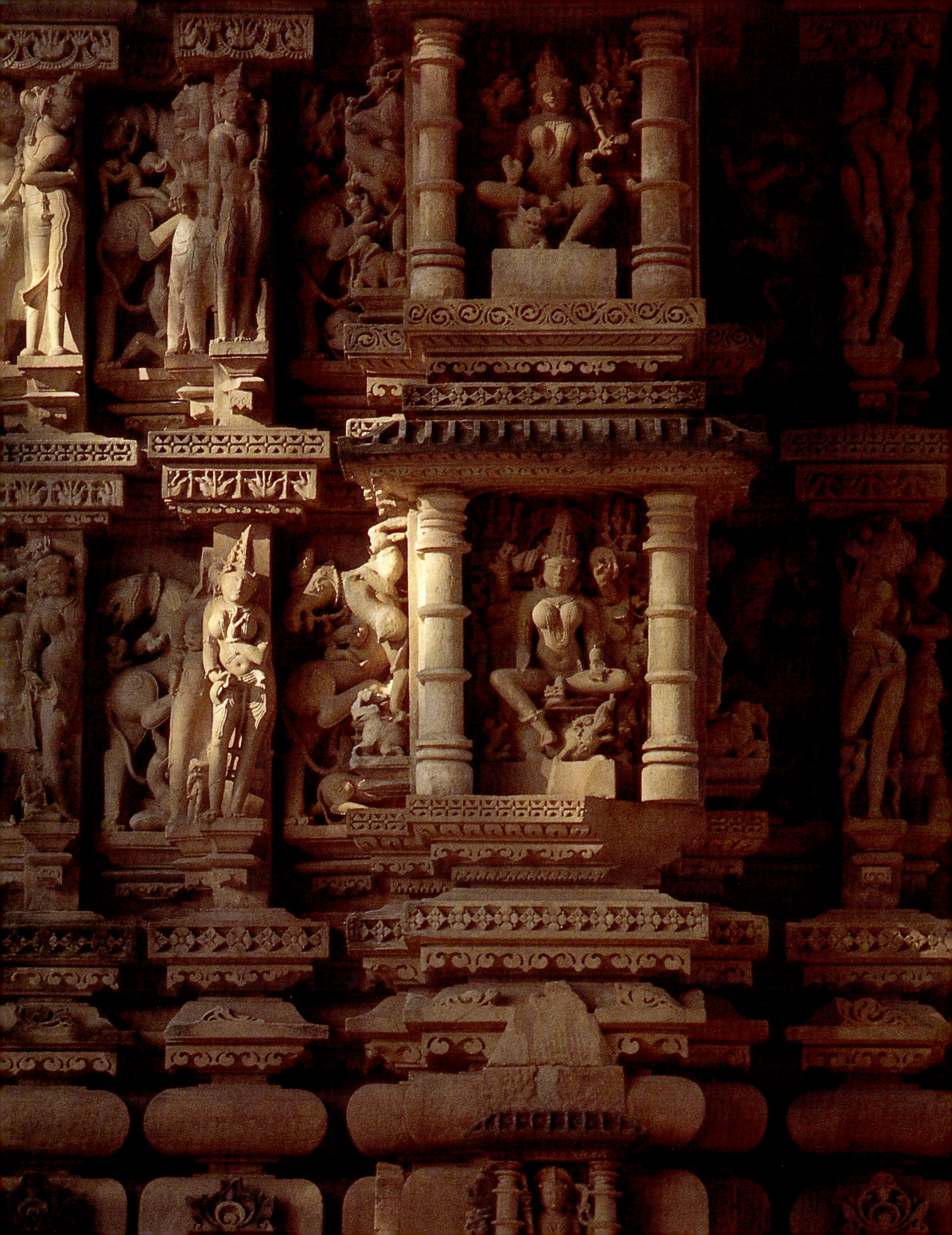

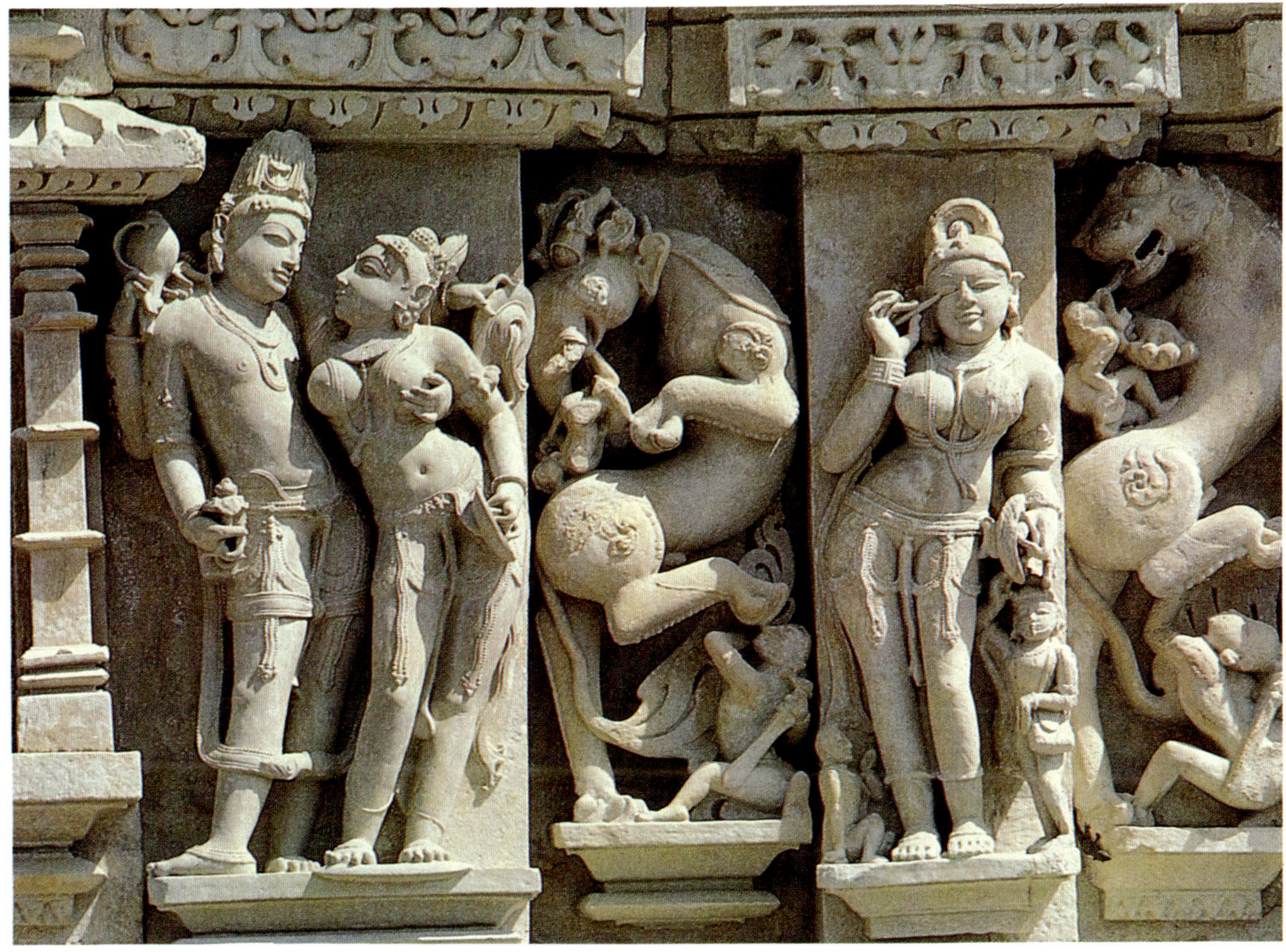

An exquisite example of sculptural art of Khajuraho : Lord Vishnu, the preserver, holds a conch in His right hand which echoes the sound of creation, and the disk of destruction - 'Sudarshan Chakra' in his left hand. He embraces His consort Lakshmi who holds a mirror as She gazes at the Lord's face. The panel also has an Apsara applying Kohl to her eyes flanked by the mythical Shardul — a combination of a horse and a lion, on her left, and a rather more unusual one of a horse and an elephant on the right. *Page 106* : The outerwall of Adinath Temple is adorned with exquisite sculptures of Hindu goddesses and celestial beauties. *Pages 104-105* : The Chaturbhuj Temple.

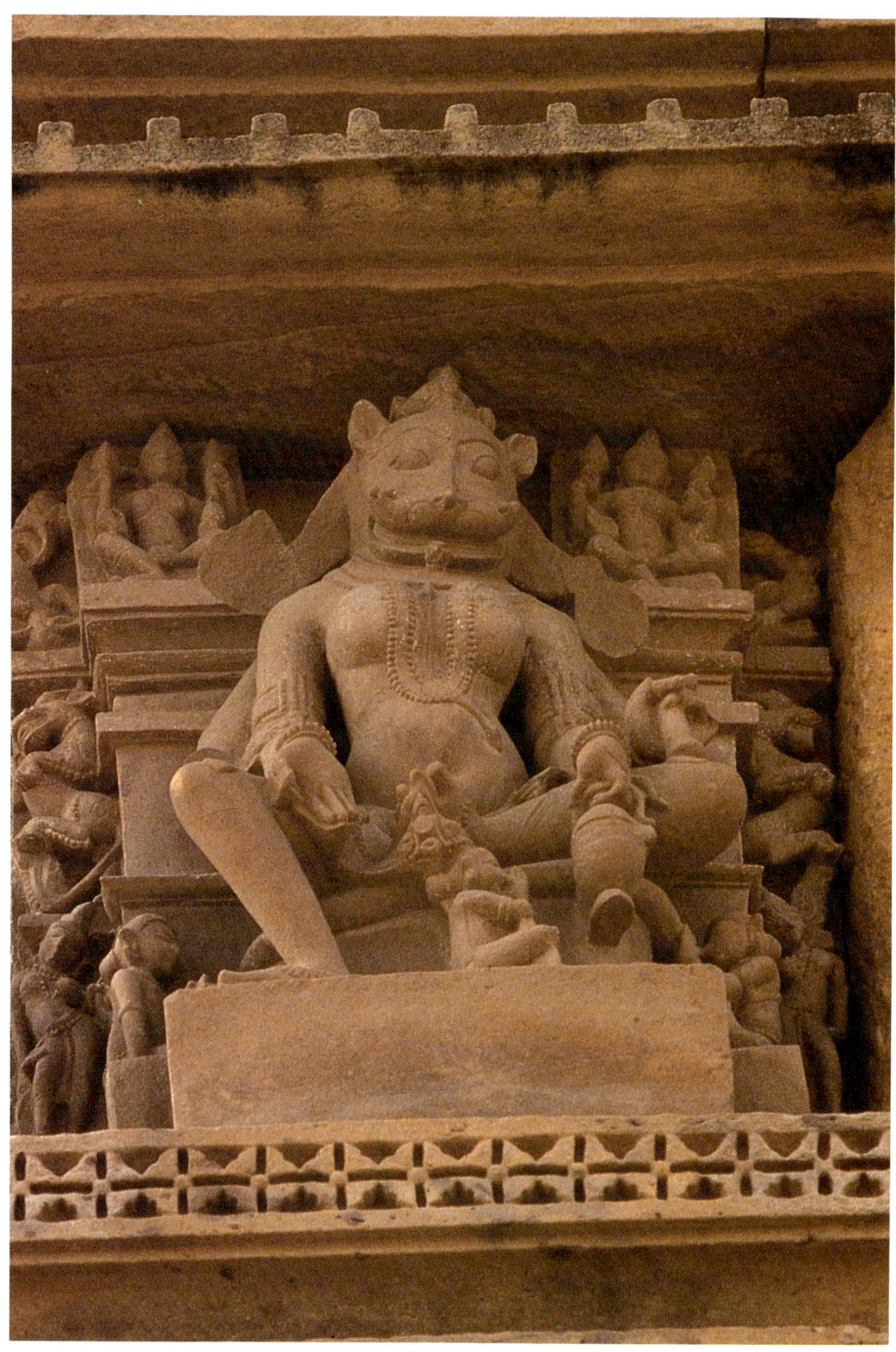

The architects of Khajuraho have visualised different aspects of life in a unique way. Even the lion-headed Narsingh, an incarnation of Lord Vishnu, has been portrayed in feminity. *Page 109* : Ardhnarishwar - the incarnation of Lord Shiva who is half male and half female. *Pages 110-111* : Lakshmana Temple - Platform's frieze showing a war procession. Camels shown here are exception amongst animal motifs depicted elsewhere in the Khajuraho temples.

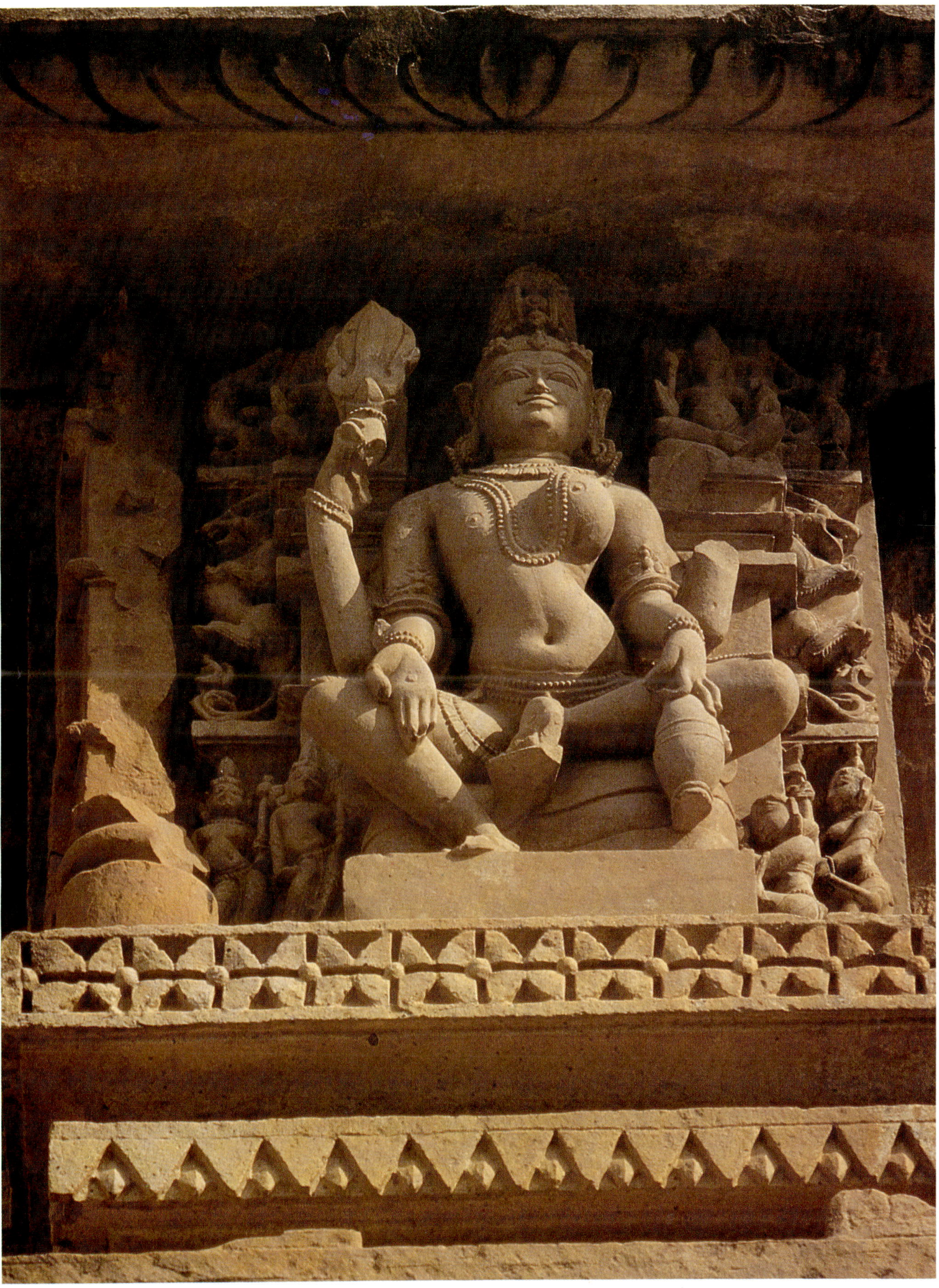

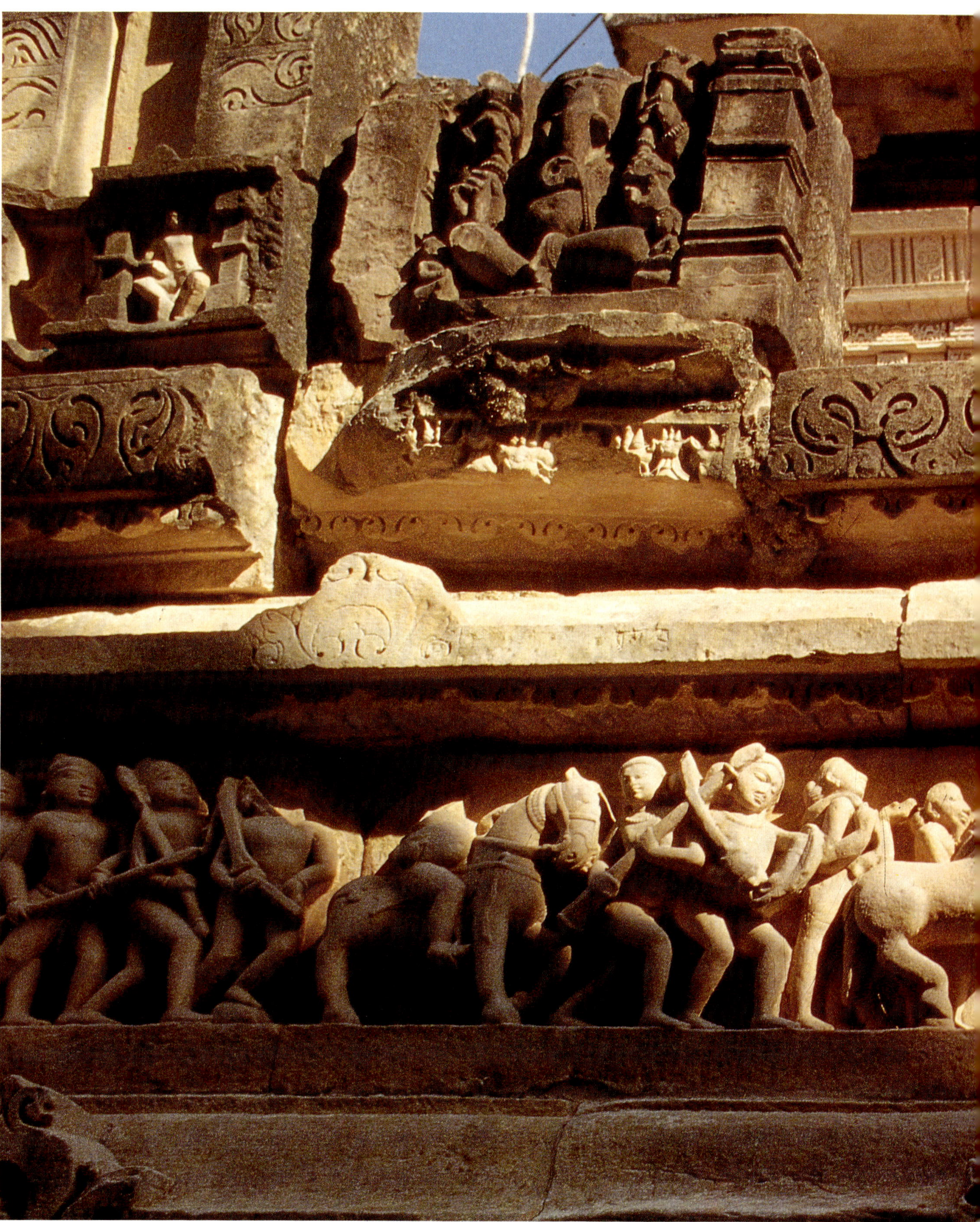

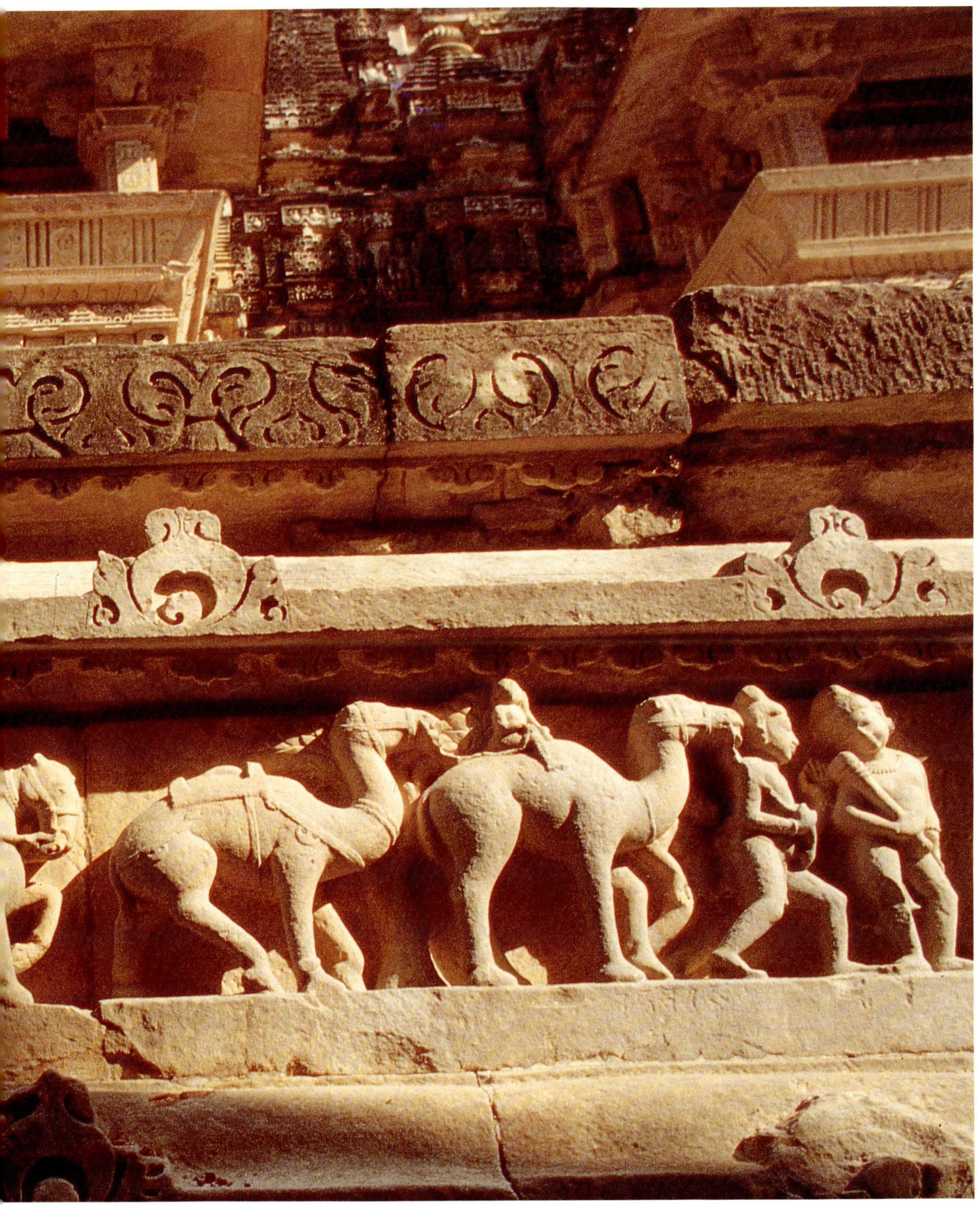

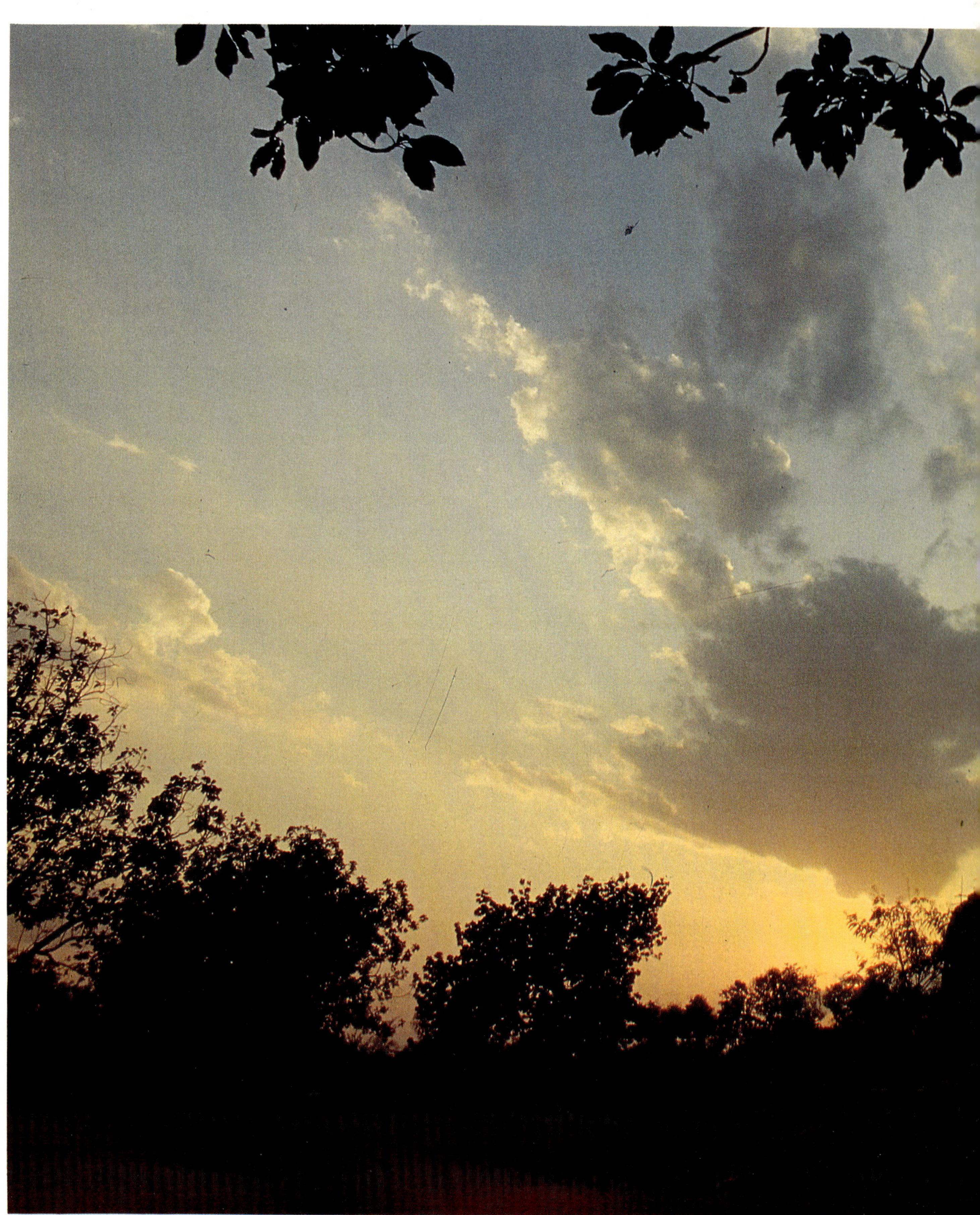

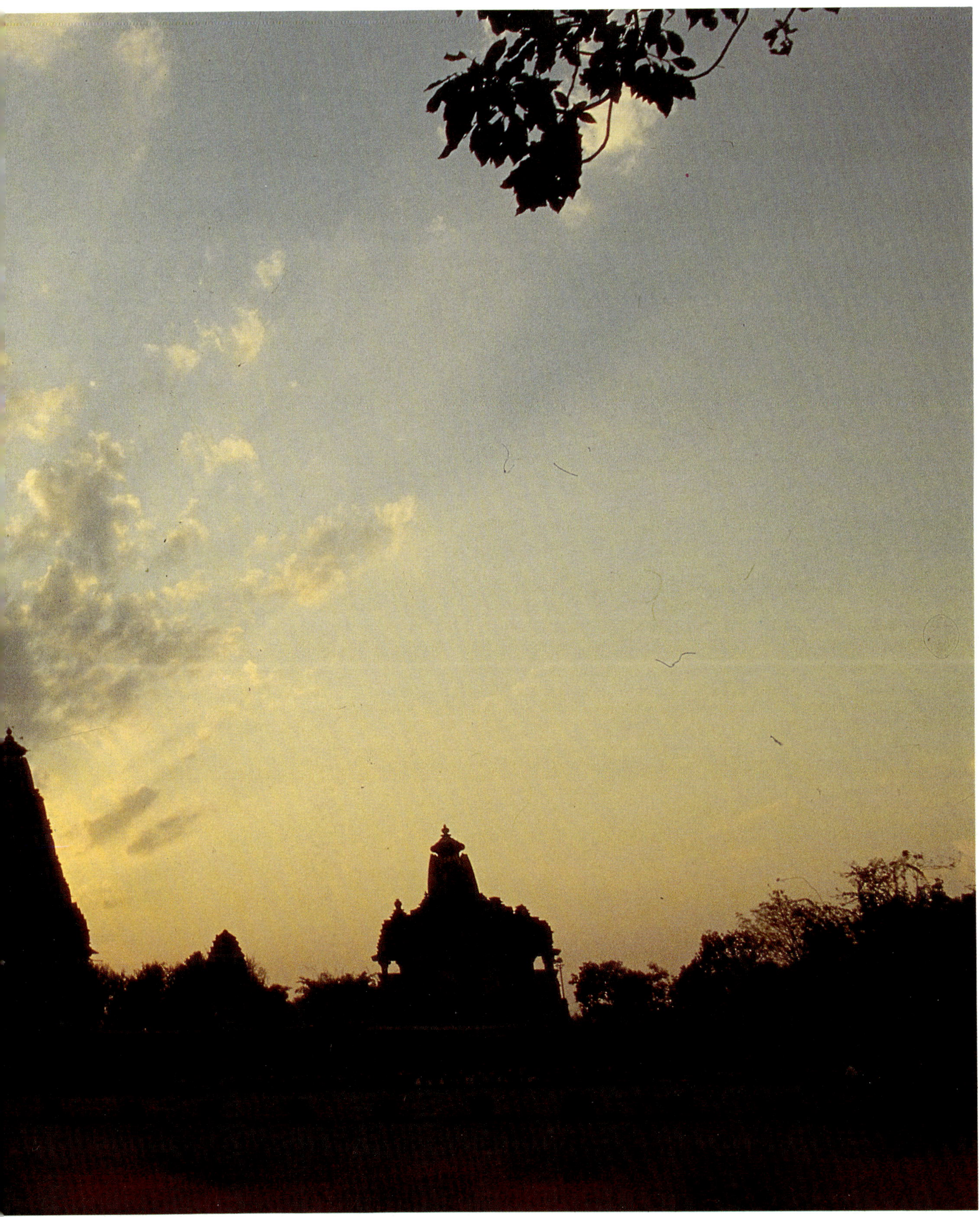

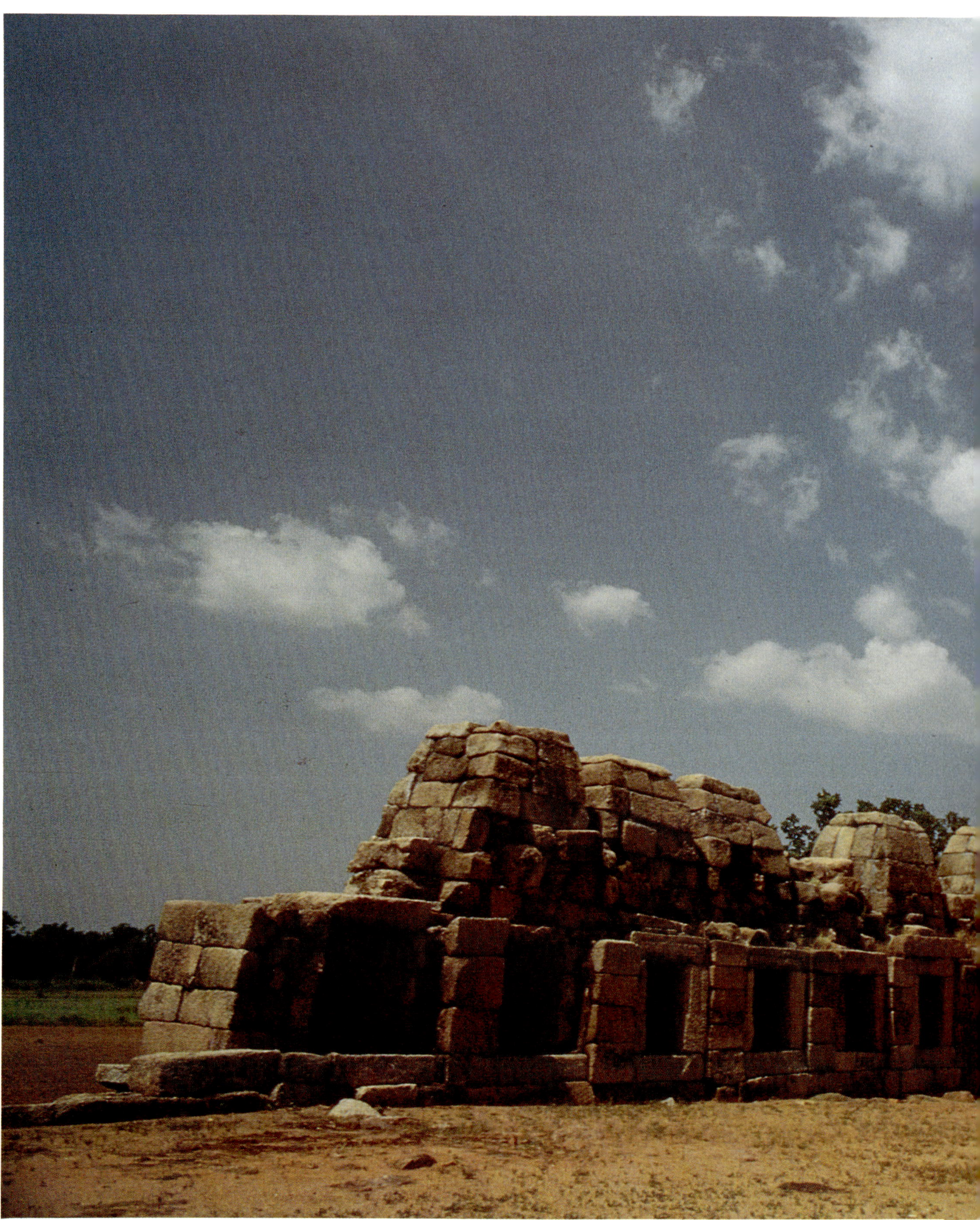

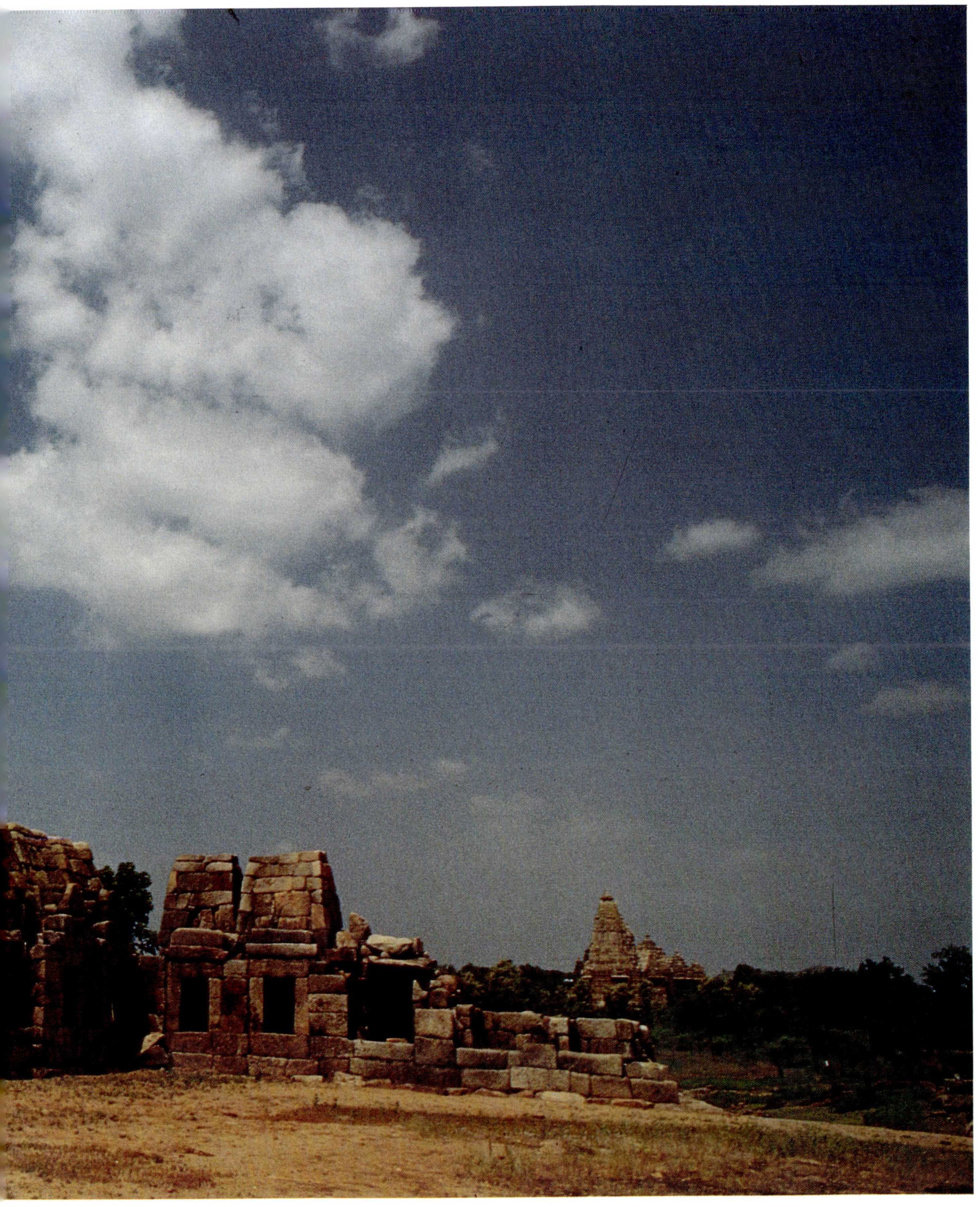

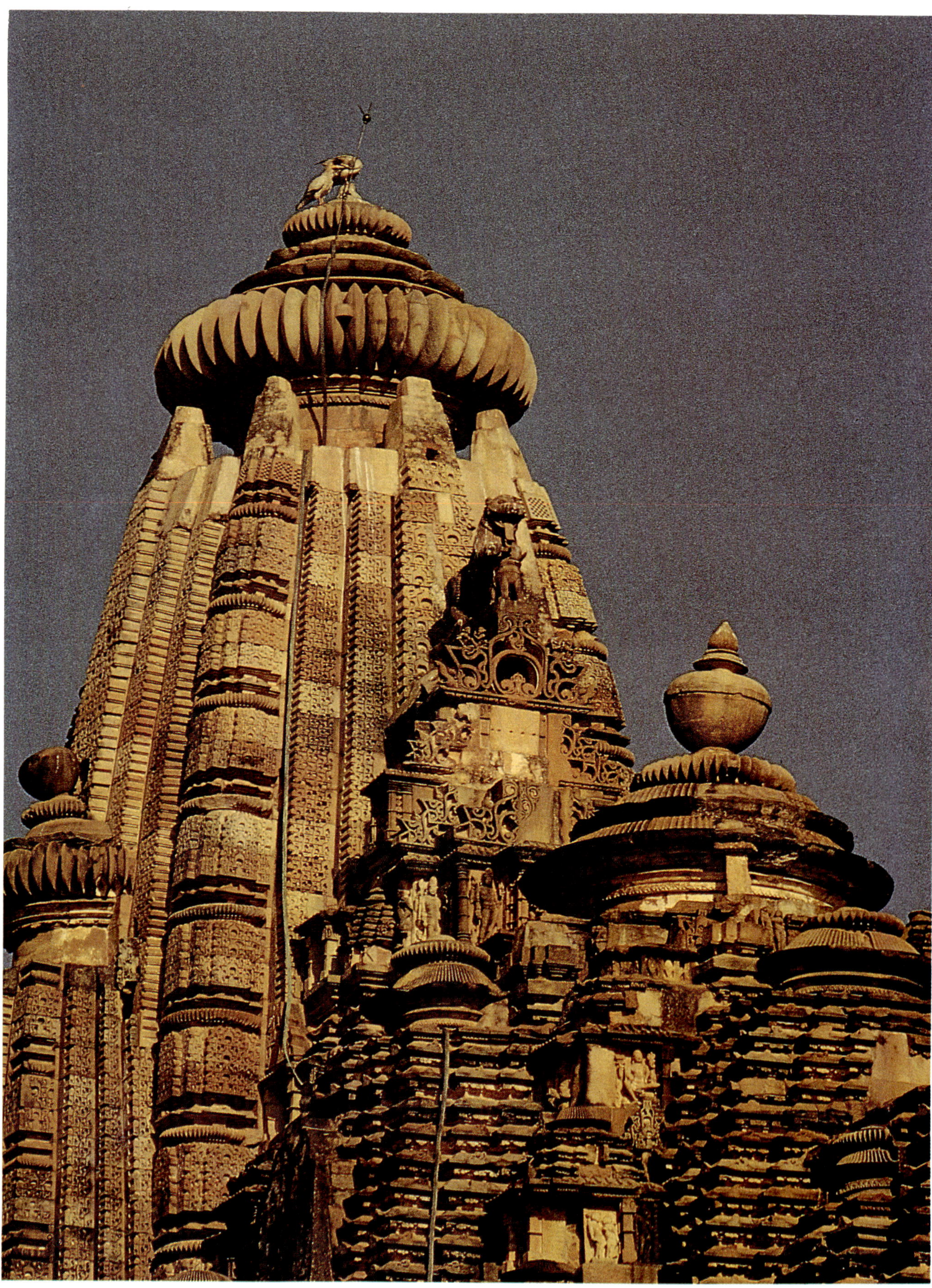

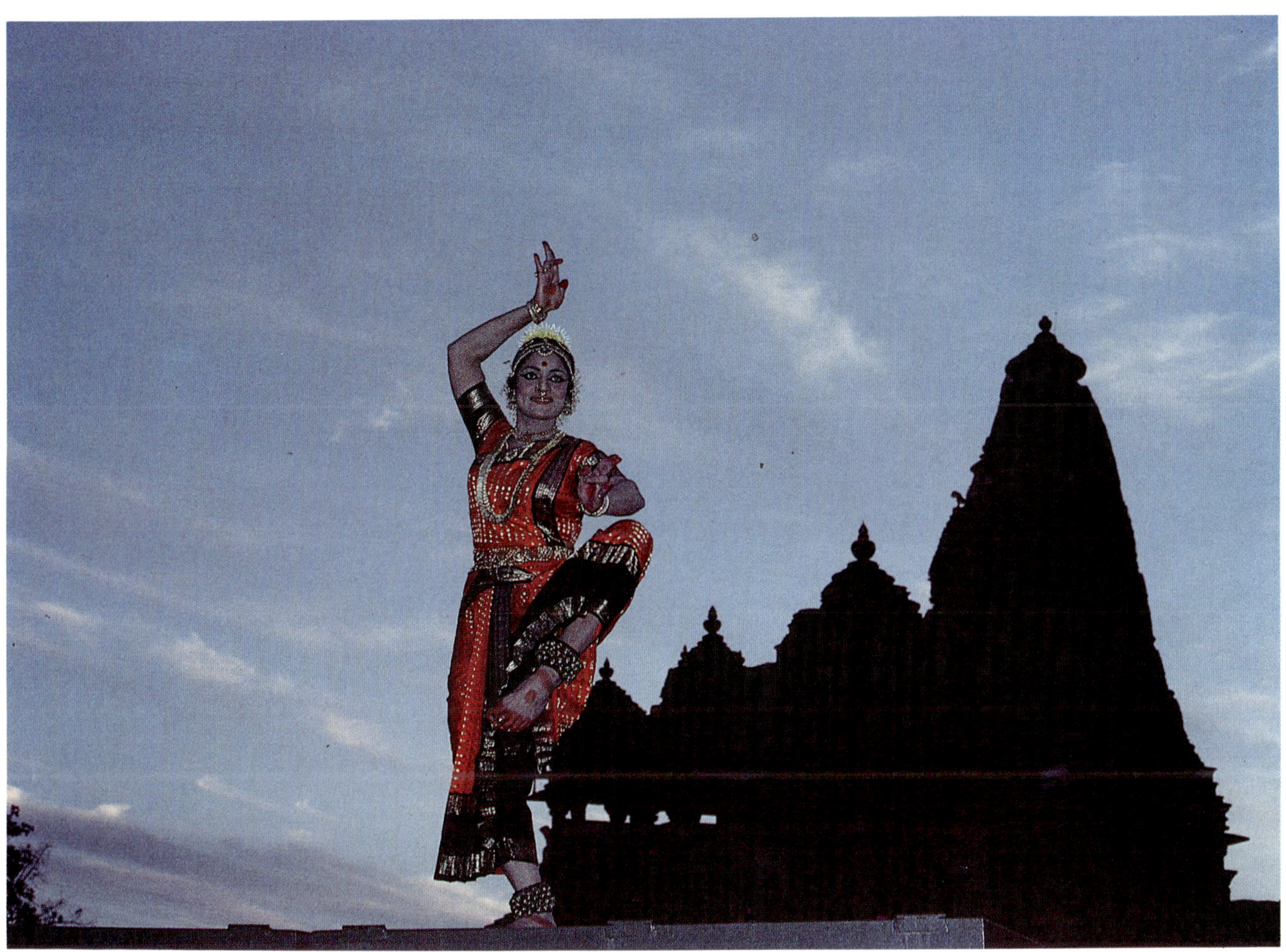

S. Kanaka, an exponent of Bharatanatyam, trying to assimilate the rhythm of Shikharas of Kandariya Mahadeo temple. The 'Shikharas' (spires) have one or two or three inverted lotus blossoms and 'Kalash' vase placed in ascending order on the exterior top of the temple. These represent the celestial palace of Shiva, the Mount Kailash, and also have a hidden expression of Hindu philosophy of life — the gradual ascent to self-fulfilment and ultimately attain liberation - 'Moksha'. *Page 112-113* : Not only the human beings even the God gets astonished to see the exquisite Khajuraho sculptures! *Pages 114-115* : Chaunsath Yogini Temple.

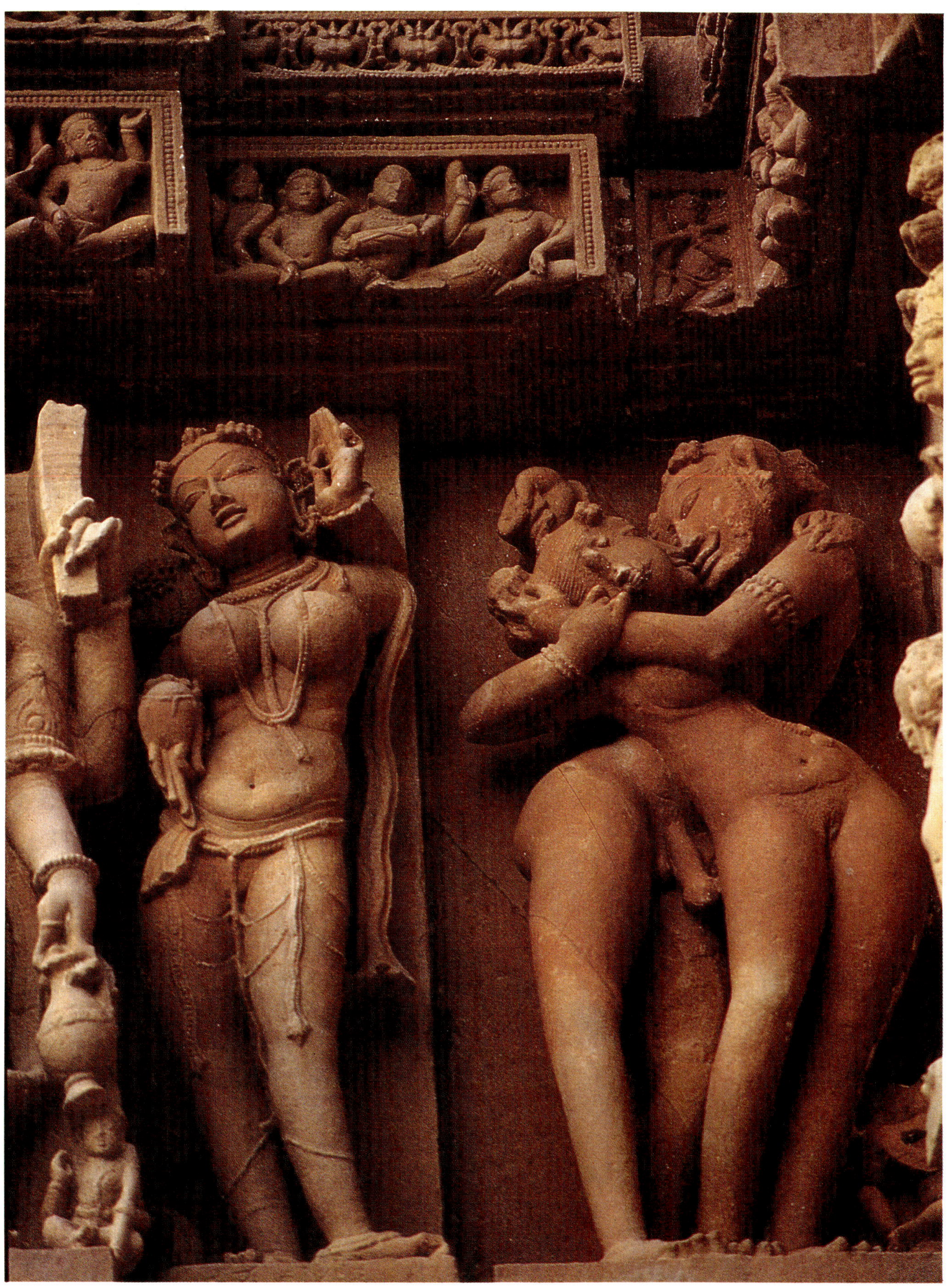

E R O T I C A

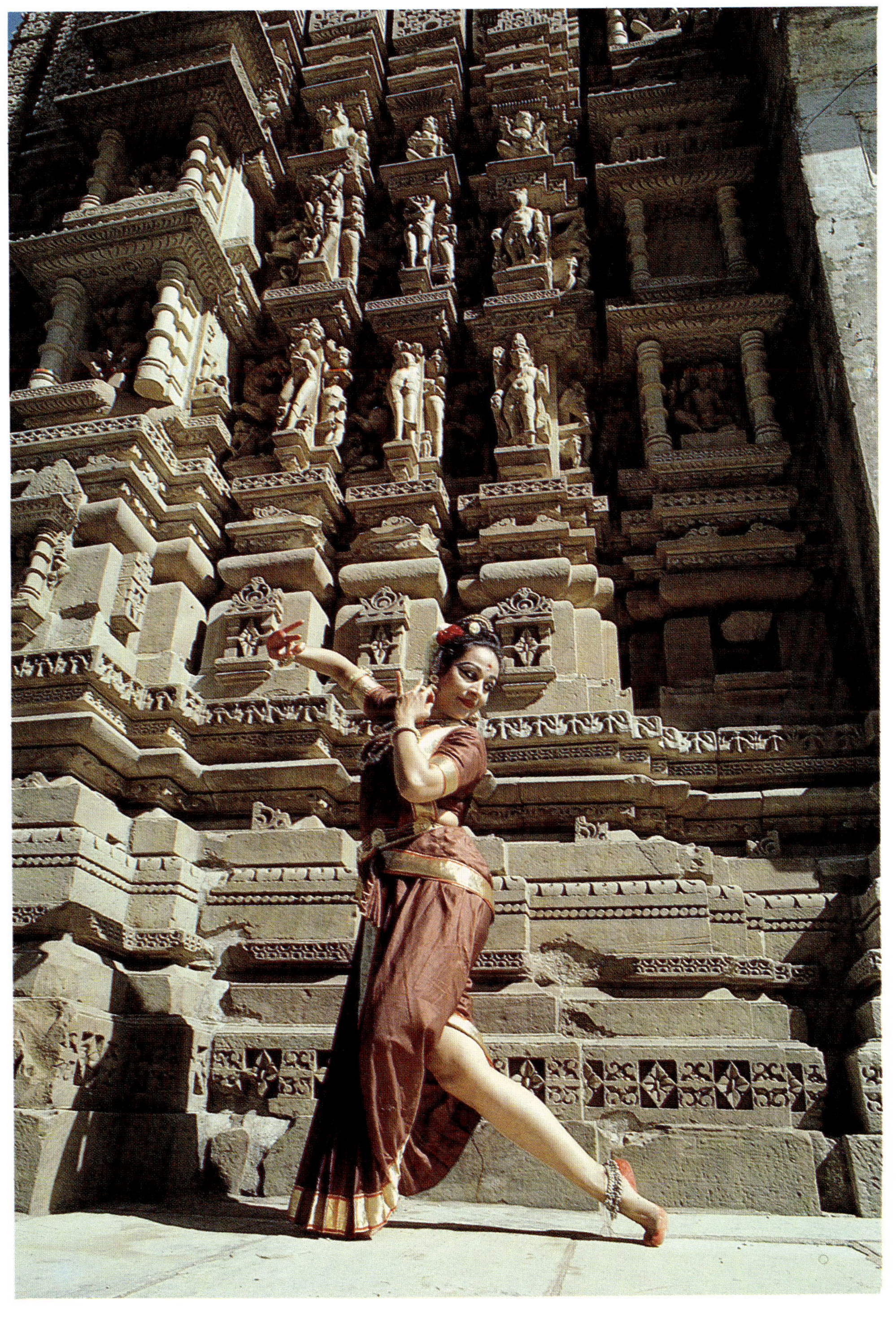

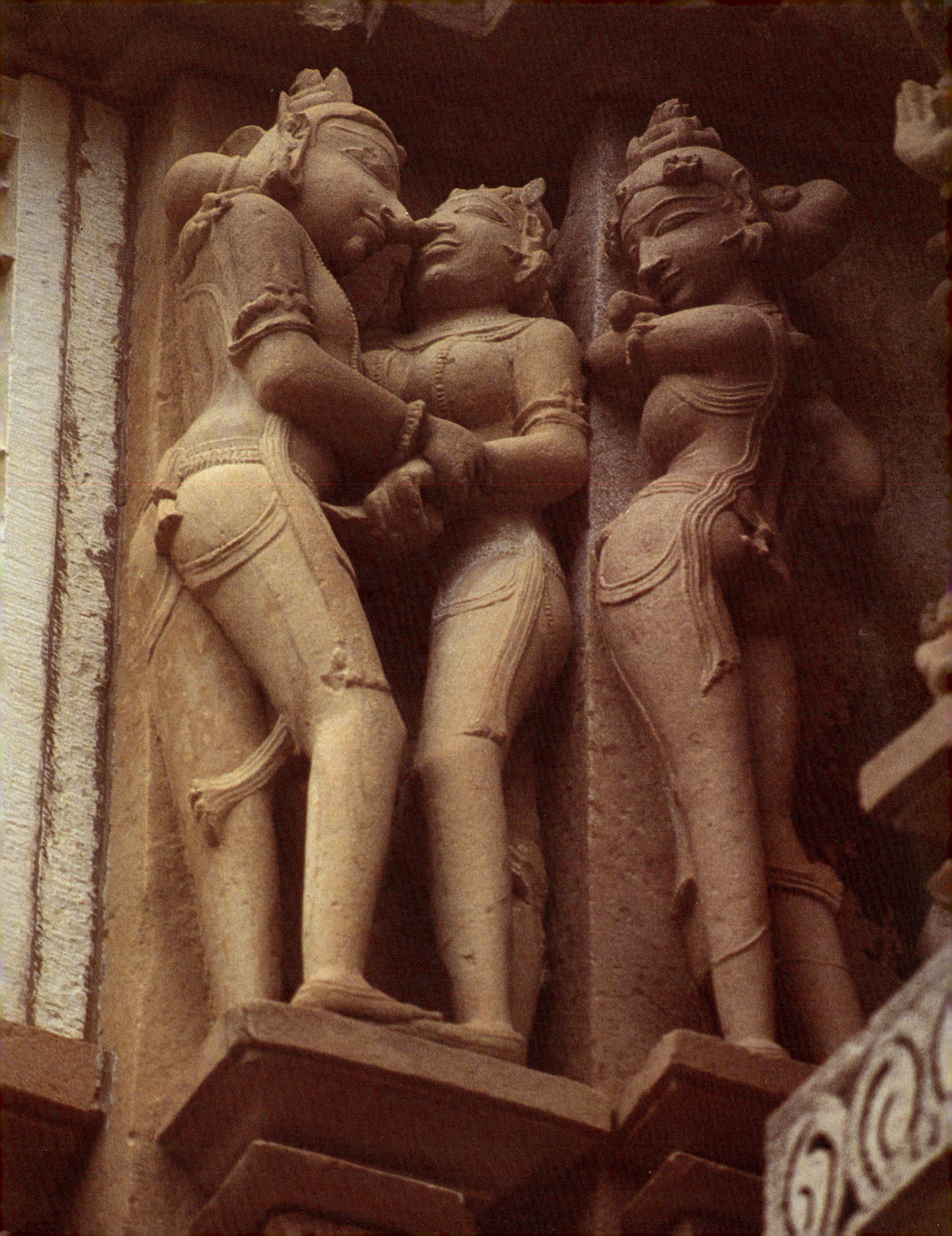

E R O T I C A

Erotic images of apparent human delight chosen to adorn the temples put forth exquisite example of art but simultaneously, created question marks in even amongst westerners' mind whether these were favourable to chastity? One of the most appropriate explanations is given by Jawahar Lal Nehru in *Discovery of India* — "Indian art is so intimately associated with Indian religion and philosophy that it is difficult to appreciate it fully unless one has some knowledge of the ideals that governed the Indian mind. In art, in music, there is a gulf which separates eastern from western conceptions."

The codes and ethics of life ascribed in the ancient literature, the Puranas, assign each Hindu god a female counterpart, the Shakti, who complements his power. Parvati, the consort of Shiva, is also worshipped in the form of Kali and Durga, when she plays the part of a mother-goddess. Likewise Laxmi, the consort of Vishnu, the god who preseves the universe, and so many other gods and goddesses form energy partnership. In Shiva worship the Lingam-Yoni symbol, popularly known as the Kundi, the male aspect Lingam is never complete without the matrix, the Yoni, the creative force in its feminine aspect. The union of the two represents the act of creation 'genesis'. Thus, the absolute is manifest in multiple forms but is again resolved into oneness.

A curious mind seeking a single interpretation of the mithuna (erotic) sculptures adorned in Khajuraho temples soon discovers that none exists. Both the pro and against interpretations are never short of logic. For example, Christian theology contains the sexually negative tenets of immaculate conception', virgin birth, and celibacy of priests and nuns, while India's civilization — being both spiritual and sensual — irradiates the union of man and woman with bliss. Erotica images are timeless expression of bliss wherein the fire of life, the energy of the creator, is quick with the ardour of its internal source and at the same time throbbing with the pulse of time. Presumably, some caravan forgotten by wandering gods and goddesses, must have turned to stone. The fallen fragments may be of the stars, with a covering of erotic imagery — caressing, copulation, orgasm and lust.

Many interpretations have been given to justify the placement of erotic sculptures on Hindu temple walls. Contrary to the tendency to dwell on such a controversial subject, and to produce long texts loaded with wordly adorations and abstract irrelevancies, my humble effort is not to offer any original explanation but an attempt to put forth the most common hypotheses.

The erotic expressions are symbol of Shakti, the supreme power — both sexes in one God, representing the 'oneness' of God, or the magic syllable 'Om' or 'Aum'. These are representations of supreme bliss. *Brihad Aranyaka Upanishad*, one of the Hindu scriptures, explains- "In the embrace of his beloved a man forgets the whole world — everything both within and without, in the same way, he who embraces the self knows neither within nor without."

Mulkraj Anand, in his book *Kama Kala*, says, "With that characteristic genius for elaborating the highest sanctions, the ancient Hindus, therefore, accepted an anthropomorphic view of God, in which not only is human sexual pleasure exalted as the joy nearest to God in realisation, but every thing in life becomes divine, every action becomes when properly understood the concrete expression of some universal law....."

The mithunas are temptations to lewd thoughts, put there expressly to be overcome by the devout. Temptation being very close to the 'cleansing' theory, the mithuna images are generally placed on the exterior of the temples. Can truth be indecent! If the devotee is blinded by his carnal appetites in these outer expressions, he must return and achieve self-control, for he is not worthy of 'Moksha', the liberation. The erotic sculptures are the touch-stones to test one's renunciation whether his urge of chastity is genuine. If some objects or senses are available but you disown, you reach the state of detachement which is pre-requisite for 'liberation' — being dissolved in the supreme.

One cannot deny the theory of innocense when the then man was very close to nature. Erotic images might have been just innocent depiction of a human activity in the same way as other expressions of hunting, war, dance, music and supplication.

The other perspective of the thoughts leads to the fact the man has always been conscious towards security of life. As per beliefs, the eroticas were meant to resist the evil effect of the jealous gaze of spectators, to ward off the evil spirits and to protect the monuments against lightning, cyclones and the like. It is noteworthy that there is no obscenity in the sculpture of sacred images worshipped within the sanctum or elsewhere.

Alain Danielou considers erotica an object of amusement to the people and attract them to the temples. The common man is attracted by suggestions of sensuous pleasure. He will visit the dark corners and examine it from plinth to architrave. He will walk round the pillars and reach the inner shrine. But in doing so, smelling the flowers and the incense, seeing the sacred lights, hearing the bells of worship, he will be overshadowed by the influence of the sacred place.

Sexual curiosity is one of the chief causes of perversion of mind. If spiritual progress is to be made complexes must be resolved and the mental faculty made healthy. The temples were used both as a place of worship and centres of social contacts and learning. Hinduism taught the enjoyment of the senses, rather than the denial of them. Get saturated with the pleasure of life, reveal the mystery of senses, realise them and then achieve detachment for libration, the ultimate stage of life, Moksha. Hence Hindu thought has always insisted upon the importance of sex and its physical manifestations. Sexual education through images was considered a useful means of mental clarification so that no latent longing remains in the mind that may later prove a hindrance to spiritual progress.

Erotic expressions on the temple walls are straight forward representations of ritualistic orgies or Yoga postures, which help to change subtle centres of the body and so attain harmony with it. The erotic postures are of Tantra or Kaula significance. Tantra describes the rules for the worship of 'Shakti' the female aspect of the godhood as per sacred scriptures. Hindu doctrine of procreation of the universe through the union of the energy partners, male and female, positive charge meeting the negative charge representing the act of creation — 'genesis' is a quite scientific in approach. Kaula and Kapaliks were predominant during the Chandela dynasty which must have influenced the marvelous art of Khajuraho sculptures.

Khajuraho's erotica images form merely a small part of its sculptural treasure, though they are the chief reason for its fame. The Chandela legacy has maintained a perfect balance between the physical and the spiritual aspects of life. However, everyone is free to appreciate the Rhythm in Khajuraho Sculptures as per one's level of understanding and knowledge.

The sculpture art of Khajuraho has in store the kind of surprises for the observer willing to look beyond the obvious. The outstanding point of these sculptures is the tension of passion resulting in taut muscles, firmly closed lips and half closed rolling eyes. Image of physical passion in a position reminiscent of a certain chapter of *Kamasutra*. Sometimes the sculptor seems to want to suggest rather than reveal. Indian ancient texts advocate the feminity to be expressed by fullness of breasts, belly and hips, to symbolize fertility, carnal pleasure and perfection. The jewels adorning the body serve only to emphasize the roundness of curves. Homage to the rhythm in the body movements, and expressions of women portrayed as mother, mistress, celestial beauty are also the homage to the eternal power of creativity of the supreme. Whether erotic or not, all the sculpted images on the Khajuraho temples emit an energy, a lust for life, power, grace and gaiety. The sculpture art of Khajuraho depicts the rhythm of eternal bliss prevailing in each and every stone piece. Perhaps nowhere else in the world has such a hymn to the beauty of woman been sung. The Apsaras, celestial nymphs, carved on the temple walls many a time turn her back on the visitor as if inviting him to follow her to move to eternal heights. According to the Hindu theory of creation, the Adidev (The God in beginning of univese) was neither male nor female. Overcome by loneliness, the creator divided 'the' self into two equal halves - Purush (male) amd Nari (female), so that each remained complementary to the other. A couple is a symbol of the duality of god and nature, such as light and shadow, and even as Atma (soul) and Parmatma (divine), their unity signifies the essential unity of the universe. Erotic expressions in Khajuraho art depict a perfect balance between the physical and the spiritual. The legacy of Chandelas, like any other masterpiece of art, claims the ultimate interpretation lying embedded within each individual as a personal understanding and appreciation. Thus, Khajuraho has been rediscovered by artists, scholars and other enthusiasts. Though there have been a few who perceive erotica as degradation of values in that period, many of them agree that it embodies the synopsis of Indian Philosophy!

Mithuna, (Devi Jagdamba Temple, 11th Century AD) : In a close sexual embrace, the female partner grips the top knot of her lover, the act being reciprocated by him. The rhythmic flow of their bodies and the movement of the hands are emphasized, while the minimum clothing and ornaments show the firm flesh of their bodies.

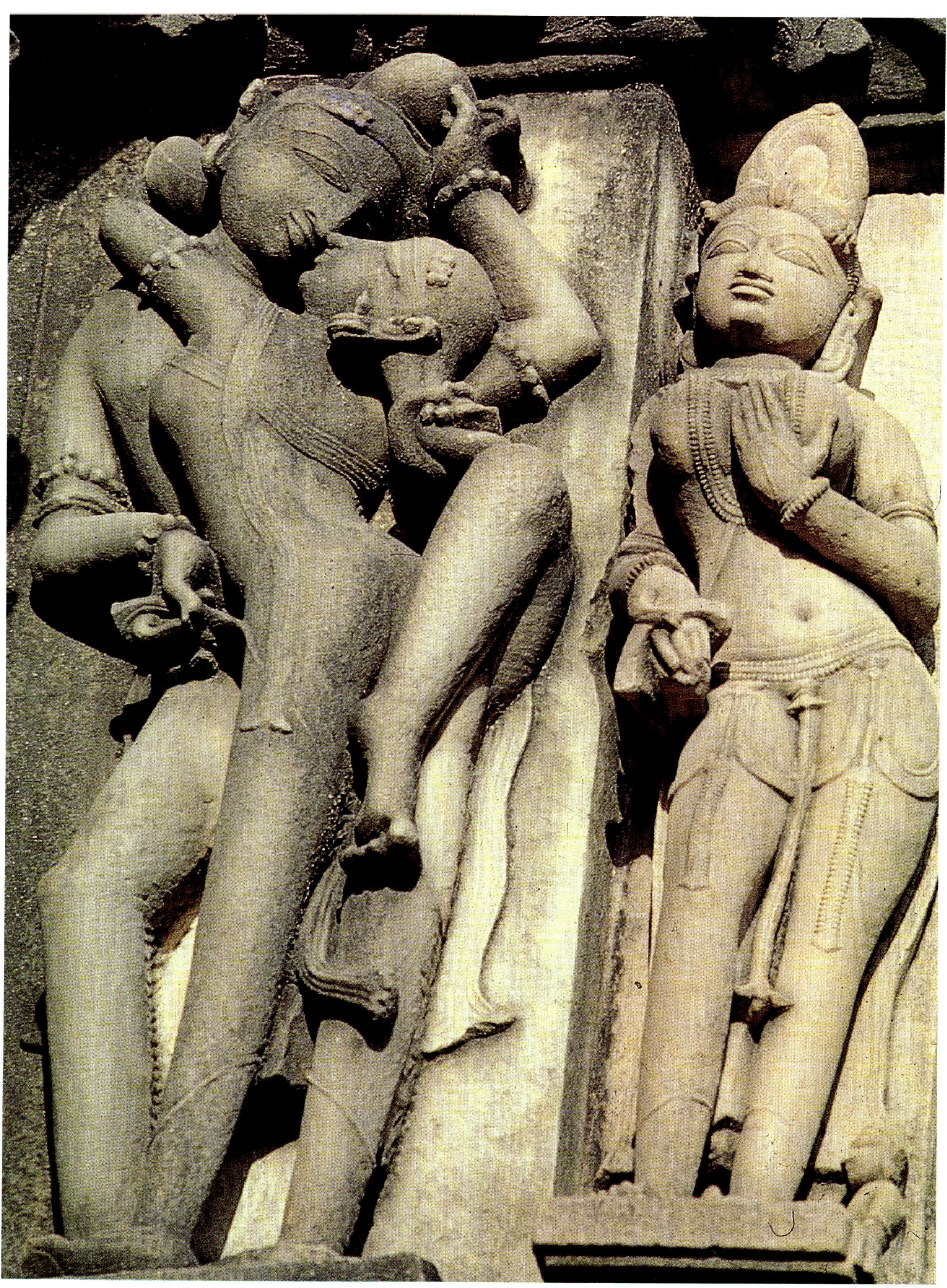

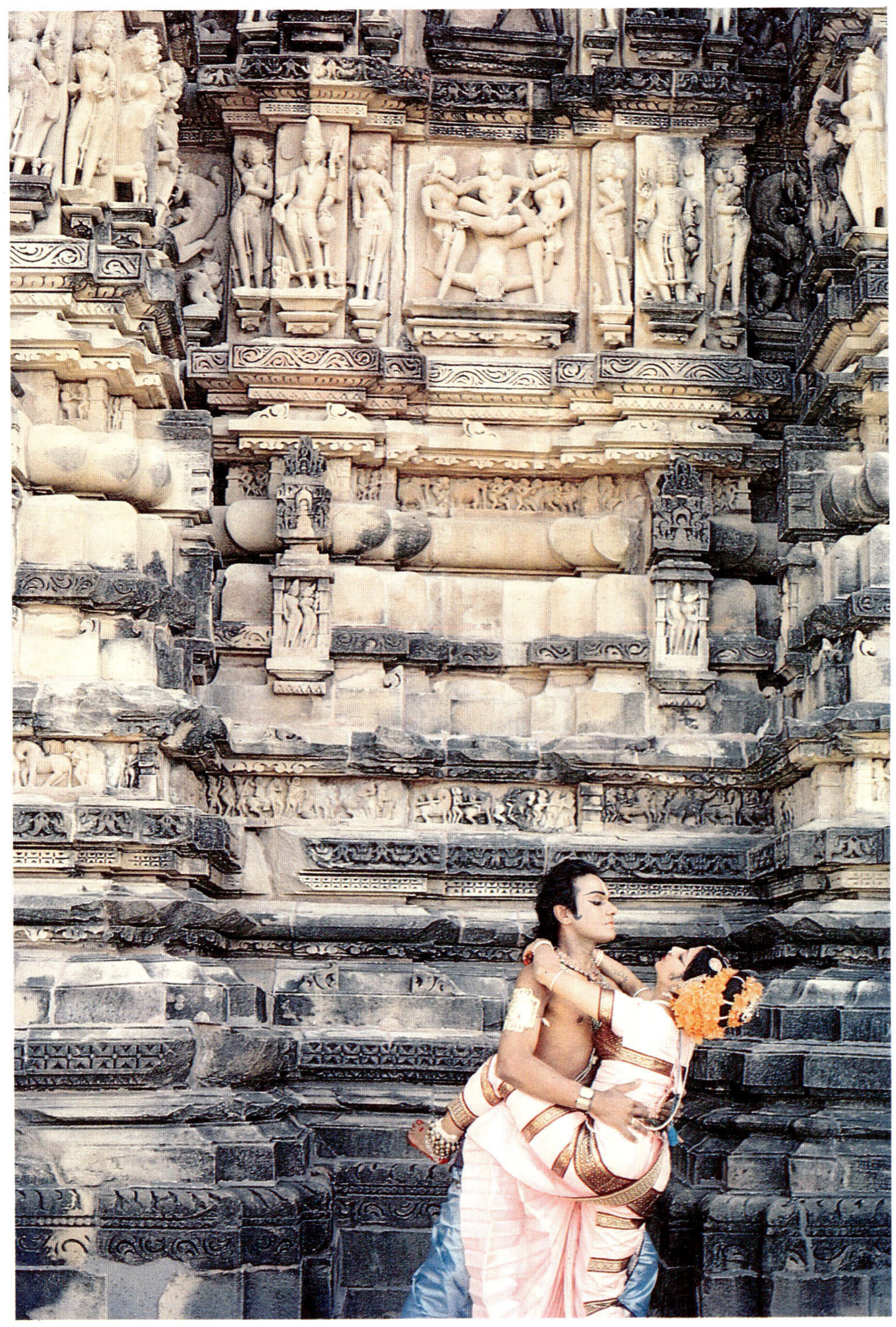

The dancer couple Raja and Radha Reddy depicting a chapter from *Kamasutra*, the ancient text written by Sage Vatsayana, 4th century A.D., which describes the art of love and sex. The dancers juxtapose their postures with the carved erotica adorning the temple walls.

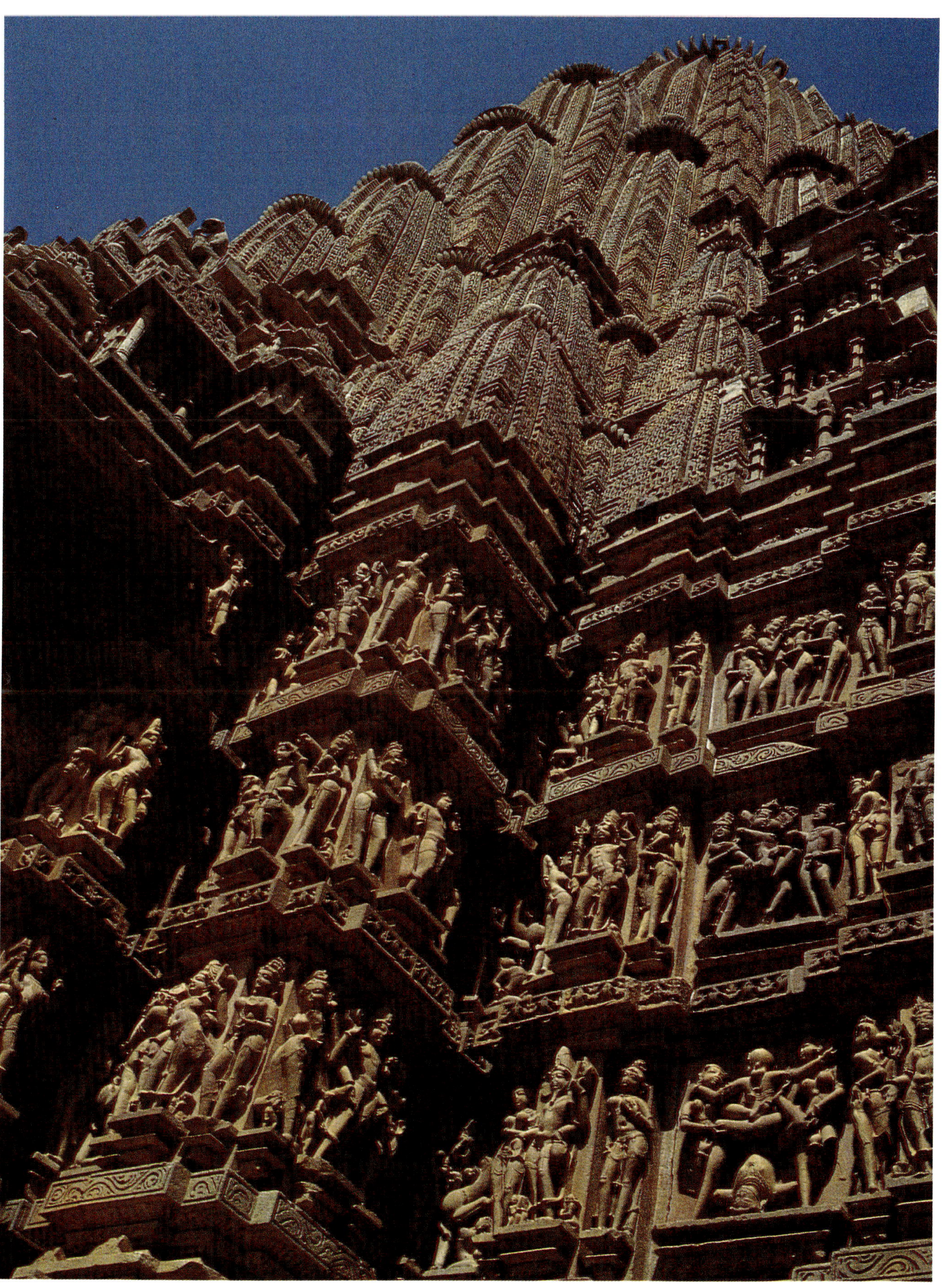

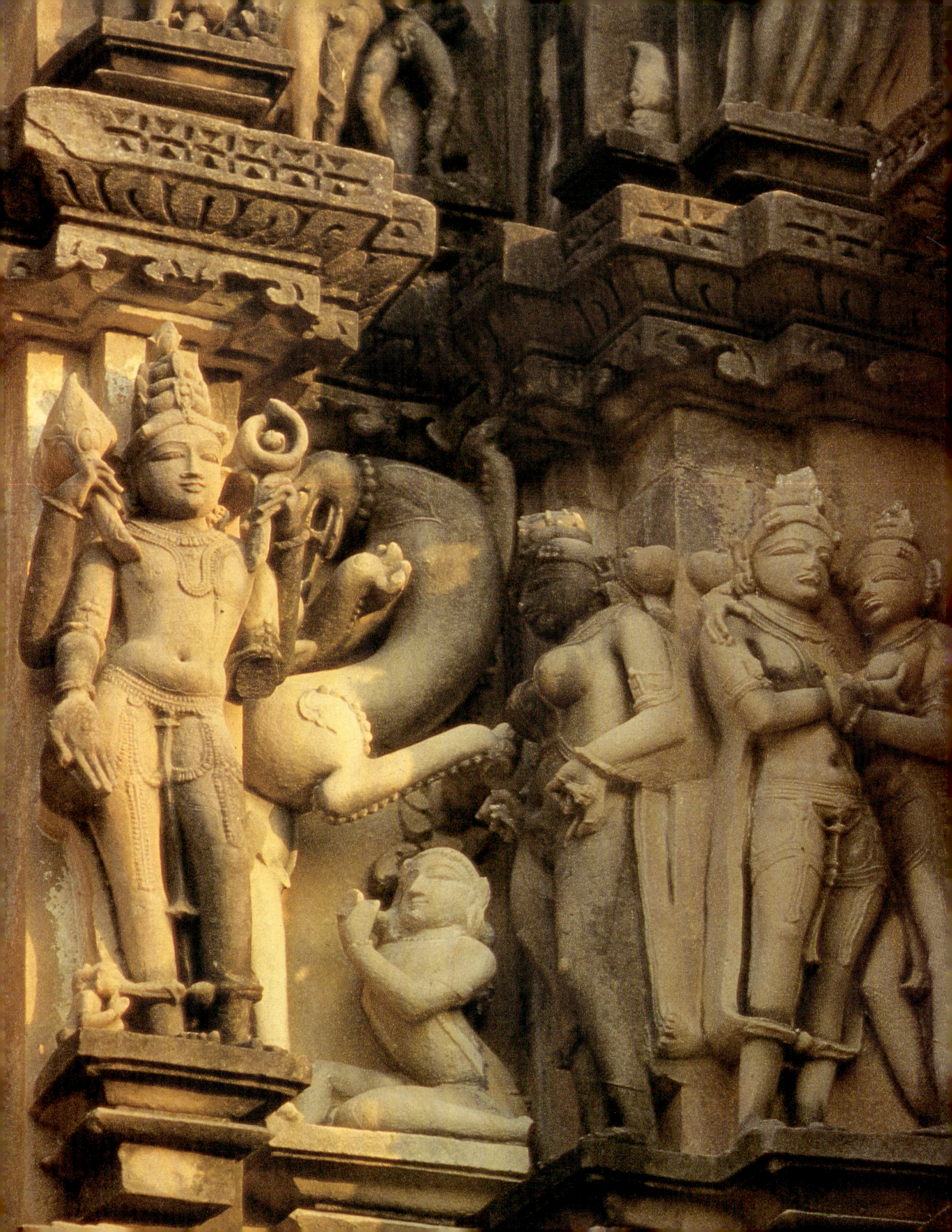

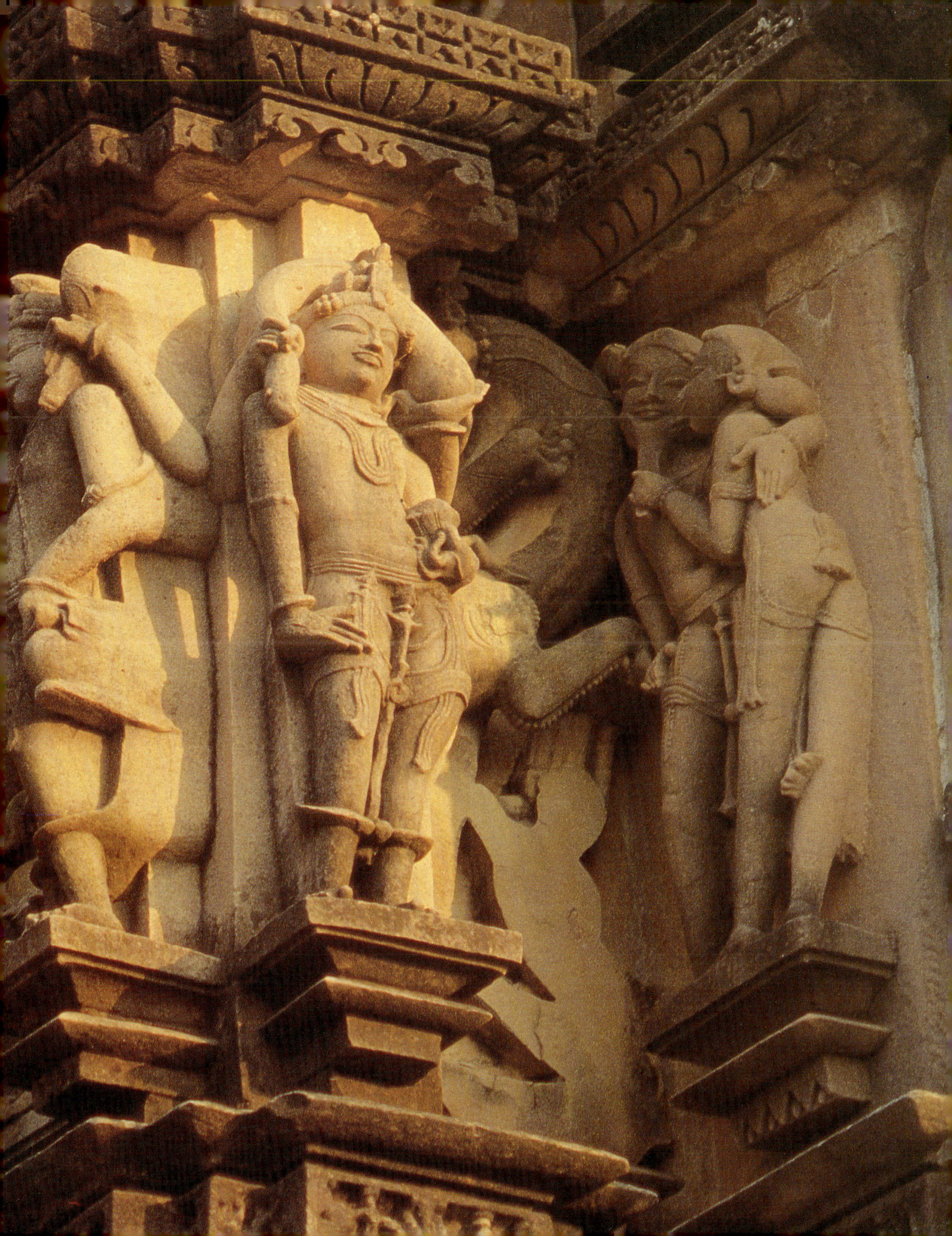

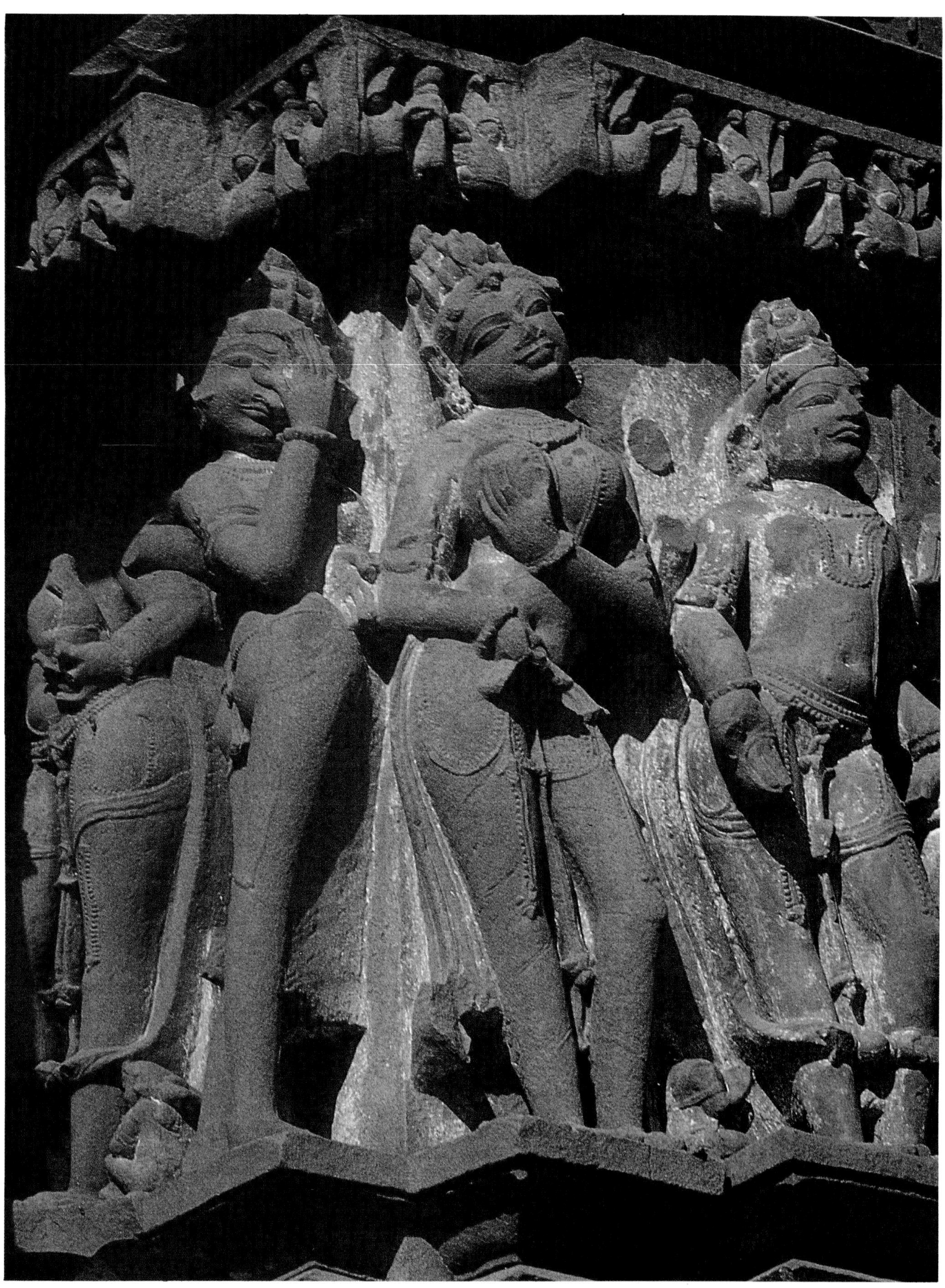

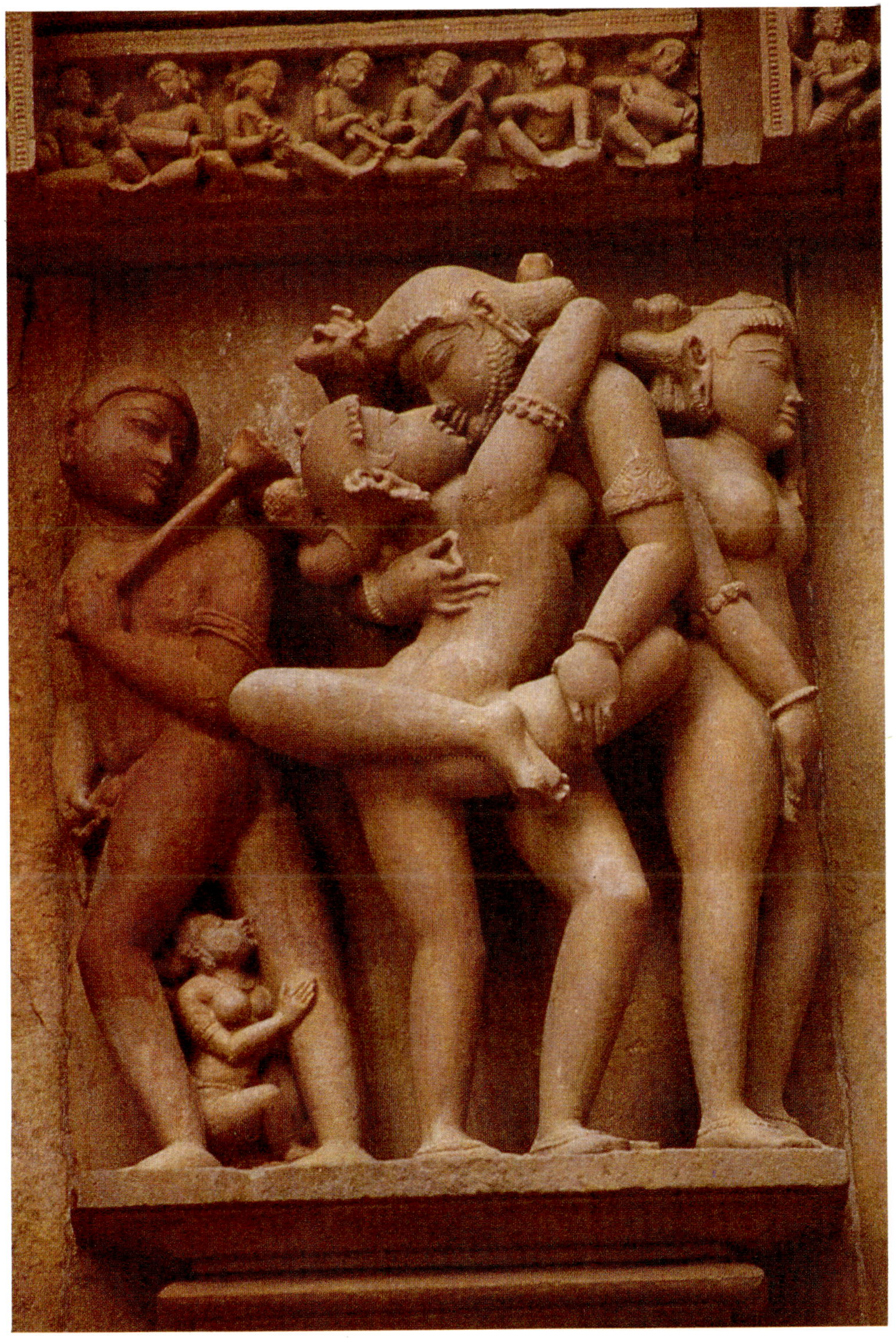

The erotic art of the Khajuraho temples is basically artistic depiction of senses rather than crude eroticism. The sculptor has captured even minute details of human body movement, the tension of muscles and vivid facial expressions.

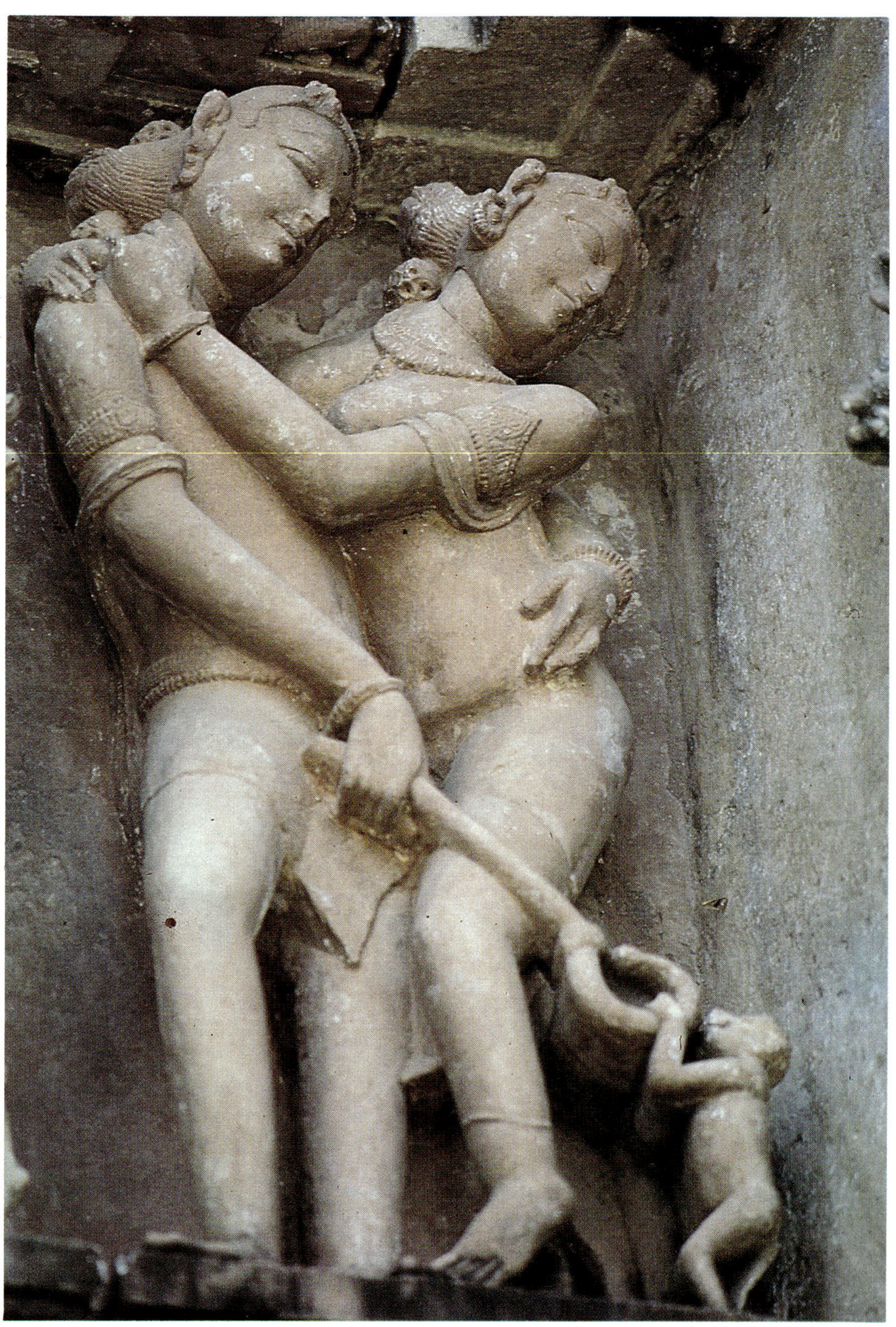

An exquisite sculpture adorned on the north wall of Lakshmana Temple which depicts a couple playing with a monkey. The sensual images in Khajuraho sculpture art is homage to the rhythm in the body movements, expressions of women portrayed as mother, celestial beauty or mistress are also homage to the eternal power of creativity of the Supreme.

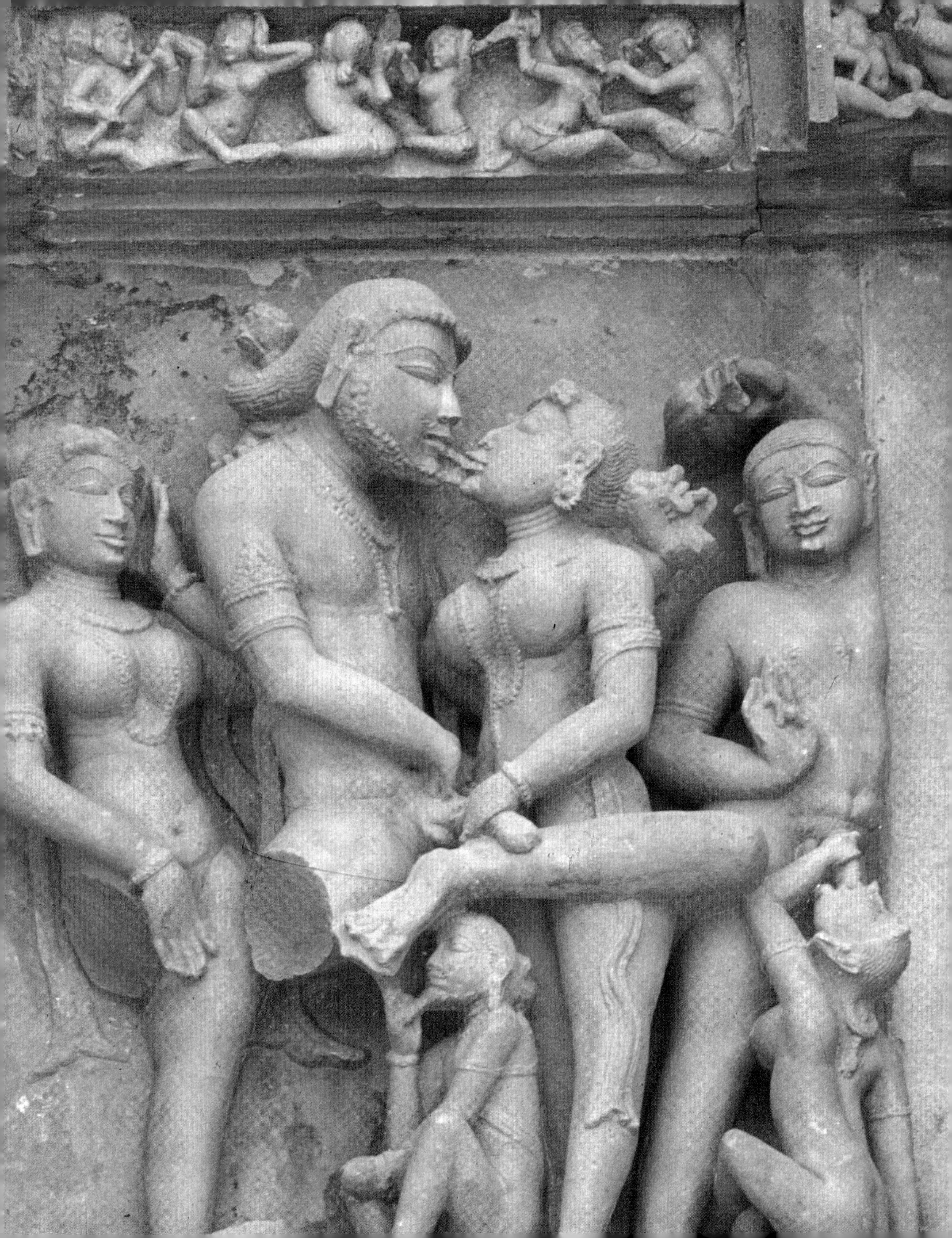

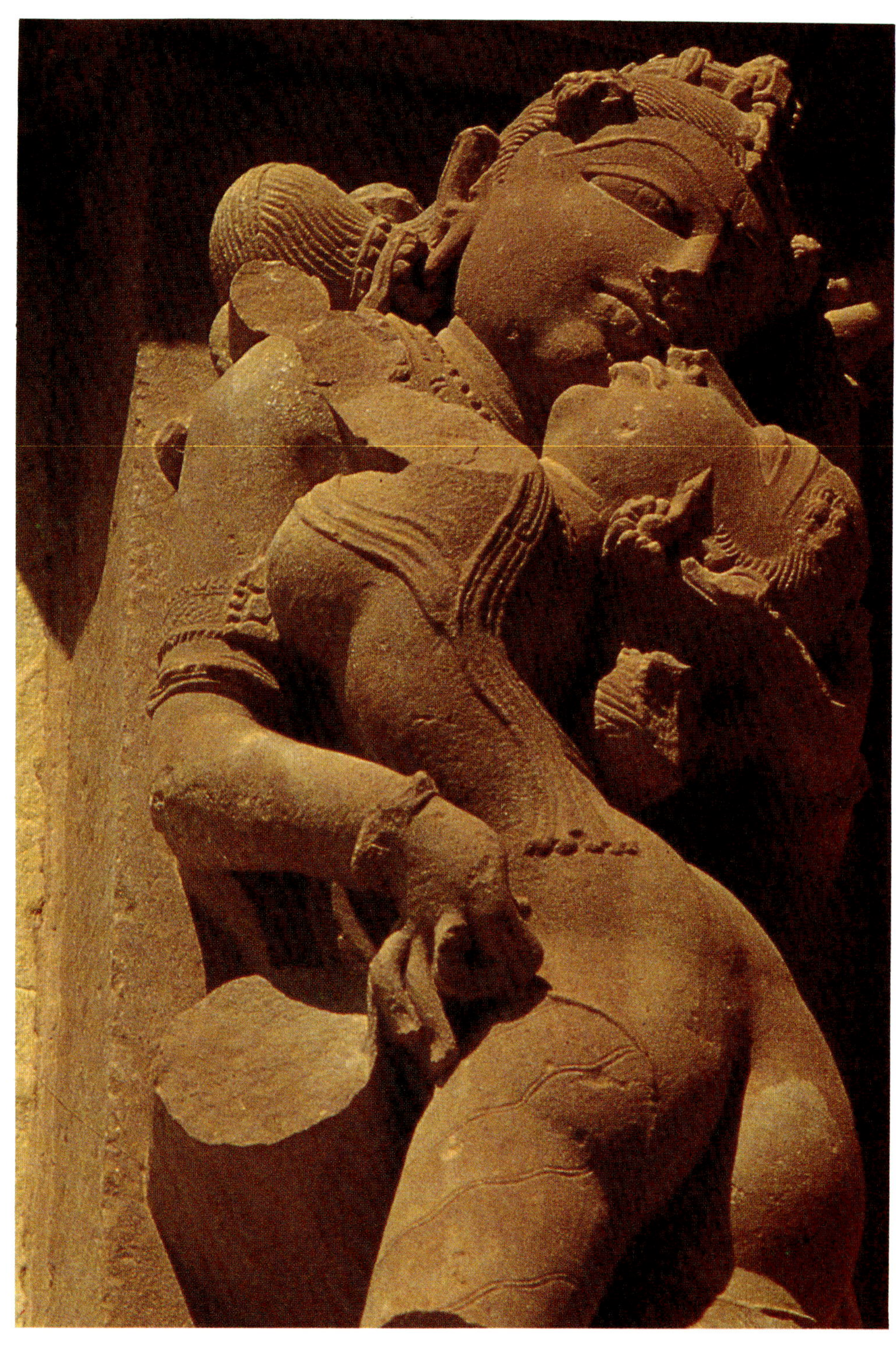

The fond embrace — the ultimate bliss of union with the divinity!

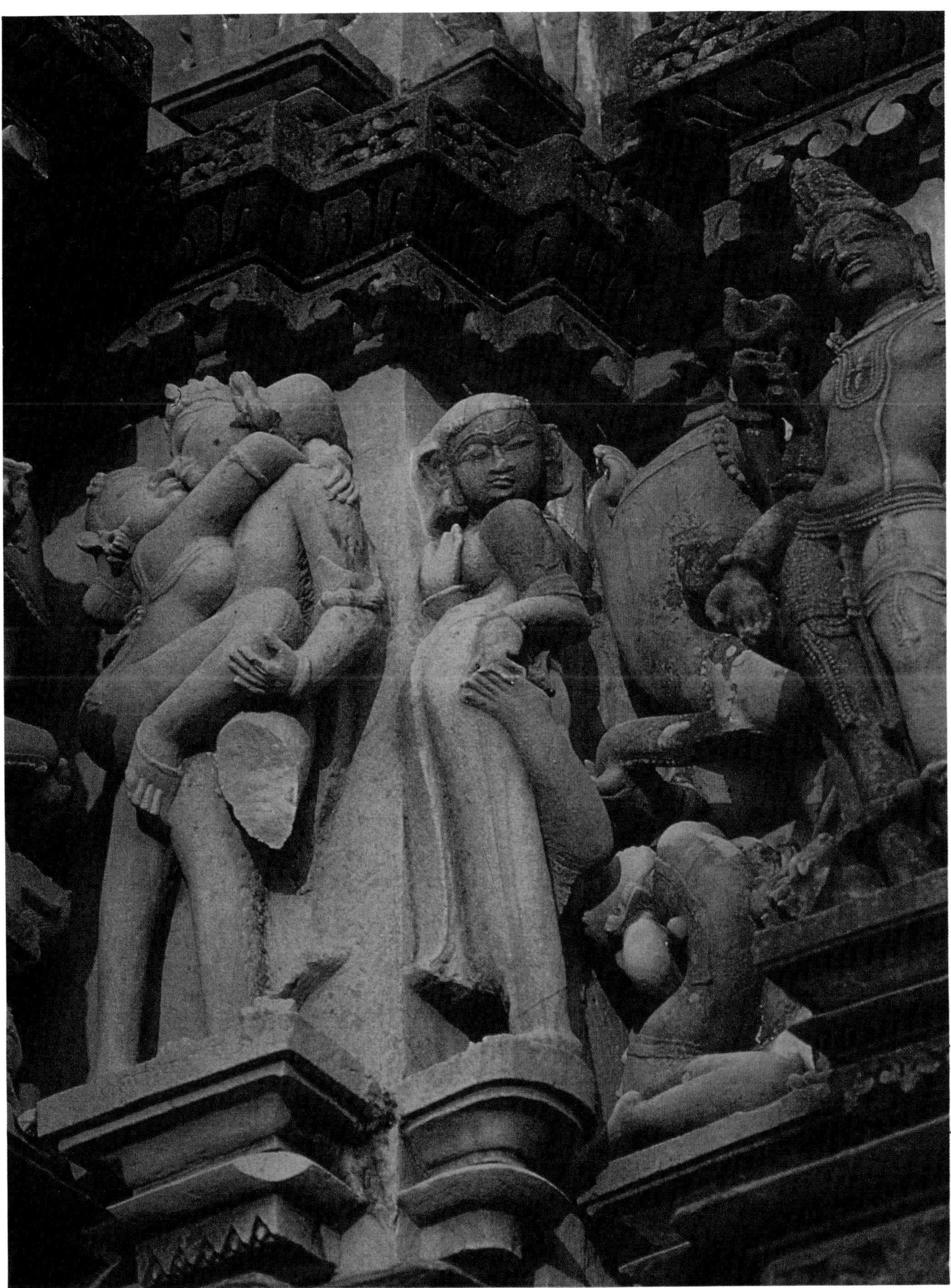

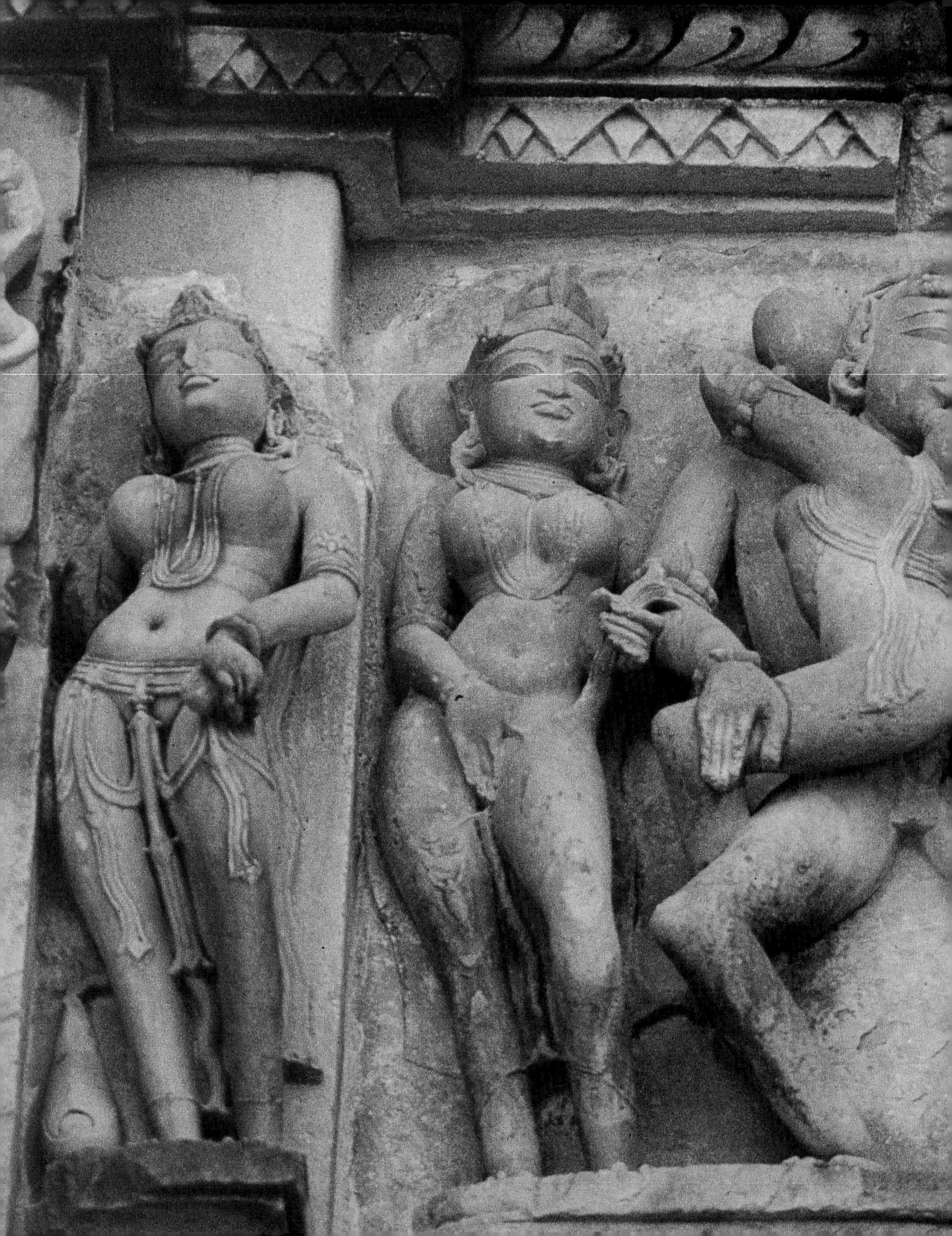

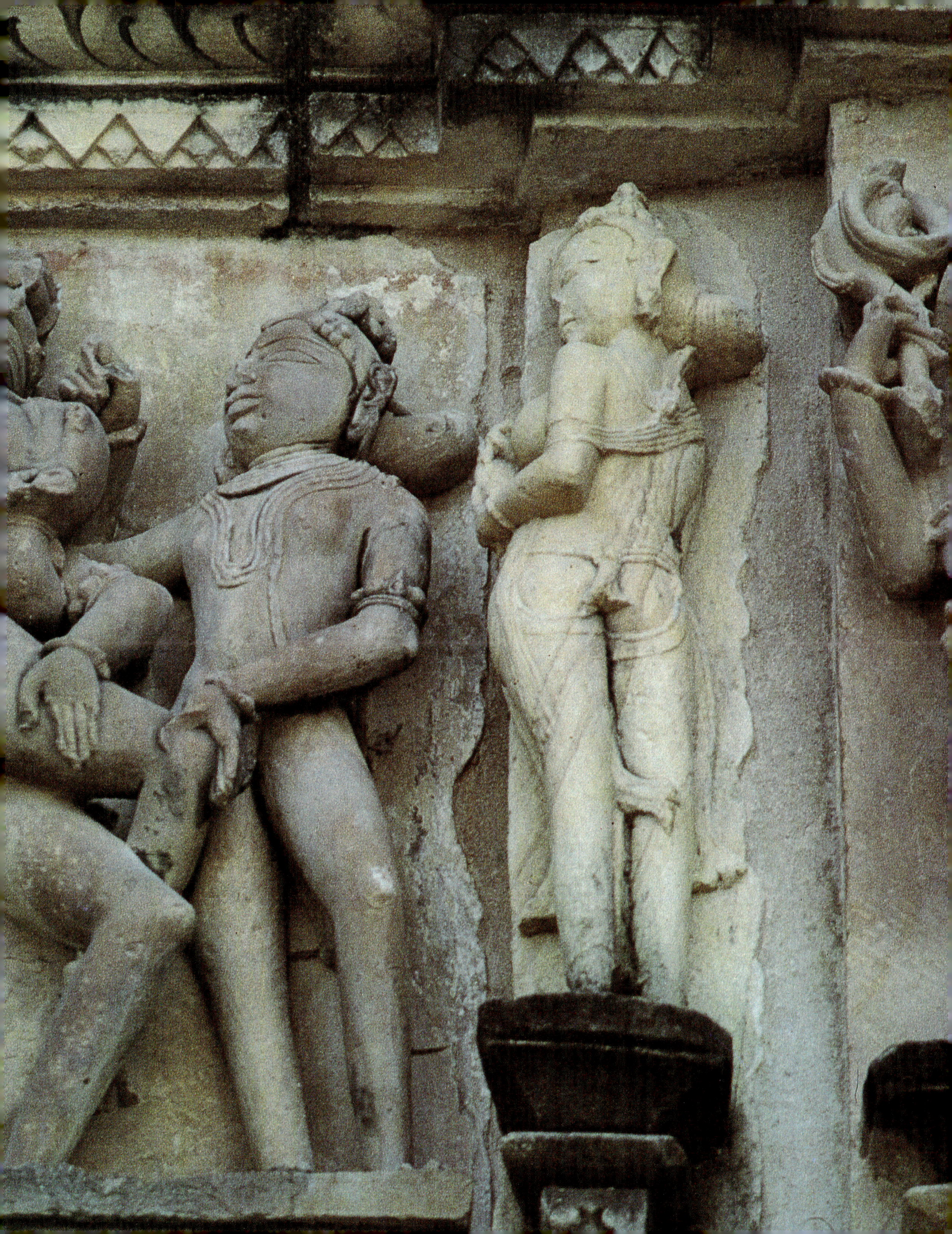

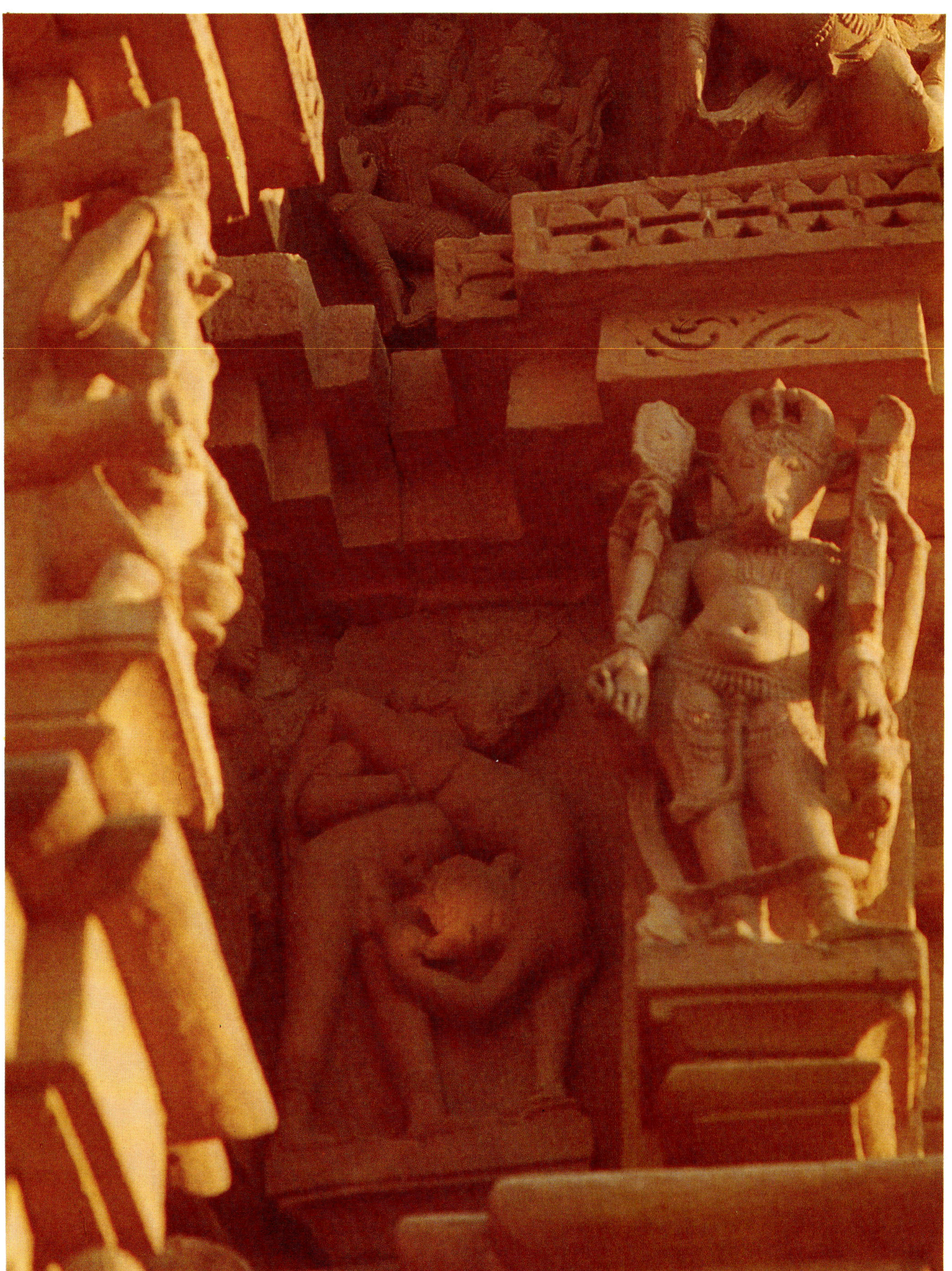

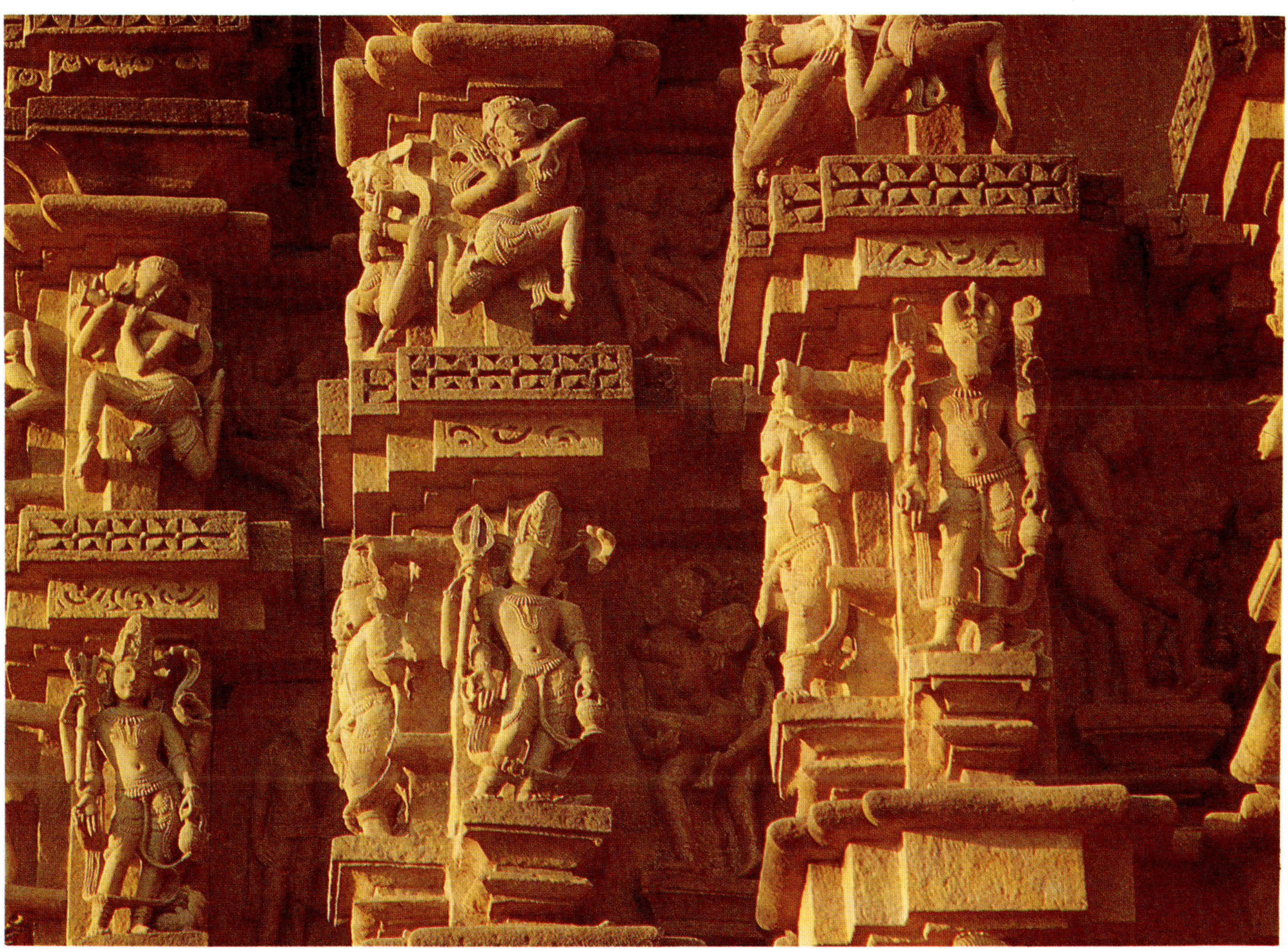

Duladeo Temple's outer wall has been adorned with three rows of sculptures. The top row has spirited figures of flying and dancing Vidyadharas (angels), some of them perform acrobatic feats, carrying garlands, brandishing weapons or playing musical instruments. The lower rows are decorated with figures of divinities, Dikpals and nymphs while erotic couples are in middle row. Erotic carvings flanked by divine images express concurrence of the Supreme.

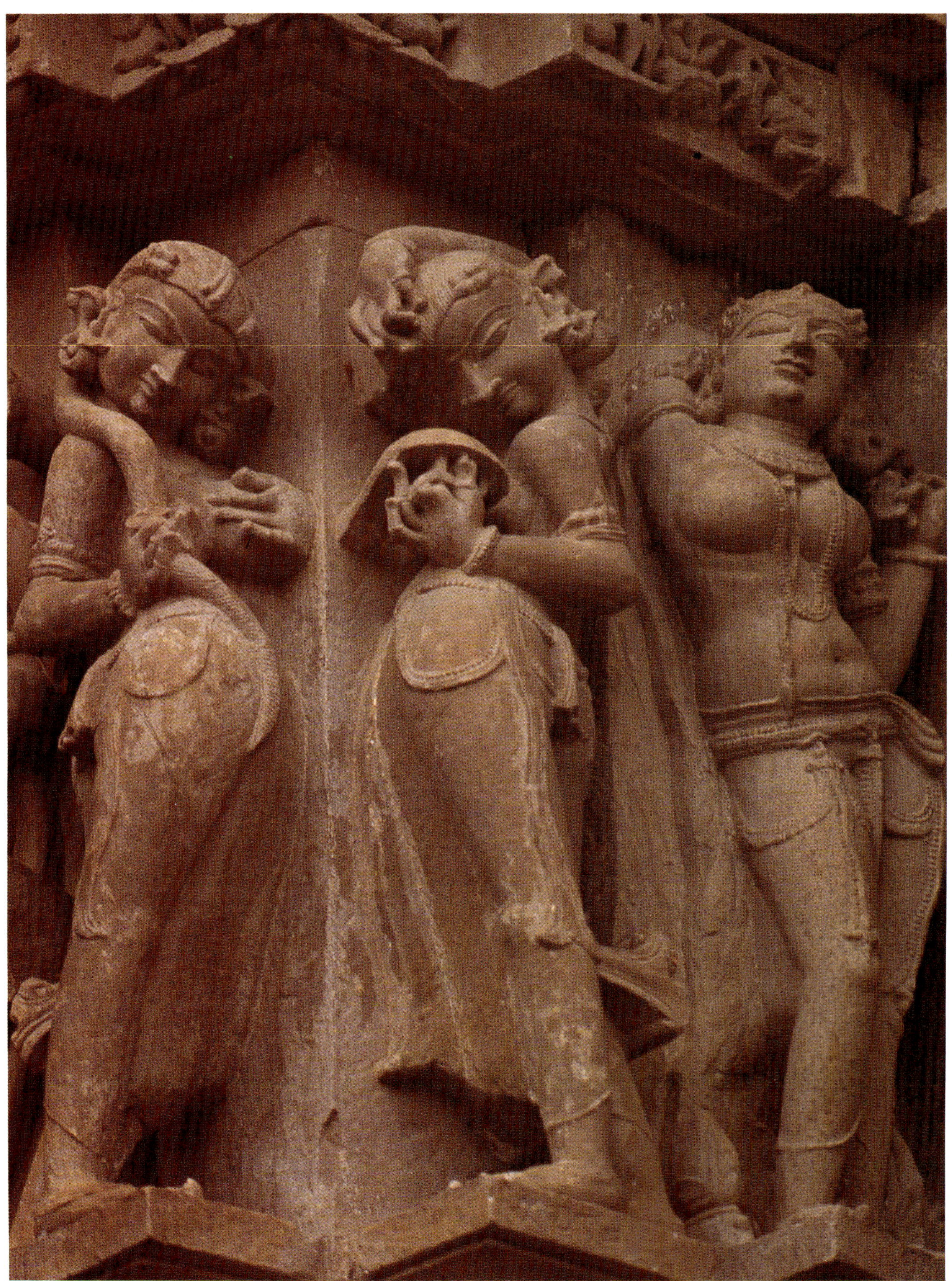

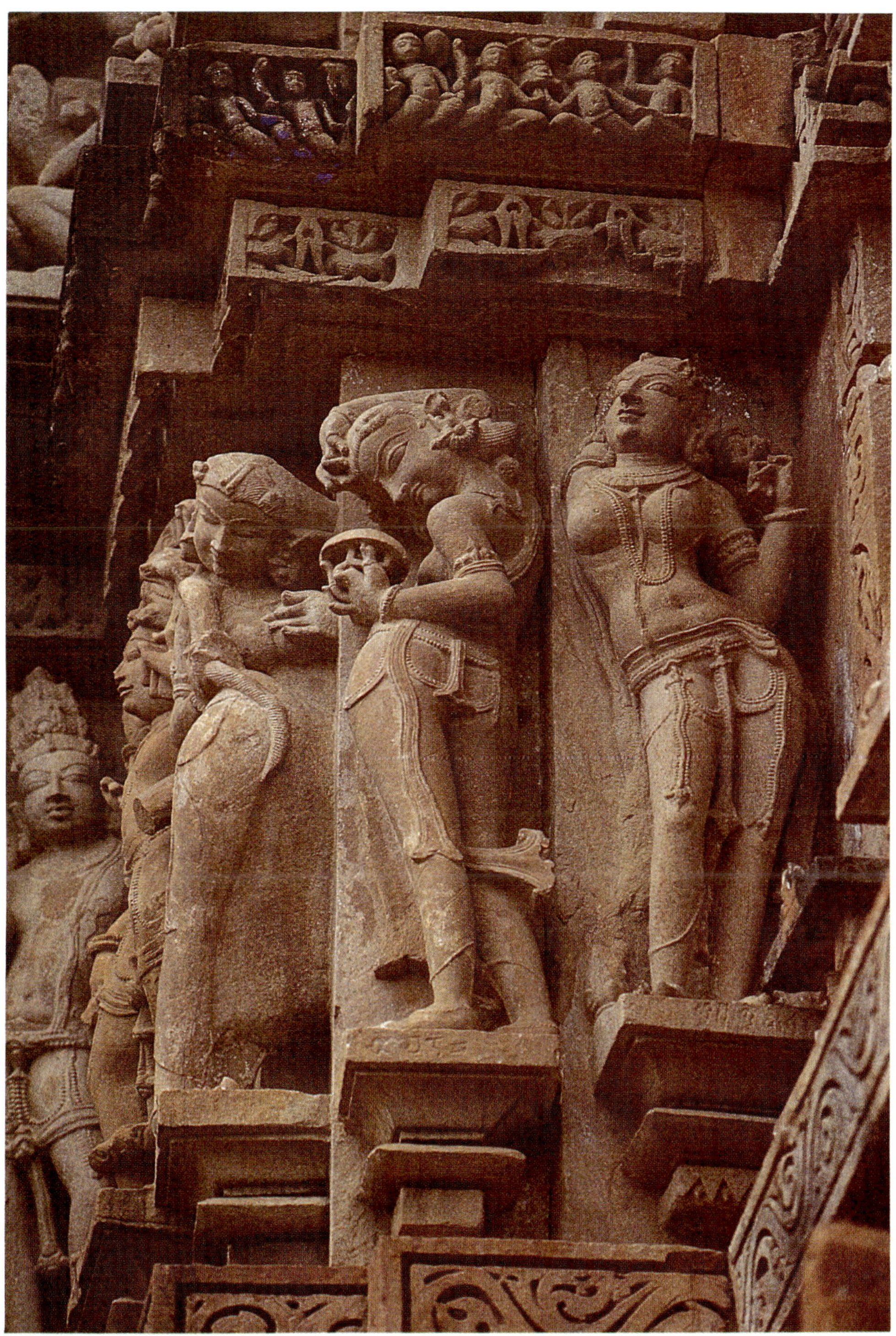

The physical passion in tune with certain chapters of *Kamasutra*. Indian ancient texts advocate the feminity to be expressed by fullness of the breasts, belly and hips, to symbolize fertility, carnal pleasure and perfection. The jewels adorning the body serve only to emphasize the roundness of the curves. With every movement of the eyes of the beholder a new perspective is created in the Khajuraho sculptures. Even the course of Sun from east to west provides a new dimension to their meaning!

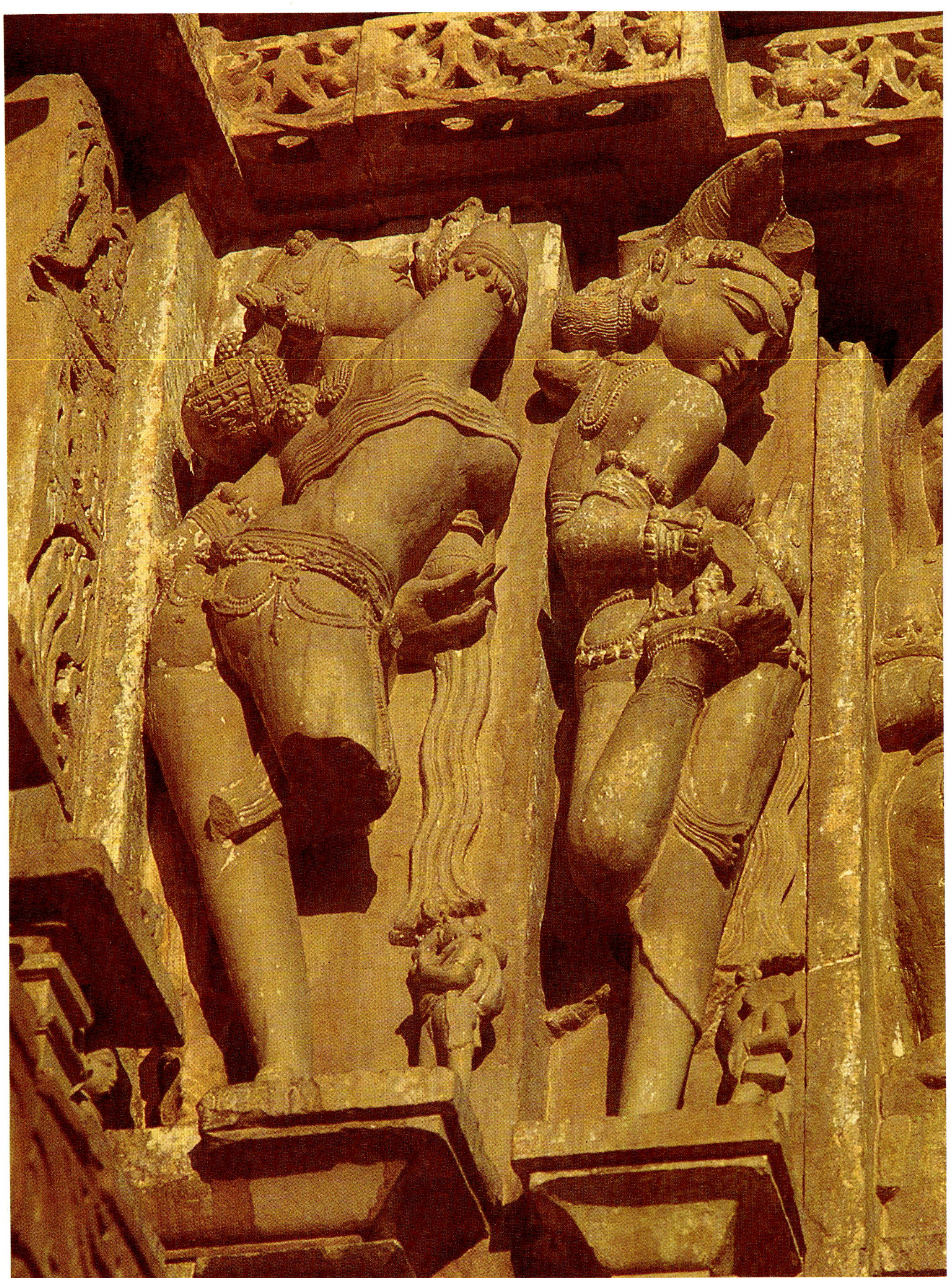

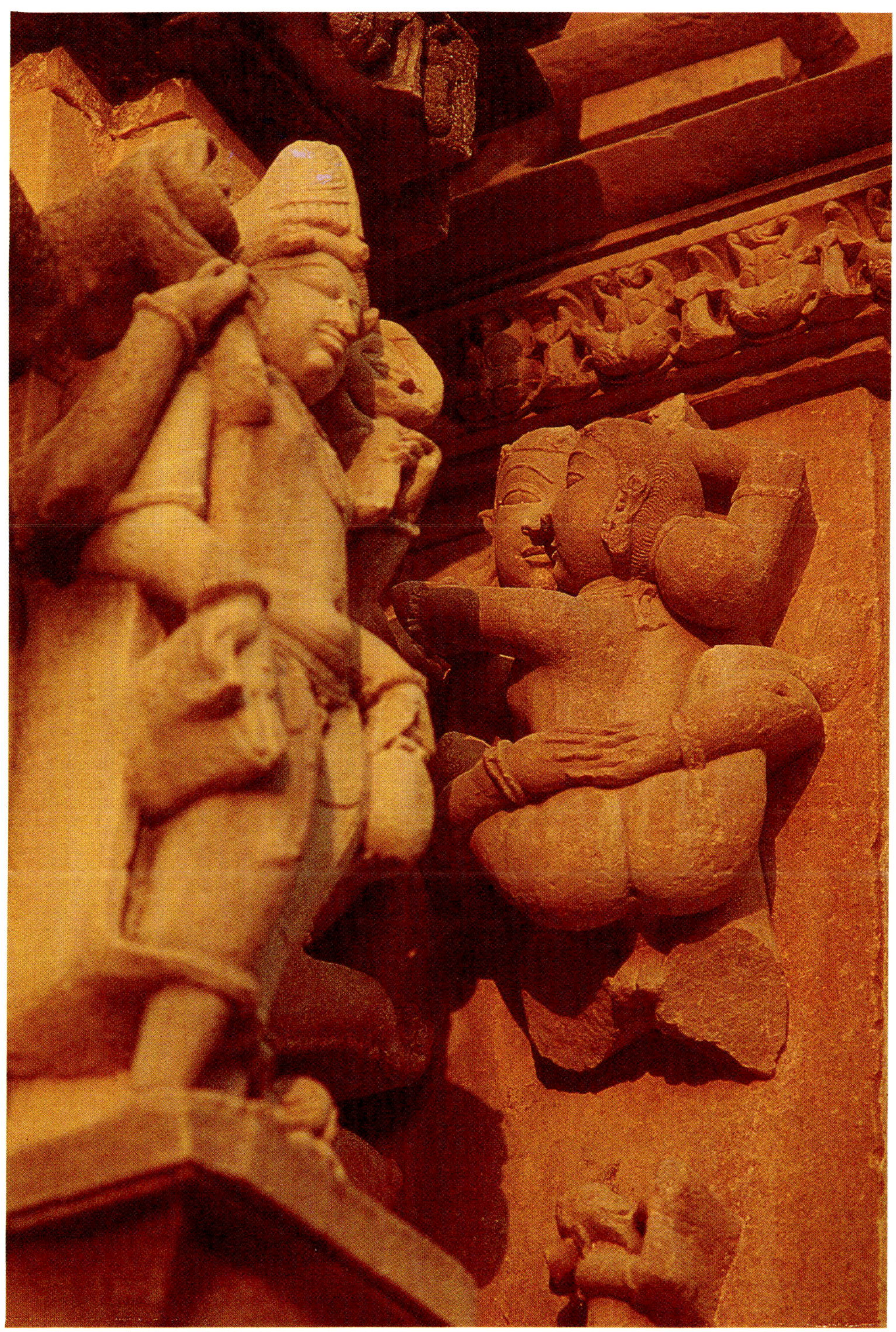

Ritualistic orgy : Lakshamana Temple terrace, 10th Century A.D. : In the myths of the Kaula-Kapalikas wine and women were supposed to act as a means of liberation. This resulted in the most gross kind of sensual excesses in the name of religion and Tantrik Yoga. These friezes depict 'Bhairavichakra' in which all decencies are thrown to the wind, Exotic love-play, Amrachushaka or fellalio, the mare and horse posture and Kakali posture.

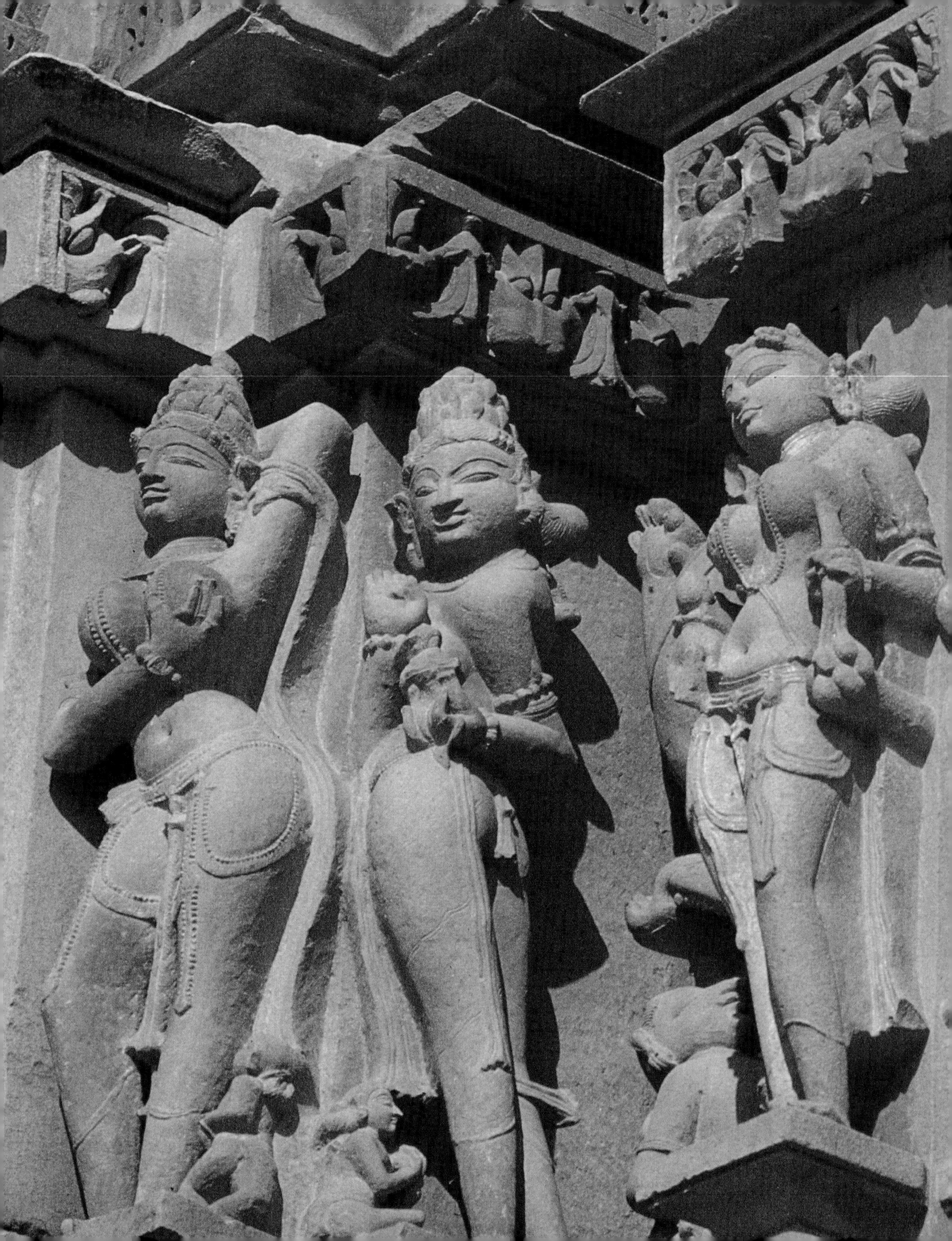

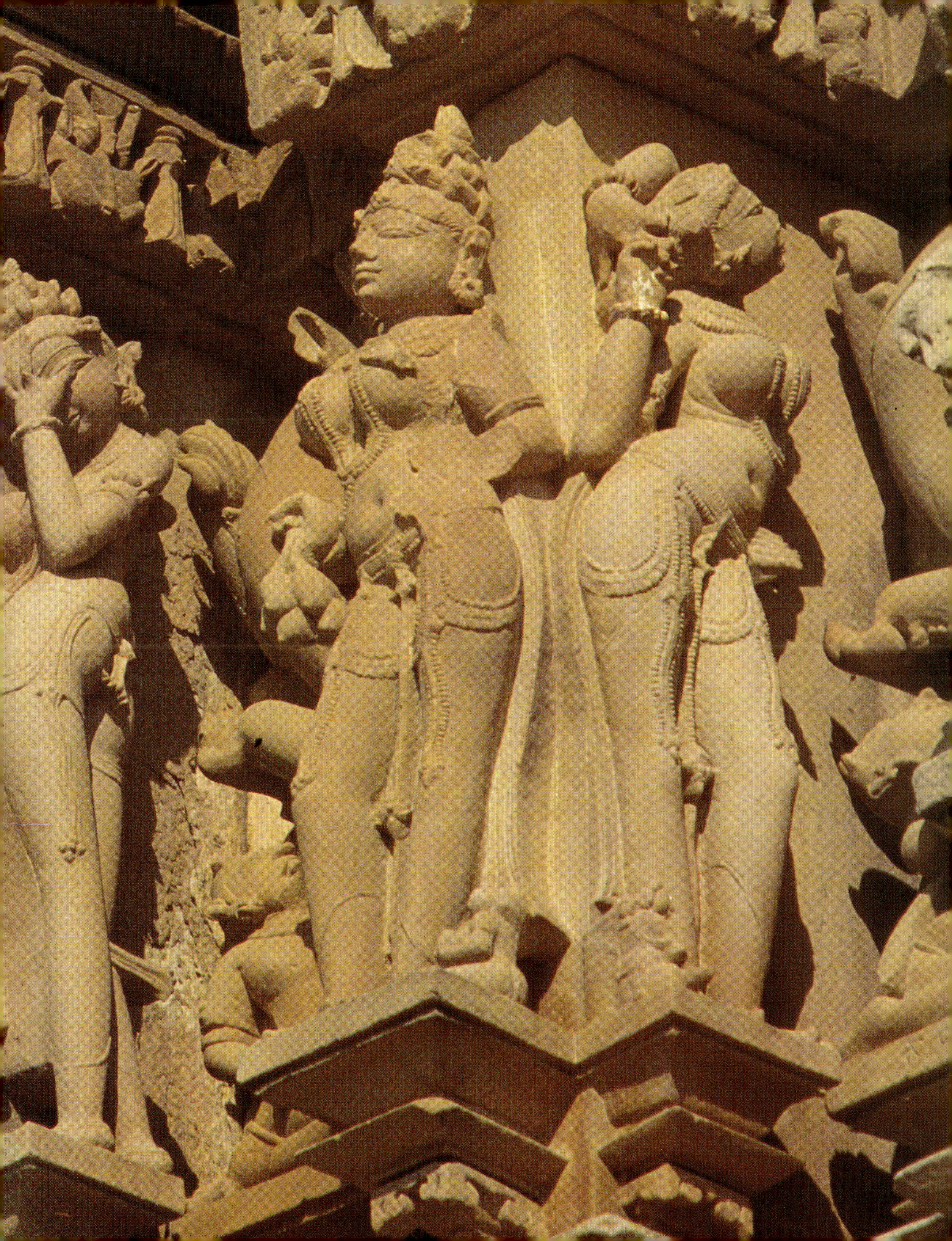

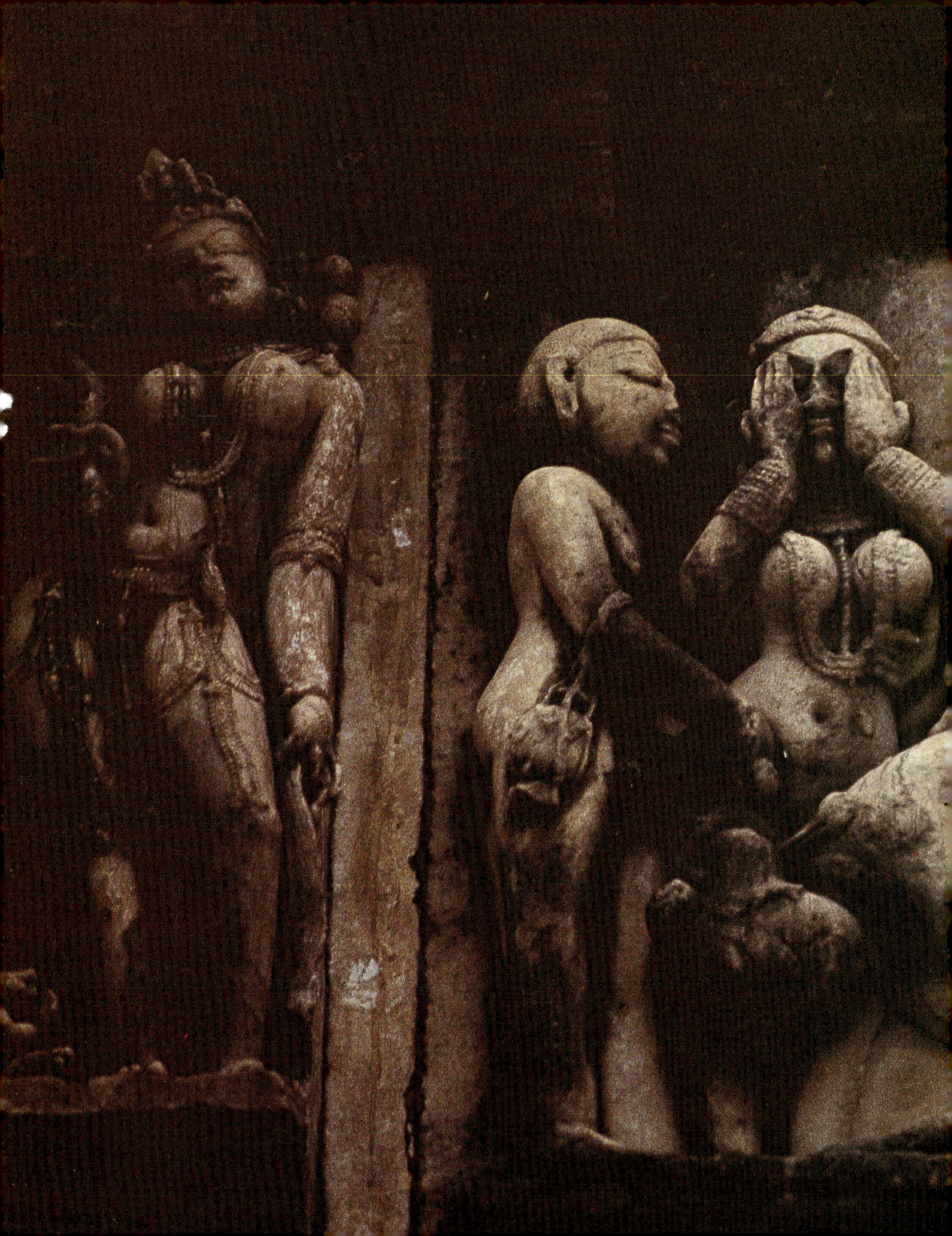

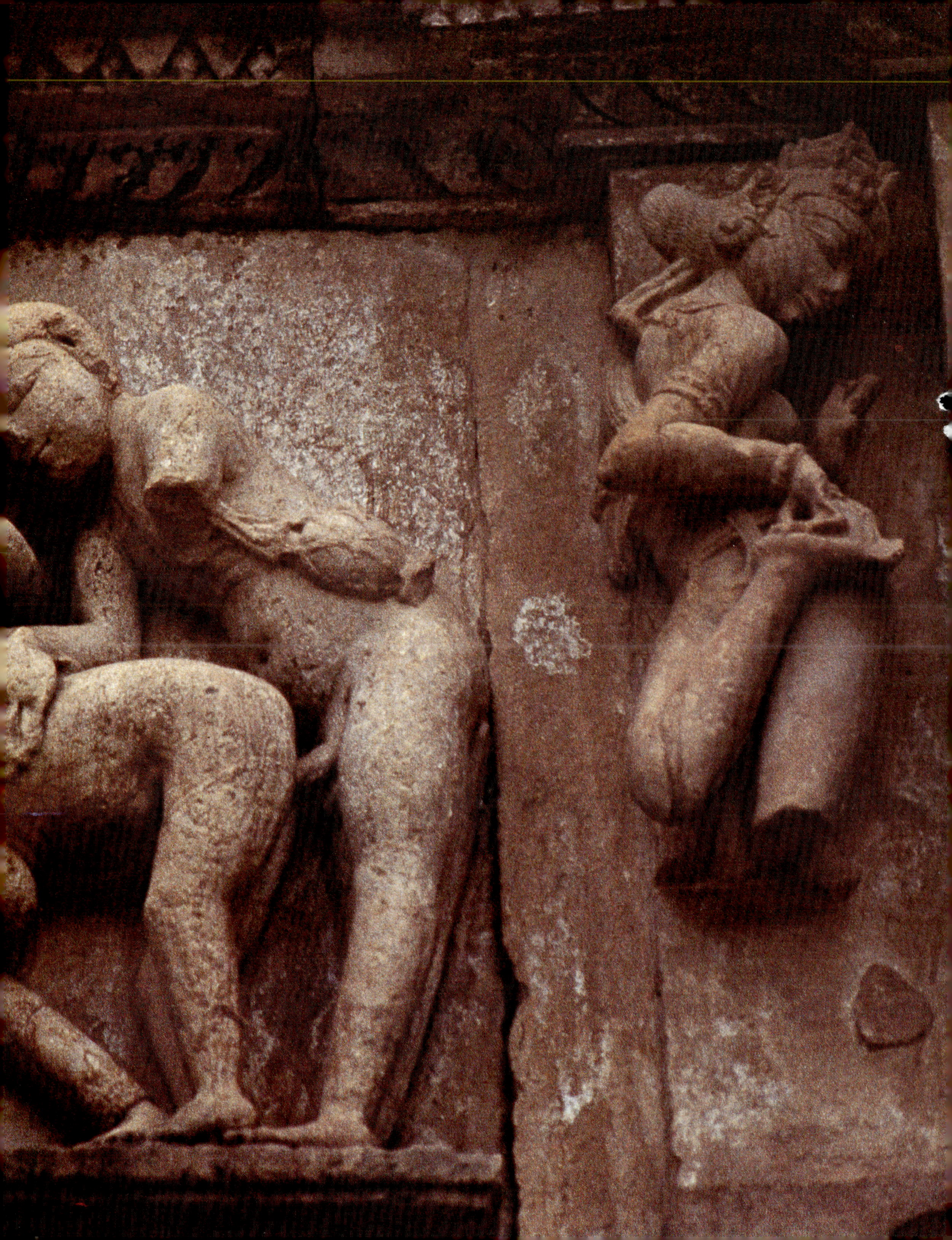

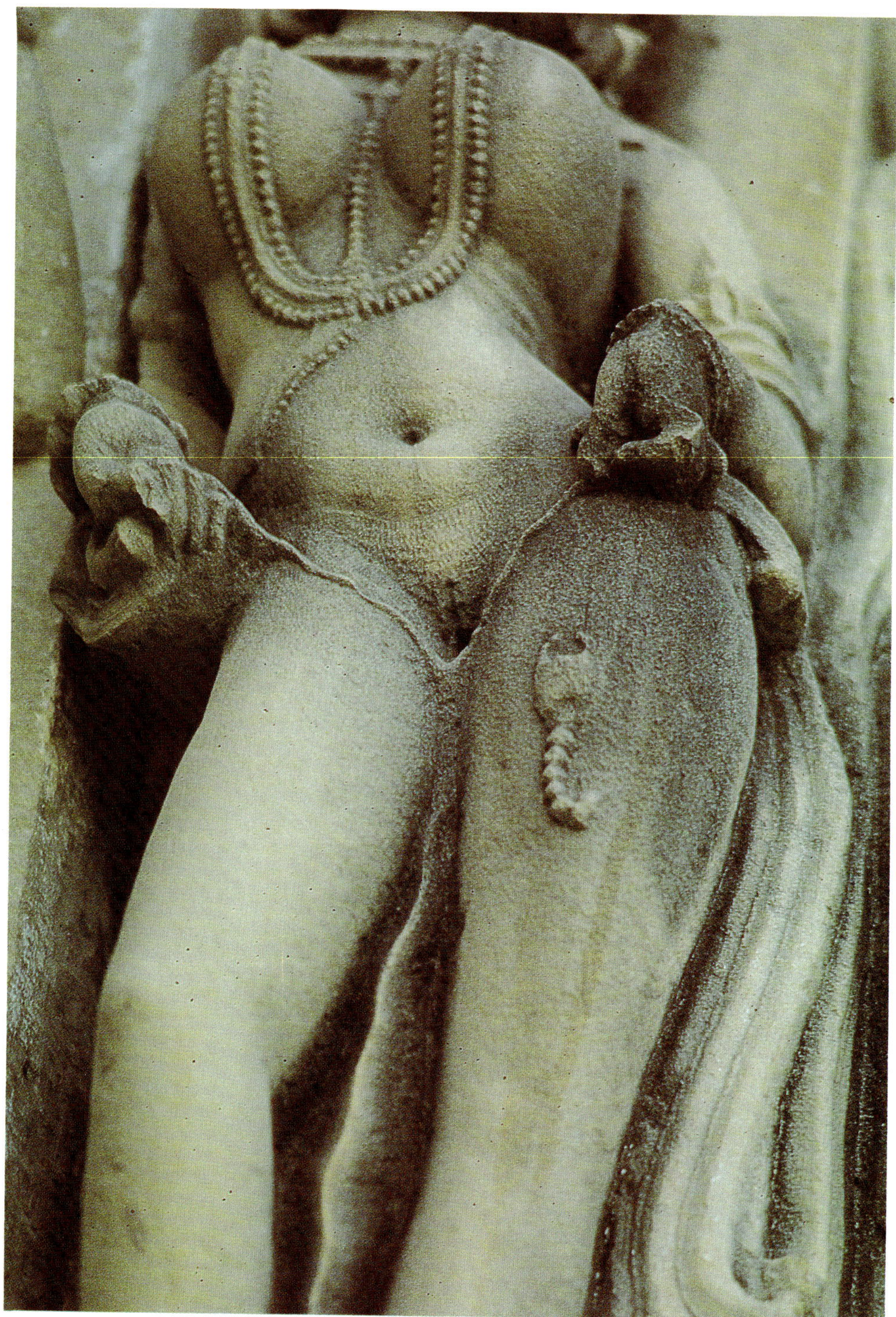

The Apsara disrobing her lower garments, the scorpion on her thigh symbolizes passion. Whether she is afraid of the insect, or she is passionate? A sculpture showing the minute details of her body and the folds of clothes is placed on Devi Jagdamba temple's north wall. Do they resemble the present day skin touching jeans in any way! *Page 149* : Even the geometric design of the temples depicts the rekindling of energy forces. 'Tantra' has its root in the Sanskrit implying the feel of cosmos within the body. All the energy forces present in nature are also present in the body in the condensed form. Hence, Tantra philosophy advocates the human body being the shortest way leading to salvation.

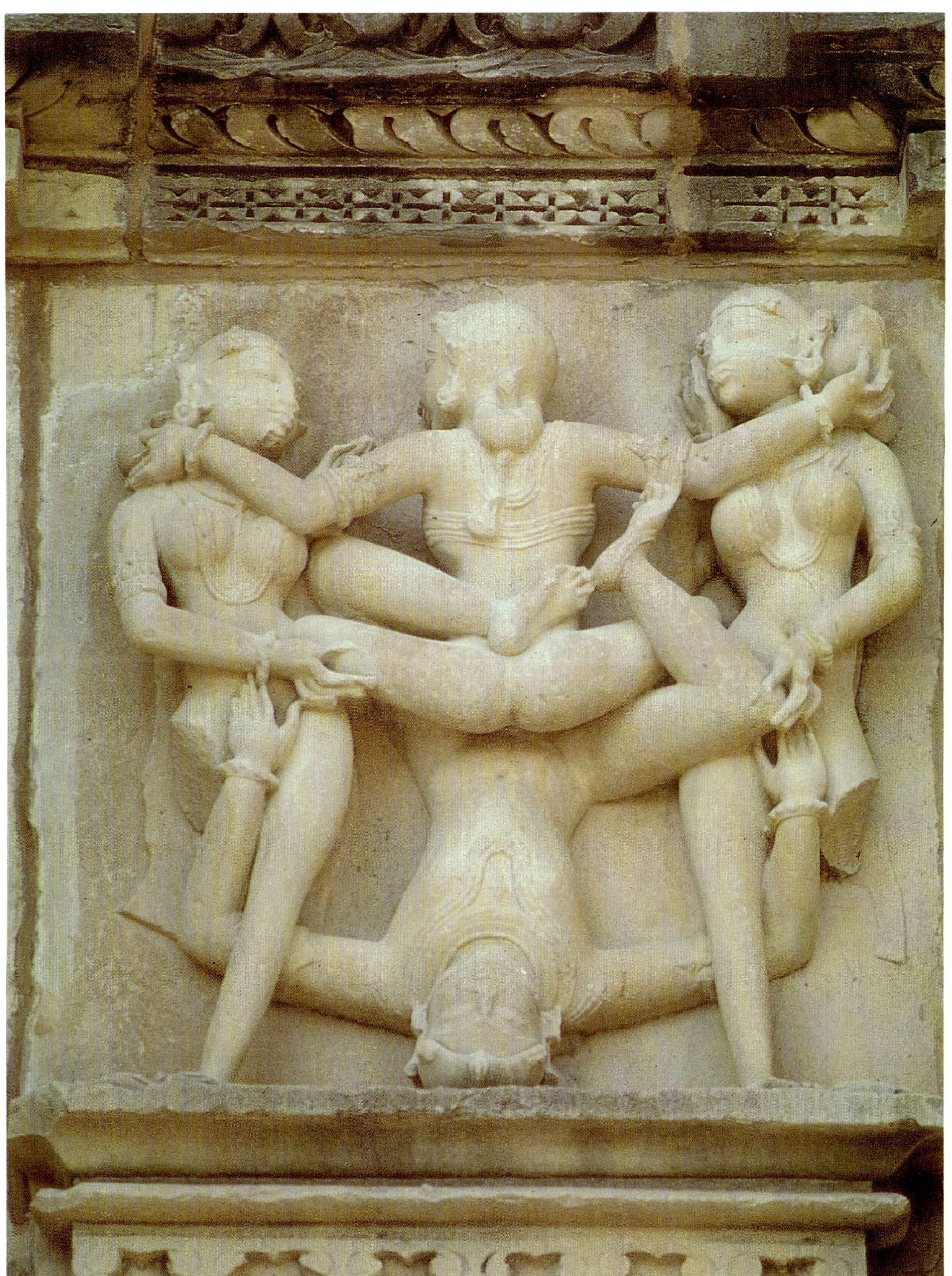

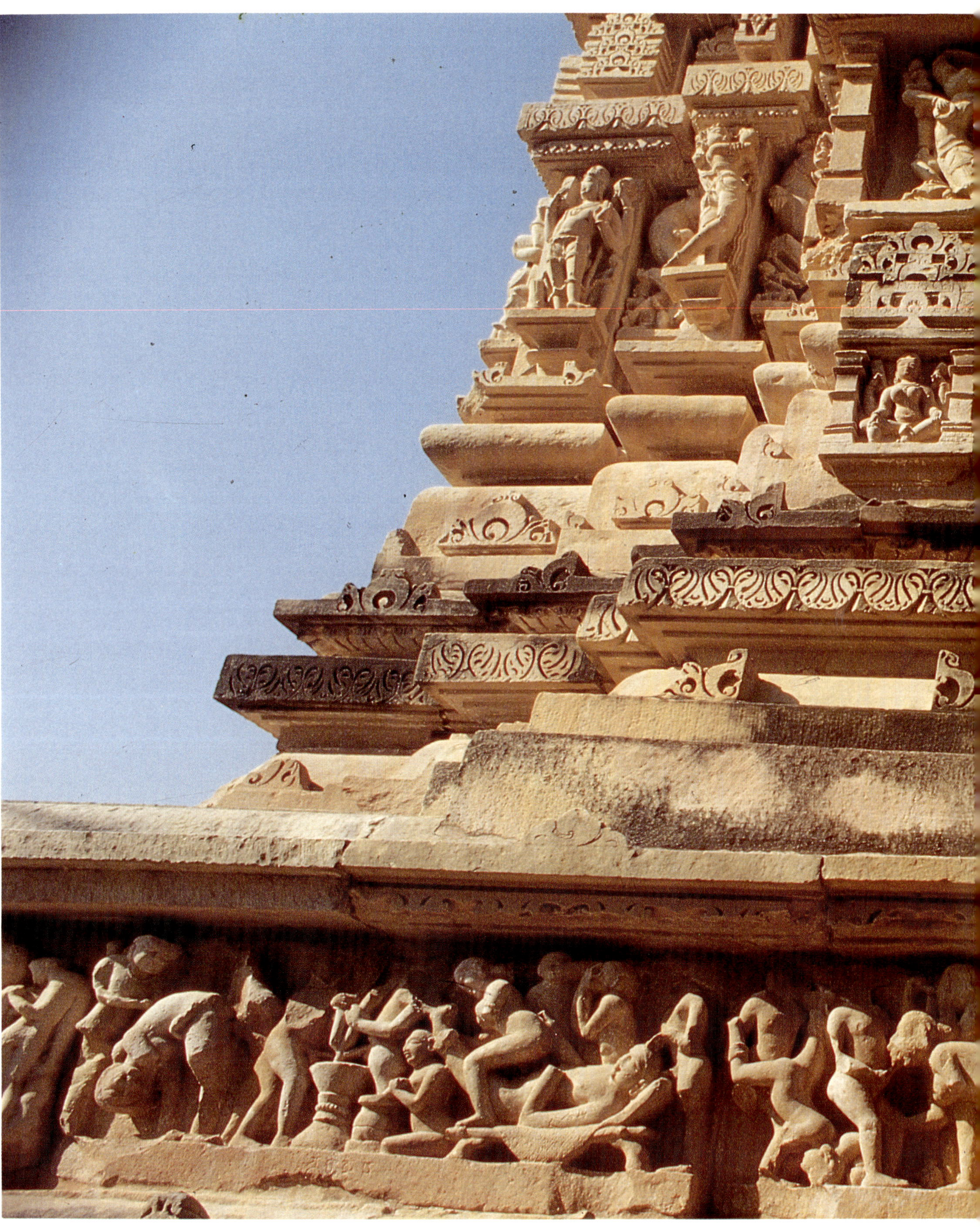

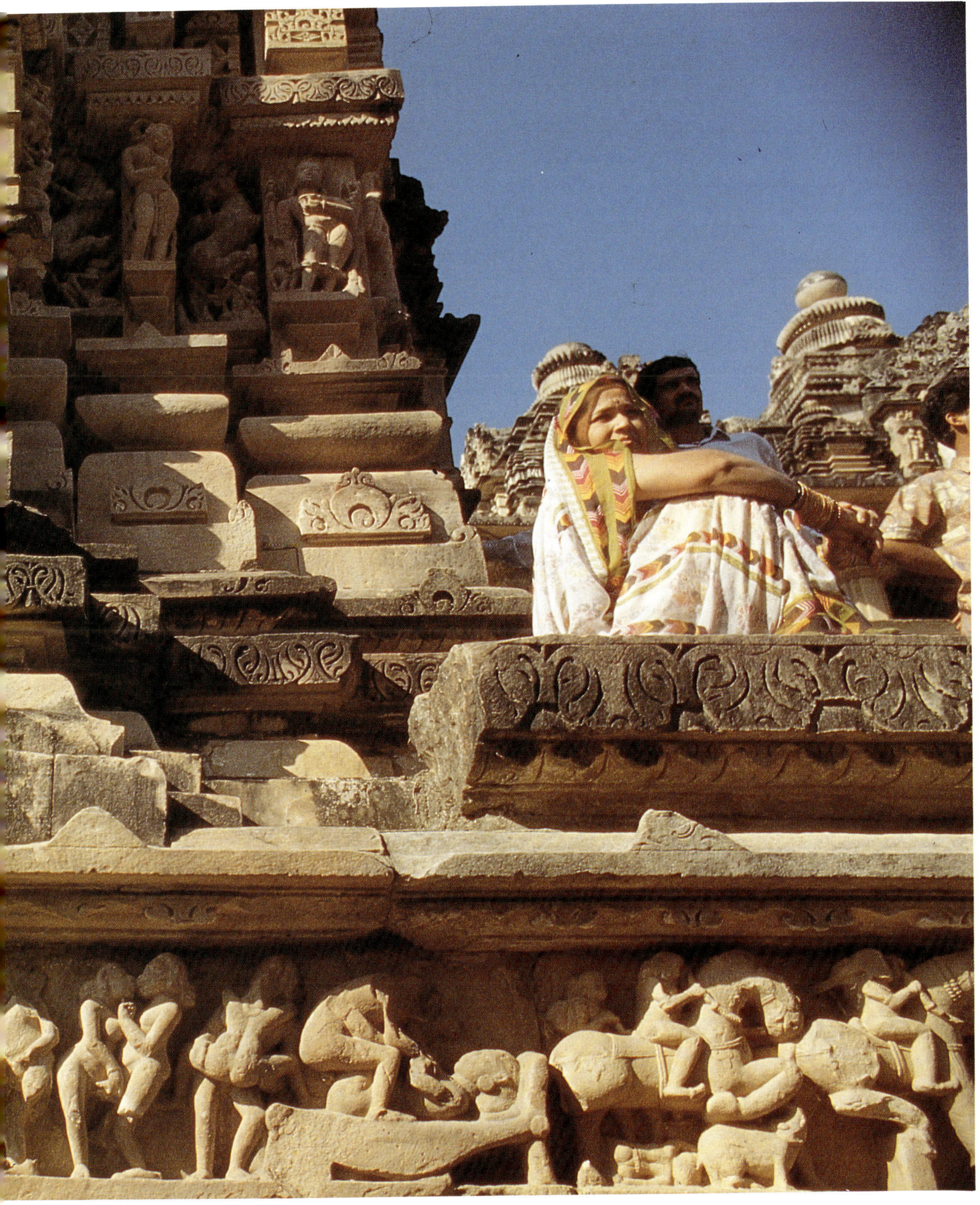

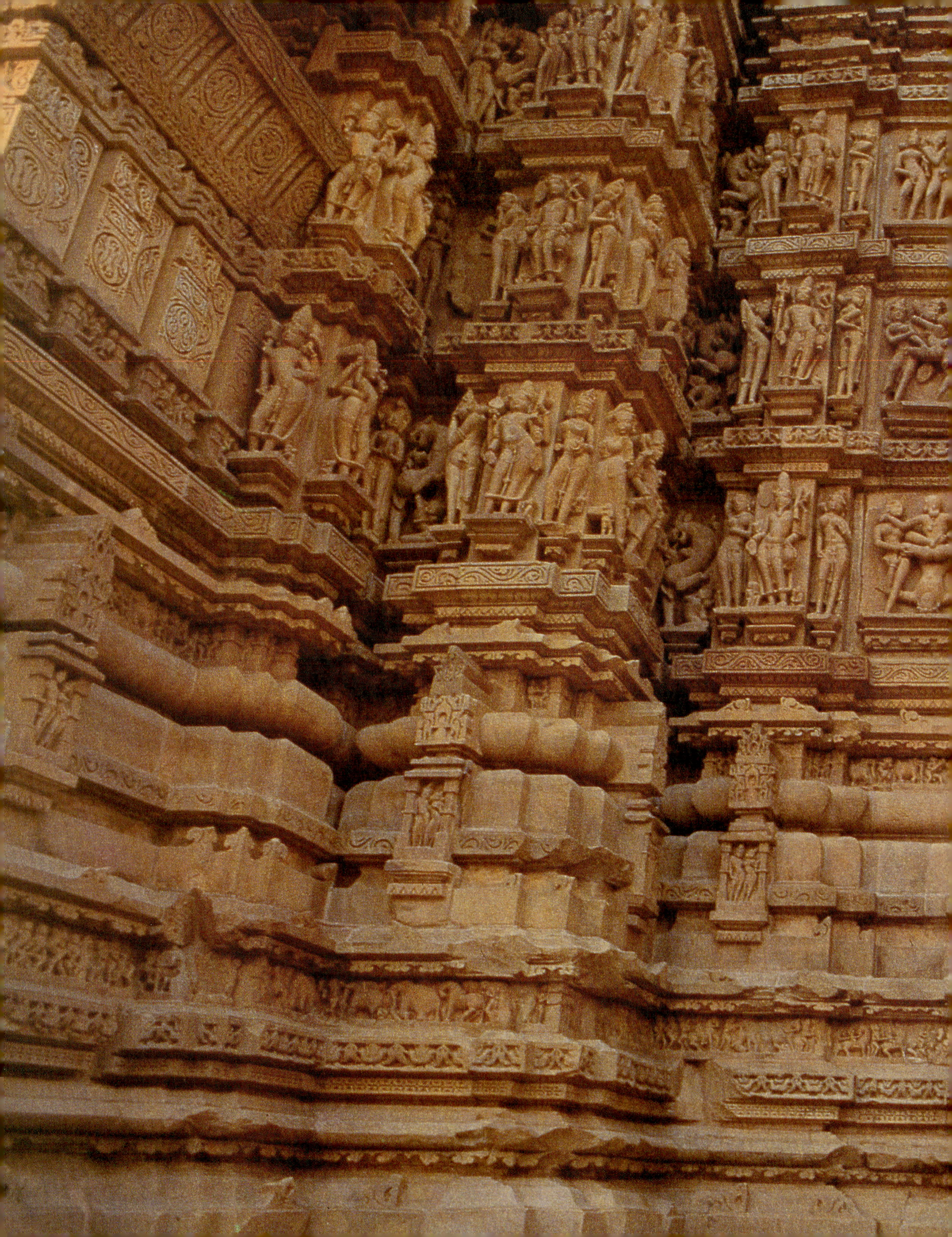

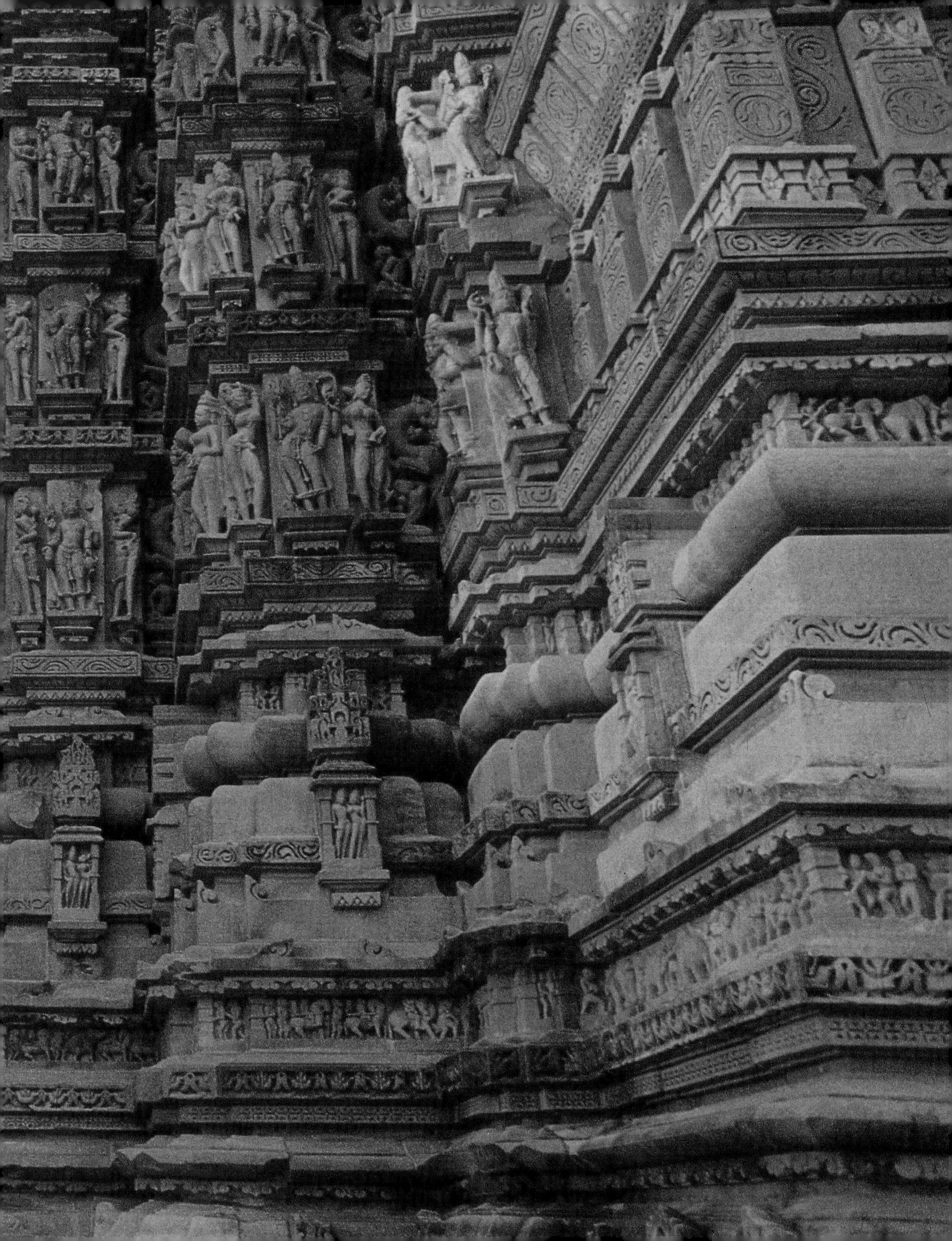

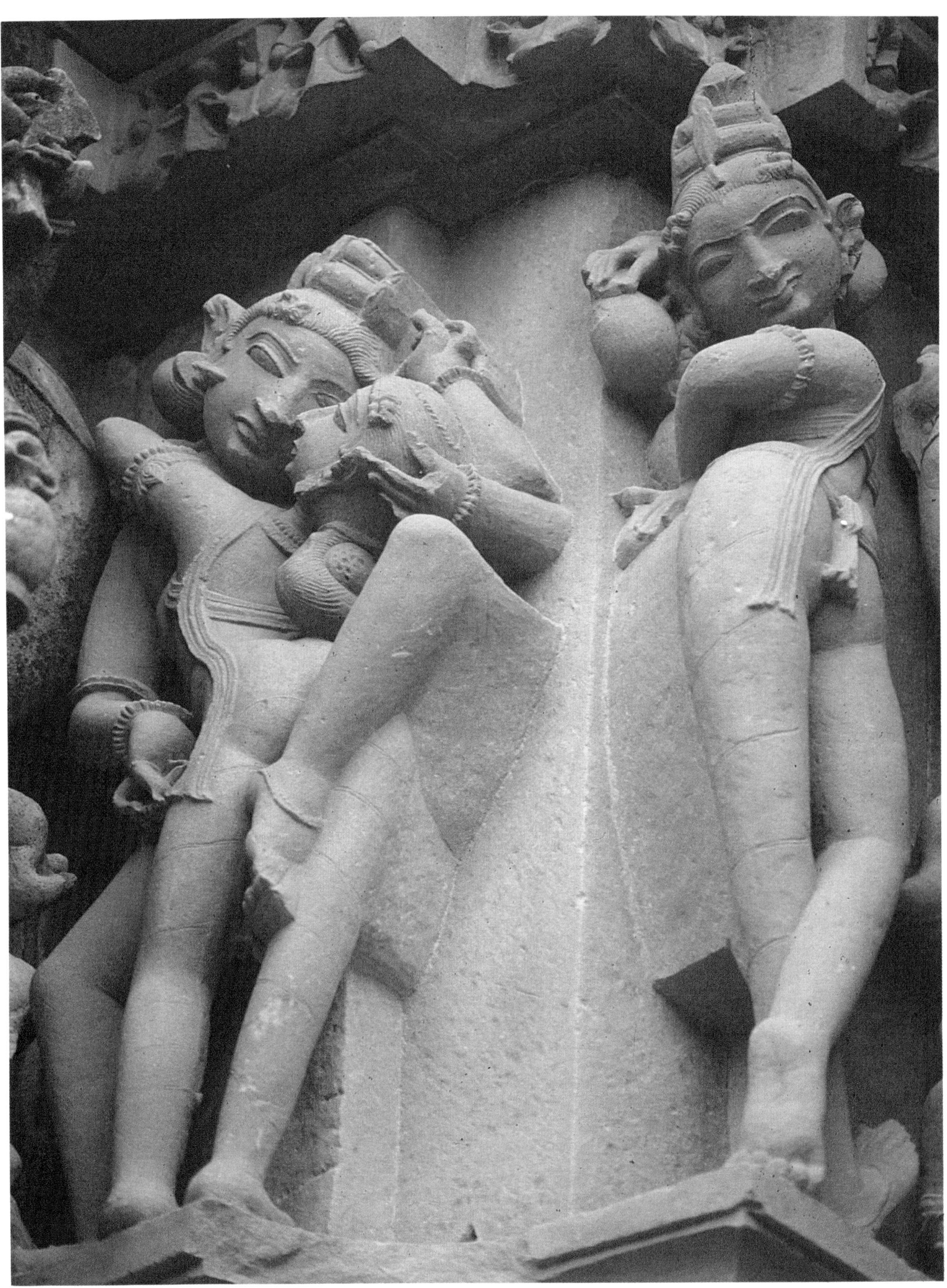

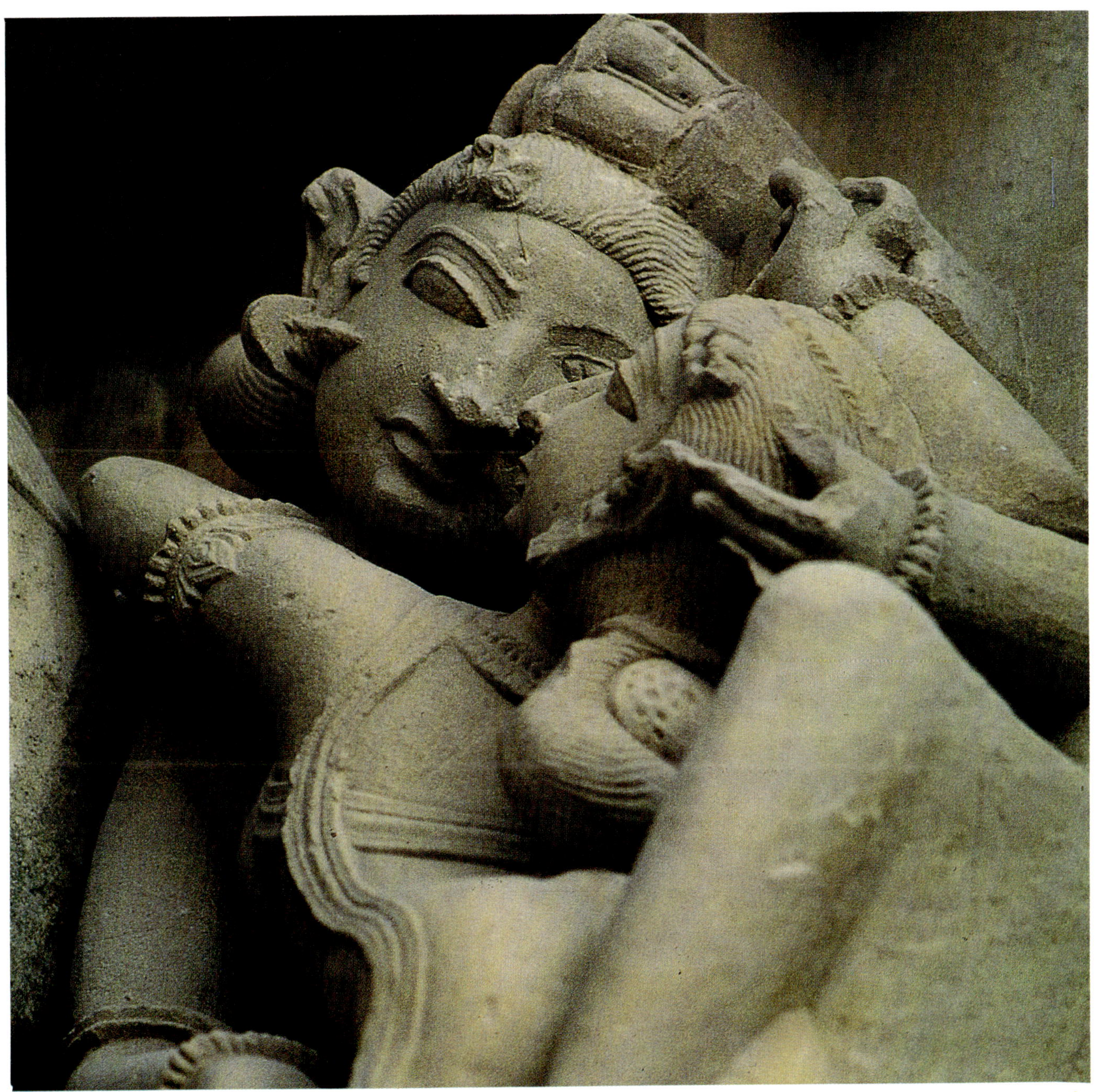

An amorous couple. Devi Jagdama Temple, 11th Century A.D. : The vigorous movement of the female partner portrayed. Her left arm holds her partner's neck tightly and her right hand clutches a lock of his hair. Clutching the hair in sexual congress to enhance the emotional intensity of the act is enjoined in the *Kamasutra.* The sculpture art of Khajuraho depicts the rhythm of eternal bliss prevailing in each and every stonepiece. Whether erotic or not, all the sculpted images on the Khajuraho temples emit an energy, a lust for life, power, grace and gaiety. Perhaps nowhere else in the world has such a hymn to the beauty of woman been sung.

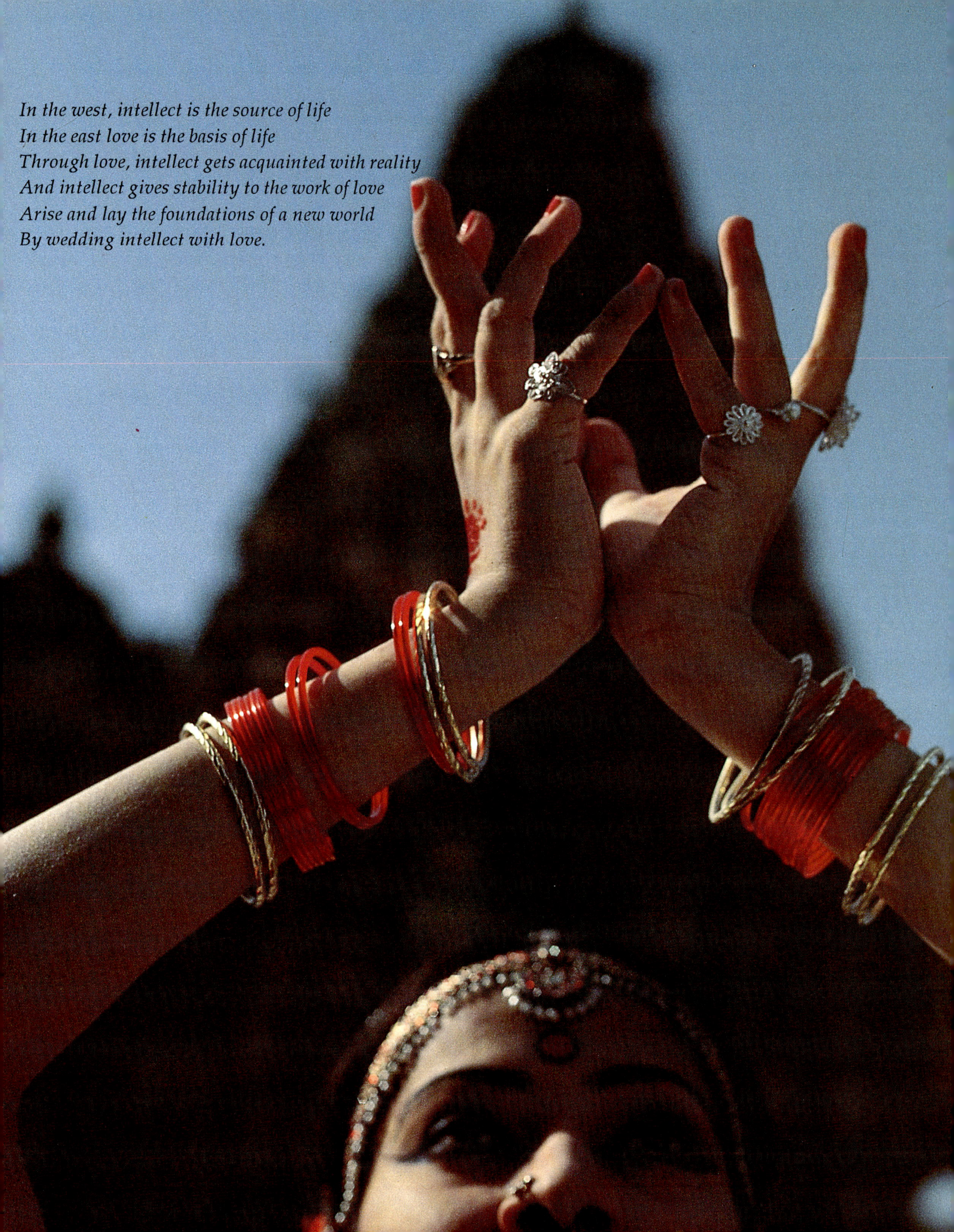

In the west, intellect is the source of life
In the east love is the basis of life
Through love, intellect gets acquainted with reality
And intellect gives stability to the work of love
Arise and lay the foundations of a new world
By wedding intellect with love.

THE LANDSCAPE GEOMETRY OF KHAJURAHO

Indian mythology admits the whole earth as one complete temple as also the human body. Shiva is considered to be the lord of three mythical realms — *Dev-lok, Bhu-lok and Paataal-lok* (the heaven, the earth and the nether worlds), and controller of the five life substances — *Prithvi, Jal, Vayu, Agni and Akaash* (the earth, water, air, fire, and space). Shiva as cosmic dancer controls the cosmic rhythm of time evolution and dissolution. Legends admit the Khajuraho a sacred place where the cosmic marriage of Shiva was performed. On the eve of Maha-Shivratri the Matangeshwara Temple becomes the venue of celebrations of Phalgun Krishna - 14th, i.e. 14th day of dark-half, waning, in February/March each year. Hence the Matangeshwara temple serves as the naval base from where various sites converge to form alignments in the sacred landscape geometry of Khajuraho. Chandelas guided by the astronomer-priests and archeologists must have observed an order in nature corresponding to the aspect of physical reality. In May, 1996 a field survey was conducted using Garmin-45 receiver to map out the differential global position system measurements using detailed topographical charts; c.f. Rana P. B. Singh, "Sacred Territory of Khajuraho: A Search in Landscape Geometry, The Lay Hunter (Cornwall, London). This study mapped out 56 water pools and ponds, while according to local traditions the number would have been 64 in the ancient past. The water-pool symbolises the union of the sun (fire), the earth and the water, parallel to that of the heaven, the earth and the nether worlds. Each temple must have had a pond or pool.

The location of survived 25 temples and ruined sites have formed a series of alignments and correspondences in landscape, its roots go to the ancient wisdom of perceiving the earth spirit. The perceived order in Nature is transferred on the landscape by the location of these sacred sites making an orderly network of alignments. This is represented by a series of circles and its superimposition and a series of triangles too. The Matangeshwara temple serves as the navel-base from where various sites converge to form alignments. The three core-sites of respective groups forming circle and symbolizing the respective mandala: for the Western group the Matangeshwara, for the Eastern group the Javeri, and for the Southern group the Duladeo. The three spots in the eastern direction forming the arc of the boundary are Chaturbhuj, Mahishasurmardini and Dantala hill peak.

The Western group of temples symbolically form a simple *yantra* (cosmic design) with three forms of Shiva - Matangeshwara,

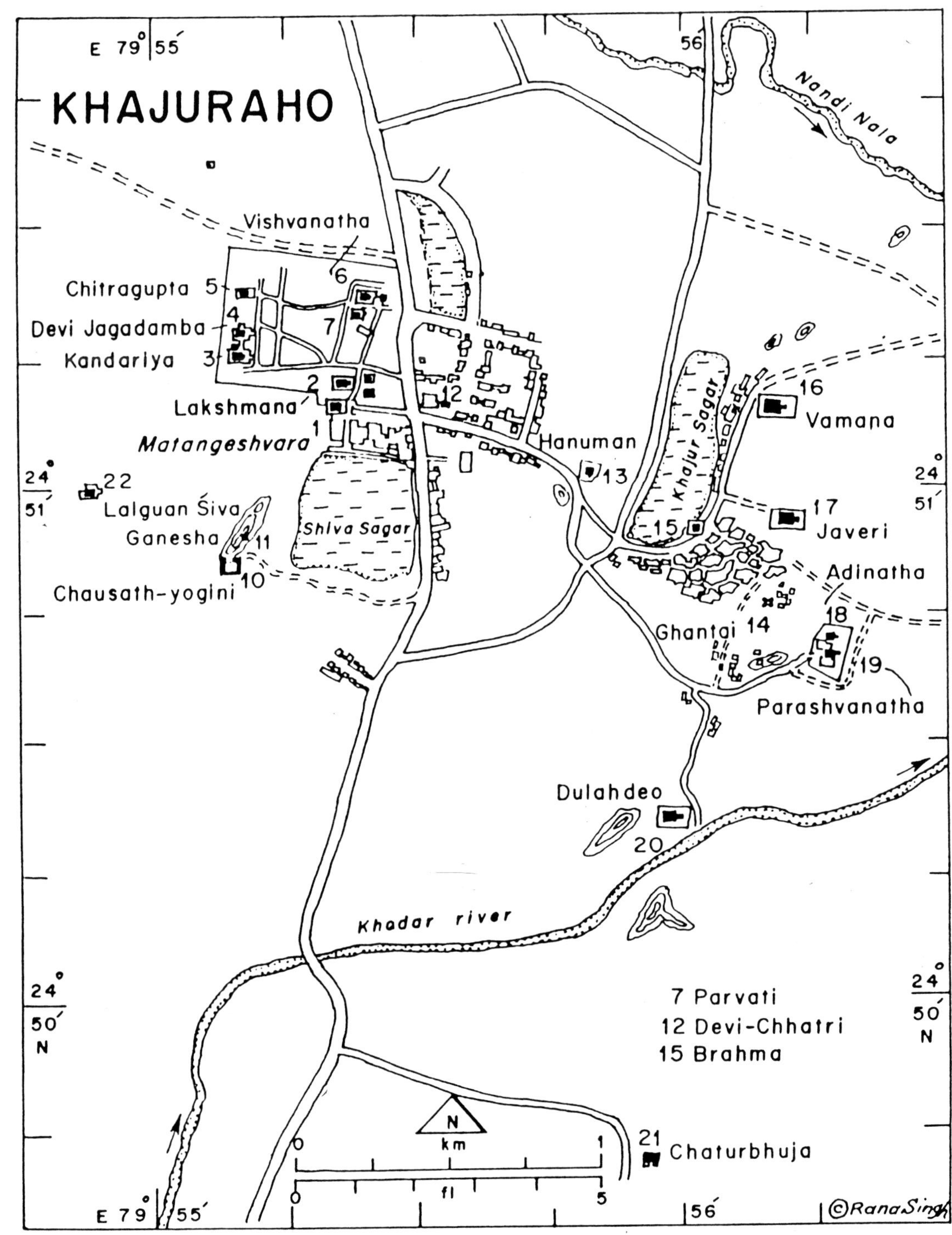

Chart 1 (*"Sacred Territory of Khajuraho: A Search in Landscape Geometry"*, by Rana P. B. Singh)

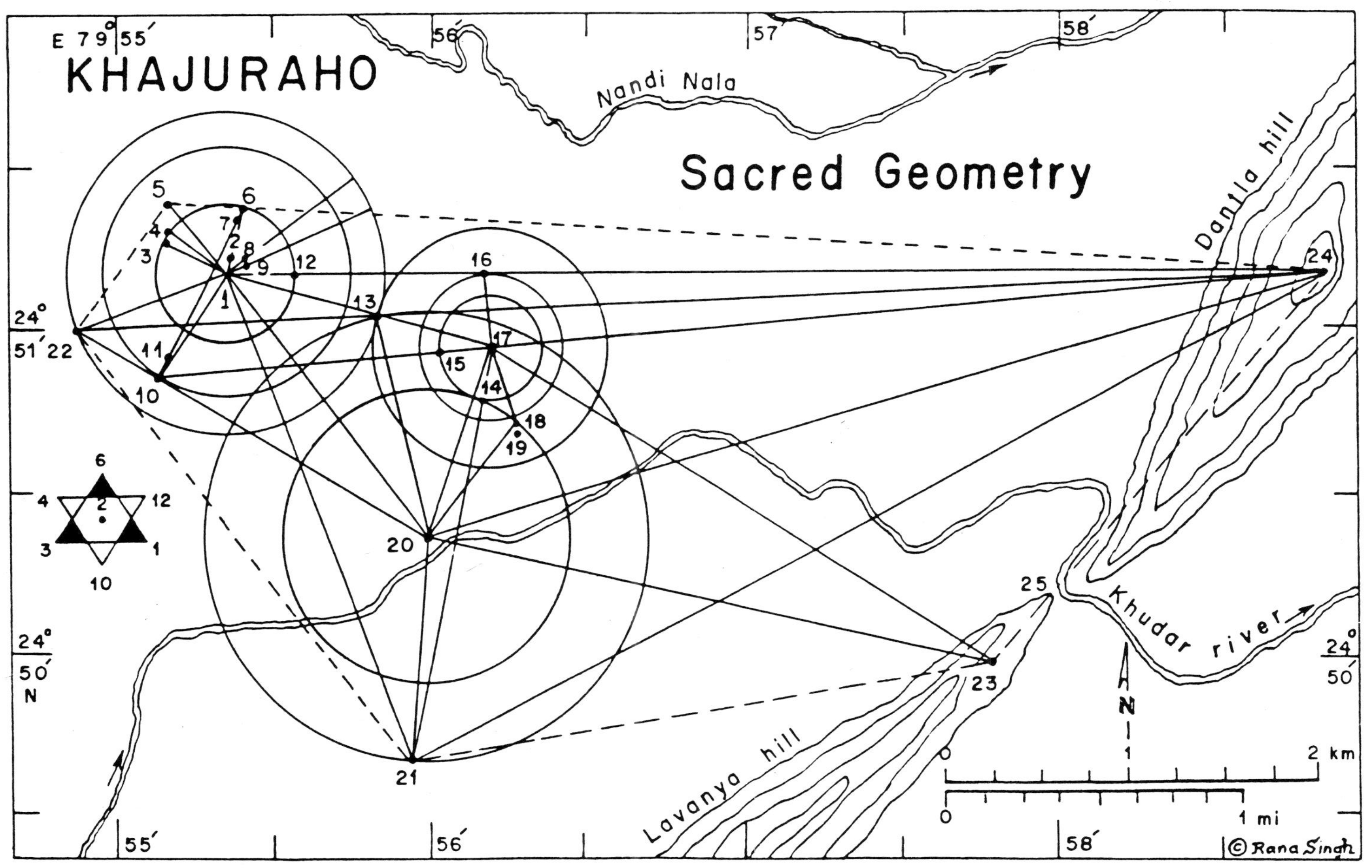

Chart 2 (*"Sacred Territory of Khajuraho: A Search in Landscape Geometry"*, by *Rana P. B. Singh*)

Kandariya and Vishvanatha — male/matter symbol, and the three forms of Devi goddess - Devi Chhatri, Chaunsath-yogini and Devi Jagdamba — female/spirit symbol. At the centre of this *yantra* lies the Lakshmana temple (probably be Maha Lakshmi originally). The centre, thus, symbolizes the integration and synthesis of matter and spirit, resulting to the creation of energy.

At the meeting point of the circumferences of the three mandalic territories lies the shrine of Hanuman (no. 13) who symbolizes the acculturation and interconnectedness between Vaishnavite and Shaivite traditions. Hanuman standing at this site and facing the south protects the devotees from the curse of the Lord of Death, Yama, who lives in the realm of south.

The alignments between Matangeshwara and Dantala hill peak is identical to the east. The doorways of Lakshmana, Kandariya and Vishvanatha temples are facing a little south-east with an azimuth of the sun on the occasion of Shivratri held close to their construction period. This shows the importance of the festival of Lord Shiva's marriage and its directional association with the Datala hill peak. This way the cultural tradition has preserved the natural correspondence of the historical past. This is visible at the multiple layers in the complex network of alignments and mandalic form reconstructed in the sacred territory of Khajuraho. The sacred territory of the Khajuraho represents a form of mandala in space where all the temples and shrines make the reference points of alignments.

The landscape is also a text of history and communication where the past serves as an institution of the mind as revealed and mythologized by the ancient seers and sages. Born of the five basic elements in cosmos — the earth, water, air, fire, and space, the Hindu divinities are omnipresent — still alive, of course invisible. The Khajuraho temples seem to be a devotional effort of ancient sculptors to make the Gods visible!